Starting as a copy boy on the Scottish Daily Express, Harry Conroy has developed a colourful career in print journalism. From news reporter covering court cases and crime, fires and funerals, he moved on to write on financial affairs and the politics of the newspaper industry came to loom large.

He played a leading part, as General Secretary of the National Union of Journalists in the industry's tensions of the 1980s, not least in the cataclysm that was Wapping.

In pursuit of journalists' interests and of a free press he fought to free the Beirut hostage John McCarthy and he actively challenged the Thatcher Government's attempts to discredit journalists over the Death on the Rock episode.

In the open and newsy style that his hallmark, in Off the Record Harry Conroy tells how the big stories are written and he reflects on the present state of the newspaper industry.

Harry Conroy currently writes business and financial columns for the Herald and Evening Times and runs his own public relations consultancy.

Off the Record

a life in journalism

Harry Conroy

Argyll
publishing

First Published 1997
Argyll Publishing
Glendaruel
Argyll PA22 3AE
Scotland

British Library Cataloguing-in-Publication Data.
A catalogue record for this book is available from the British Library.

ISBN 1 874640 67 X

Typeset & Origination
Cordfall Ltd, Glasgow

Printing
ColourBooks Ltd, Dublin

To my wife Margaret,
daughter Lynn and sons Ewan and Stuart,
for all the hassle I caused them.
To my son-in-law Adrian who was worth going to England for
and to my new granddaughter Kaitlin – she is a beaut!

Acknowledgement

I must place on record the assistance the late Mike Smith gave me in checking the facts of my trade union activities. Mike, who died after a long illness, was a trade union organiser with outstanding integrity and ability. I miss him still.

Contents

I. Go Man Go

MY JOURNALISTIC CAREER began on the features desk of the Scottish Daily Express as a trainee sub editor. I had already done extensive training to attain this position, having worked for a year on the paper as a night messenger, more accurately described as a tea boy. I was put in charge of the radio and television page which was produced to a strict format and I had to write the description of the programmes as well as give the composing room the typesetting instructions.

It was not, to be honest, a very exciting job and I became bored with it in a very short time. After all, Coronation Street even then started at 7.30pm on the same nights every week. My official hours were 10am until 6pm, but because of my bad timekeeping these were changed to 11 to 7, and at one time I was threatened with 12 to 8, if I did not get myself into the office on time. Perhaps it was youthful overconfidence. I was twenty years old and afraid of no one.

In the early 1960s, the Scottish Daily Express, along with the rest of the Beaverbrook empire was in its heyday. Almost 2,000 people were employed in Glasgow's Albion Street offices producing the Evening Citizen, Scottish Daily Express and the Scottish Sunday Express. The Daily Express reigned supreme over all other daily newspapers in Scotland, occupying the position that the Daily Record now holds. Circulation peaked while I was there at 650,000.

Iain McColl was editor of the paper, the best editor I have ever worked under. He was an elder of the Church of Scotland and the paper in those days was famous for its campaigns against the idea of bishops in the Kirk. McColl produced a lively paper and attracted to it the best team of journalists in Scotland – money was no object, and staffing levels did not matter. If the paper spotted a talented journalist they went out and hired him or her no matter whether there was a vacancy or not.

My career as a journalist was not the fulfilment of a boyhood dream. After leaving Lourdes Secondary School in Cardonald Glasgow in the summer of 1961, I achieved my ambition to become a trainee laboratory technician despite several setbacks. I suffer from eczema and had failed in my attempts to get other positions in laboratories because of my skin complaint. However, I learned how to conceal my hands during interviews so that the doctors would not spot my skin complaint, and by this subterfuge eventually managed to get a job as a trainee laboratory technician in the Haematology Department of the Southern General Hospital in Linthouse, Glasgow.

I can recall one of the doctors who interviewed me commenting that he had interviewed me for a previous vacancy several weeks before, and that I must be keen. What he did not remember was the reason why I had been turned down, and I got the job. However, as I should have realised, the doctors soon spotted my problem once I was actually working in the laboratory. They sent me to a skin specialist in the hospital, but after several visits it was decided that nothing could be done for my complaint, and in an understanding manner they told me that I would have to look for another job. I was heartbroken but had no other choice except to start job hunting again.

My mother spotted an advert in the Evening Citizen for trainee journalists and I wrote away. I was interviewed by Jack Campbell, managing editor of the Scottish Daily Express who explained the job on offer was that of night messenger. This entailed working night-shift in the Express, running messages for journalists to the library, canteen and caseroom. After a year, if you were thought suitable, you would be offered a job as a trainee journalist, but there was no guarantee and you might have to find another job.

It was at this interview that I first proved my suitability for a career in journalism – I resorted to a piece of conmanship. Any job applicant knows that there is no point going along to an interview and telling those interviewing you that you just wanted a job and it didn't really matter what it was. I therefore didn't tell Jack Campbell that I needed a job. Instead I told him that my life's ambition had been to work as a reporter and that I had submitted articles to the Govan Press. He pointed out that I already had a secure career and insisted that I talk to my parents before taking on the risk of a job as a night messenger which might only last a year.

The next day I phoned Jack Campbell from the public telephone box outside the Southern General and told him my parents had agreed. The truth was I didn't explain to my mum and dad the "risky" nature of my new employment.

I started work as a night messenger at 6.30pm on Monday, February 6, 1962. It was not what you would call an auspicious start. No one appeared to be expecting me. I was only in the building about ten minutes when Douglas Carmichael, who was in charge of the copy boys, approached me, and asked if I had my letter of appointment as Mr Campbell could not remember hiring me. Fortunately I had the letter in my pocket.

For twelve months I ran up and down the stairs of the Express fetching tea, collecting cuttings from the library, taking copy to the caseroom. It was not a pleasant job. You were treated as the lowest form of life, at the beck and call of reporters, photographers and sub-editors who, when they wanted anything, merely called, "Boy". At 19, and 5ft 10ins tall, I looked down on the majority of them but had to bite my tongue and do what I was told.

The worst part of the night was after 10pm when reporters would return from their break in the pub and send you upstairs to the canteen to fetch them a meal. In the canteen as a night messenger, you automatically went to the back of the queue if someone arrived behind you. This system operated on the basis that the production staff had a limited meal break while you had all night to wait to take your order back down to the editorial department. Then when you eventually arrived back you got a rollicking from the reporter or sub editor for taking so long. It was a dog's life.

I was only in the office half an hour when I received my first ticking off. Big Jim McAuslan, the night production editor, was passing the copy desk where the wire copy from the Press Association was sorted out into stories. I was standing watching what was going on with my hands in my pockets. McAuslan growled, "If that's the way your going to stand around, you won't have much of a future here."

Big Jim had a gruff exterior, but looking back I realise that he kept you on your toes as part of your training. However, he had a bad habit of continuing to read whatever was in front of him while he was giving you instructions and it was often difficult to catch what he was saying, but he didn't take kindly to being asked to repeat himself. I can remember one occasion when he grunted something to me and all I could catch was "library". I said, "Pardon," but after he had repeated his request I was still none the wiser, but realised I didn't dare ask him again.

There was nothing for it but to go to the library where I told the night librarian that Big Jim wanted something, but that I hadn't a clue what it was. I figured that all I could do was wait and sooner or later Big Jim would phone asking where I was. I asked the librarian to say that there were a number of copy boys being attended to and to ask what particular file was it that he was looking for. After fifteen minutes the call came and the librarian explained that they were busy and enquired which "Boy" he was looking for. Big Jim replied "the one looking for such and such cuttings" which I then took to him.

My spell on the night messengers was a great introduction to journalism. You learned your way around the building and became familiar with how the other departments worked. Other than former night messengers working as journalists you knew the building better than most, including senior executives.

This was illustrated early one morning when Big Jim could not get the telephone operator to answer the phone. In those days direct lines were not common and the operator was a vital link in communicating with the outside world. I was ordered to go up to the phone room which was in an eyrie right at the top of the building and find out what the operator was doing.

I had a good idea what I would find when I reached the phone room and I was correct. There was the lone operator sitting with his feet up on another chair sound asleep oblivious to the little red lights flickering and the lines buzzing around him. I woke him up and warned him people were trying to get a line out of the building. I returned downstairs and explained to Big Jim that the operator had been visiting the toilet.

Then shortly afterwards Big Jim, who was in charge of the paper in the wee sma' hours of the morning, again could not raise the operator. I was ordered to take him to the phone room. I made as much noise as I could when we were approaching the room, but to no avail. There was the operator sound asleep, feet up on the chair head lolling backwards. I left Big Jim in the phone room and beat a hasty retreat.

The job also had its moments of drama, even as a night messenger. I can remember the tense atmosphere in the editorial on the night in October 1962, when the Russian ships carrying missiles to Cuba were drawing closer to the United States naval blockade. The world has probably never been closer to a Third World War, and we were kept informed of the latest developments and the positions of the opposing ships by the constant flow of wire copy from the Press Association and Reuters.

I will always remember picking up the pink slip of paper which announced that the Russian ships had changed direction and were no longer on a collision course. I handed the piece of paper to Ian MacColl who was the archetypal cinema screen editor, sitting in the middle of the editorial floor attired in a white shirt with the sleeves held up by garters. McColl immediately shouted out to the packed news subs' table and across to the reporters, "The Russians have turned back." You could feel the relief surging through the room as everyone realised the world had stepped back from the brink.

The paper had taken on six new night messengers at the same time but I was the runt of the litter – the one that they almost forgot about. None of us particularly fancied our role as message boy, but after a year in purgatory, if not Hell, we all managed to get journalist positions. My particular mate on the boys' desk (there were no girl night messengers) was Rab Patience who went on to become a sports journalist and was editor of the Saint and Greavsie programme for a lengthy spell. Another colleague, Murray Stevenson, became editor of the Paisley Daily Express.

Drew Rennie was in charge of the department I joined as a junior sub. He was assistant editor in charge of features and Alan Fielding was features editor. Rennie dreamed up the ideas and briefed the writers while Alan designed the pages and was in charge of production.

Rennie was a brilliant journalist and had under him some of the finest writers in the United Kingdom, never mind Scotland – journalists such as Brian Meek, Molly Kelly, Deirdre Chapman and Michael Grieve. Rennie did not like me, or certainly gave a good impression of not liking me. Perhaps I was too cocky for him. I was very keen and would send over articles for him to read which I had written in my spare time.

Every one went in the bin. Not once did he refer to them, not even to tell me how badly written they were! His only comment to me regarding my ability as a journalist was to put his arm round my shoulder one evening and announce to the entire features desk, "Harry has plenty of enthusiasm, but fuck all ability."

He then insisted that I join him for a drink in Tom's Bar.

Perhaps it was intended to toughen you up and prepare you for the rough and tumble of journalism, but it was not enjoyable at the time. Thankfully not everyone adopted the same attitude and I was lucky to be taken under the wing of Brian Meek, who had joined the paper as a feature writer from the Edinburgh Despatch which has since closed, and George Ritchie, a softly spoken and highly intelligent person who was in charge of the readers' letters page. I looked after the readers letters while George was on holiday and he was constantly giving me good advice and passing on his knowledge.

Brian, who now writes for the Herald, would often invite me for lunch, even when Drew Rennie was joining him. He encouraged me to continue writing and gave me tips. It was through Brian that I first encountered what could truly be described as a famous person.

The Daily Express was always signing up sports personalities to put their names to "ghost" pieces for the paper. One such person was Sugar Ray Robinson, the former World Champion boxer who came to Glasgow for a bout. Brian was writing Sugar Ray's articles and the arrangement was that they would meet for lunch in the MacDonald Hotel at Eastwood Toll on the outskirts of Glasgow.

Part of the deal was that Robinson would answer readers' questions in the paper and Brian Meek arranged that I took responsibility for this. He would take me to lunch in the hotel with Sugar Ray and I would take down the answers to the readers' letters and write them up for publication. I just sat at these lunches pinching myself to make sure that I was not dreaming, that I was actually having lunch with the legendary Sugar Ray Robinson.

This of course is one of the great benefits of being a journalist. It allows you to meet people from many walks of life, the rich and famous, the poor and the disadvantaged as well as members of the criminal fraternity.

However my main job was still to prepare the TV and radio page, a section of the paper which you would not believe would attract too much attention from those at the top. However I was to discover otherwise much to my cost.

The Beaverbrook chain of papers was in those days High Tory and there was a policy that in the run-up to General Elections the Labour Party was to be described as the Socialist Party as the powers-that-be thought this would frighten off the voters. Unfortunately no one told me about this policy.

During the 1964 General Election there was of course the usual Party Political Broadcast. When Labour's turn came along I had LABOUR PARTY POLITICAL BROADCAST appearing throughout the page, as of course it was on every channel.

I finished work as usual around 7pm and went home not realising the storm which was about to burst around me. The editor spotted the offending words when the first edition was put on his desk around 10pm that night and immediately ordered the machines to stop until the corrections were made. The following day I was threatened with dire consequences by the editor himself, if I made the same "mistake" again.

My first breakthrough in the writing field came when Gordon Reed, who wrote the Go Page which covered the pop scene, got married. Drew Rennie was acting as his best man and if my memory serves me right went on honeymoon with Gordon and his new bride. Before they departed I was told in a perfunctory fashion that I was to provide the What's On Guide for the Go Page while Gordon was away. This was a listing of what groups were appearing at the various gigs throughout Scotland.

In Gordon's absence the plan was that the paper would take the pop material from the London edition but include in the page the Scottish What's On. At least that was the intention until Alan Fielding came to me and asked what I was writing for that week's Go Page. Astounded, I said, "I'm only doing the What's On." Alan replied, "I want a Scottish story," and turned on his heel. I was flabbergasted. I had never been asked to write anything for the paper other than the few lines between the TV programmes, and although I enjoyed the music, I knew nothing about the pop scene.

It was September 1963 and luckily for me the Beatles were due in Scotland the following month, so I came up with the idea of a guide, Who are the Beatles? They had been around the charts for a year and their recording of She Loves You was just reaching the top of the hit parade. We published a photograph of the four idols with details of their hobbies, colour of their eyes, favourite records and so on. Not very original – but it gave me my first by-line in the

Scottish Daily Express, although this turned out to be a bit of a letdown.

I was really excited at the prospect of seeing my story published in the paper and I went to the vendor at Langside Bus Garage at 10pm to buy a copy of the first edition. In fact I bought six copies and quickly opened a paper to admire my work. It was a great show but the sub editor had given me the by-line of Henry Conroy. I have never been called Henry and I was furious at the deliberate mistake.

Drew Rennie and Gordon Reed did not appear to be overly impressed when they returned from holiday to discover that I had been writing stories for the Go Page, but after that I was asked to stand in whenever Gordon was on holiday or off sick. I was 20 and liked pop music. It was exciting to be given the opportunity to interview the pop stars I had seen on television or listened to on records. Among the stars I interviewed during my time helping out on the page were Rolf Harris, Marianne Faithfull and my idol, the late Roy Orbison.

Marianne Faithfull was a 17-year-old schoolgirl when I met her at the STV studios in Glasgow, shortly after her recording of As Tears Go By had appeared in the hit parade. I was taken aback when I was shown into her dressing room to be faced with the blonde teenager wearing only her bra, pants and stockings. But I showed my true professionalism and concentrated on the interview, although I had to take a ribbing from my mates back in Albion Street when I described what I had been faced with.

The Scottish pop scene was expanding rapidly in the early sixties, with live groups playing at clubs throughout the country. Many of the groups had large followings on the club circuit. Groups such as Bathgate's Golden Crusaders, Dundee's Black Diamonds, Tommy Trousdale and the Sundowners and Helene and the Kinsmen were well known on the Scottish scene. But none had really emulated the Merseyside bands and broken through into the national pop charts.

One of the first to do so were the Poets who were signed up by Andrew Oldham, the Rolling Stone's recording manager. I covered the story of their signing by Oldham exclusively in the Scottish Daily

Express and gave details of their first recording, Now We're Thru' which was to be released on the Decca label. The record appeared in the lower reaches of the charts and the group hovered on the edge of stardom for a short time but never managed to make another hit. Some of the members of the group such as Tony Miles, Alan Weir, Hume Paton, George Gallagher and John Dawson carried on in the pop scene as professional musicians with other groups.

The first Scottish group to make the breakthrough into the real big time was Lulu and the Luvvers who regularly played at the Lindella Club which was off Glasgow's Union Street. Gordon Reed had written stories about Lulu and her group in the Scottish Daily Express which had helped her to be spotted by the talent scouts from London.

I was invited along with Gordon to Lulu's farewell party in the Phonograph Club in Buchanan Street, Glasgow. Lulu had been belting her songs out on the Scottish club scene for some time. Lulu and the Luvvers first record, Shout, reached the Top Ten but their new London management ditched the Luvvers and launched Lulu – Anne Marie Lawrie from Denniston, Glasgow – on a solo career which took her to the very top of showbiz.

I became heavily involved in the Scottish pop scene and bands would invite me to come to their weekend gigs in the hope that I would write something about them in the Go Page. This was flattering for a 20-year-old, who, only a few months before, had been fetching tea as a messenger.

Former boxing champion Peter Keenan invited me to join the panel of judges for his beat group contest in the Paisley Ice Rink. This turned out to be an exciting affair. The local group from Paisley were expected to win, but unfortunately only came second, which led to the judging panel being besieged in Peter's office by angry fans. Police had to be called in to escort us safely from the premises. It gave me a small insight into how a football referee must feel when the home fans are howling for his blood.

I began to see pop writing as a possible career and applied for a vacancy with the New Musical Express, the leading pop paper based in London. I didn't get an interview, but a few weeks later, the editor of

NME phoned me to say that they had another vacancy and invited me down to meet his deputy.

The interview was arranged for a Saturday in the deputy editor's home town of Brighton, for around noon. I had only ever flown once before and had never been to London, never mind Brighton. The entire trip was an event. I flew down to Gatwick Airport and caught the train to Brighton.

I arrived in Brighton at around 12.30pm – thirty minutes late – and phoned the deputy editor at his home. He did not seem too pleased. I don't think he appreciated being asked to break his weekend and informed me that I was late, and that he was about to have lunch. He told me to meet him at the pier at the front in one hour's time.

He duly picked me up at the appointed hour but instead of driving to his home or a quiet lounge he merely drove further along the promenade and proceeded to interview me in the car. I had brought my Go Page cuttings along to show the kind of material I had written, but I'm afraid I fluffed the interview. He was holding an entire broadsheet page of the paper in front of him and asked me if had written everything on the page. Foolishly I said yes and he remarked, "including this piece, here, which has got another name on it." Without thinking I answered yes and explained that the name was a house name used by the paper to give the page a bit of variety.

Later I checked and to my horror the name he was referring to was Judith Simons, one of Fleet Street's top pop writers – a woman that he would probably know personally. Added to my late arrival, I reckoned that I had ruined any chance I had of getting the job.

Looking back, I think it was the best thing that could have happened to me. I had really only started to learn my trade. It was far too early to start specialising in a particular subject. At 20 I enjoyed writing about the pop scene but I doubt if I would still have had the same enthusiasm at 30.

A few months later, in October 1964, I left the Scottish Daily Express to join the Daily Record as a junior reporter. It was on a six month trial basis and I began to learn the art of journalism the hard way by covering fatal road accidents, fires, and crime.

2. Looking for Trouble

PAT ROLLER of the Daily Record was Glasgow's best known reporter. Whenever a journalist appeared on the scene of a story, the cry would go up from the invariable gaggle of kids – "Are you Pat Roller, mister?"

This must have been frustrating for reporters from papers other than the Daily Record. Pat had a personal column in the City edition of the Record during the fifties, sixties and early seventies under the banner, Pat Roller – Looking for Trouble. He reported the petty crime and assaults which are everyday happenings in any city the size of Glasgow as well as the good deeds performed by neighbours. He also reunited many distraught owners with their lost pets, and collected money for charity.

Every year Pat raised thousands of pounds for good causes by merely acknowledging donations from readers at the foot of his column. He was frequently asked to break open charity bottles in bars throughout the city.

But Pat was too busy "looking for trouble" to personally carry out these engagements himself and the reporters who deputised for him were usually greeted by at least one of the assembled gathering with an account of how they had personally met Pat on a previous occasion.

Such encounters could be embarrassing. For the truth was Pat

Roller did not exist! However, you did not want to embarrass the person by explaining that the column was actually written on a rota basis by the Record's general news reporters. The name was actually a play on the word, patroller, for that is what those writing the column did. They patrolled the city visiting the divisional headquarters of police, the infirmaries and fire and ambulance headquarters.

But the column was written in the first person and was one of the best-read pieces in the Record. Few, if any, citizens of Glasgow had not heard of Pat Roller, and most believed he really existed. During the school summer holidays, youngsters would hold jumble sales in aid of the Red Cross or OAP folks, and send the cash raised to Pat Roller. I can recall as a nine year old going round the former railway cottages in Corkerhill with my brothers, Bernard and Michael, collecting old comics and magazines before setting up a stall at the bus stop to sell them for Pat Roller's Red Cross.

Little did I imagine then that twelve years later I would be writing my first Roller column after joining the Daily Record in the early sixties. Each night two reporters would be allocated the task of writing the column. One of the reporters would remain in the office while the other would go out in a car equipped with a radio to do a round of calls – visiting hospitals and police stations to check if anything was happening. The reporter 'patrolling' the city would keep in contact with his office partner on the car radio, while the office-based reporter would pass stories picked up from the police radio to his partner in the car. The reporter on desk duty in the office would write the column based on facts passed to him via the radio. Deadline for the column was midnight.

It was a couthy column concerned with everyday life in the new housing schemes and the slum tenements which still existed in the city. Pat Roller campaigned for years for the removal of spiked railings from tenement backcourts. Young boys and girls were often impaled on these dangerous rusty relics of the past and the column would highlight these accidents and call for the City Fathers to have them removed.

Another Roller campaign was the call for the removal of the

derelict wash houses which still remained in the backcourts of Anderston, Gorbals, Partick and Maryhill. These Victorian structures had long since fallen into disrepair and were a magnet for young children to clamber over. But such was the perilous state of these Victorian edifices that children were regularly seriously injured when the concrete roofs collapsed on top of them.

When not campaigning on these fronts Pat Roller would be reporting house fires, stabbings and road accidents. These would be picked up either by the outside man when he called in at the ambulance headquarters, or from the porters at the Victoria Infirmary or Western Infirmary. The 'inside man' listened to the police radio and made a regular round of phone calls to the police fire and ambulance to check if anything dramatic was happening in the city. Whoever was doing the office stint was responsible for listening to the police radio, which was technically illegal and frowned upon by the police. Through the radio you could hear the Z cars, as we called them in the column, being directed to cover incidents.

This would all be done by code which only the police were supposed to know. The codes were changed at least once a year to try and keep eavesdroppers such as ourselves confused, but we soon broke the new code and could once again follow what was happening around the city. For example a call to a 1, 2 and 3 would mean that there had been a road accident, someone was injured, and an ambulance had been called. However it was often difficult to keep track of the radio messages as you answered phones, chatted to other reporters and tried to write the column. You had to be careful when calling the police not to admit that you had heard the message on their radio and instead pretend that a reader had phoned in with the information. You also had to be careful that you did not direct the editorial car to an incident so that it arrived before the police, otherwise we would have made ourselves very unpopular.

It was a game of cat and mouse. The police knew what we were up to but we could never admit it, and had to remember to turn the radio down when we were calling the police. Each Roller team would do three nights, either Sunday, Monday, Tuesday or

Wednesday, Thursday, Friday. Because of the shift teams you were very often on with the same partner and you would agree between yourselves who was going to do the calls and who was going to be the inside man. My regular partner was Malcolm Speed, who eventually became the Record's news editor, and is now the editorial manager of the Daily Record and Sunday Mail. Malcolm preferred the office end of the team which suited me.

One of the perks of doing the outside calls was that it was not all work. Normally there was a little time for relaxation in one of the city hostelries. On my very first night on the calls this almost cost me my job. Never having done the column before I did not know the routine and my driver, who had arranged to meet some relatives that night, told me that I did not have to call the office until midnight. He did not bother to explain that this was the absolute deadline for copy or that the office might be trying to contact us through the radio to pass on stories they had picked up.

We spent the evening in a bar near Cowcaddens then dropped his relatives off before I phoned the office to check in. The phone erupted in my ear with Bruce Camlin, the then night news editor bellowing, "Where have you been since 9 o'clock? Why haven't you kept in touch with the office?" They had been trying to contact me all night, so why wasn't I answering the car radio? My disappearance meant that the inside man had to write the column entirely without my help. I was ordered to return to the office and was given a good rollicking. I had not been with the Record long and my lack of experience saved me. This episode taught me the Golden Rule all reporters should obey – always keep in regular contact with your office.

The Roller shift normally started at 9pm and finished at 3.30am. The radio car would do two rounds of the city as well as being diverted to Castlemilk, Drumchapel, or elsewhere to cover a particular story. You would return to the office around midnight for your break just after the column had been completed. Then around 1am you would set out again, this time armed with copies of the first edition of the paper which you would deliver to the various police stations. This would normally take you to around 2.30am if you were not diverted on a morning story.

The Daily Record was not alone in doing this nightly round of calls by phone and car. The rivalry between the newspapers in the sixties was such that it was considered a mortal sin if you missed a late night story which appeared in a rival's final edition. But unlike the others we were the only paper which had a fixed slot to fill each night.

It was rather ironic that both the Glasgow Herald and the Scottish Daily Express had a regular calls reporter doing the job while the Record shared the duty around but wrote up a 'personal column' on the results of their patrol. You would often bump into Big Fred Robertson, the Express calls man or Ernie Purdie of the Herald. We would share titbits but of course if you had a 'goodie' up your sleeve you would look bored and say there was 'nothing doing' and then hope you didn't see them for a few weeks.

Both were real pros – Big Fred was the archetypical news reporter as seen on screen – shabby raincoat and a general untidy appearance – but he knew Glasgow inside out and had built up good relationships with the police, so he didn't miss much.

Ernie was what you would have expected of a Herald reporter of the past. Quiet, dignified and dapper in appearance. He would wear a soft hat, and doff it to the officers at the bar. The Herald was not too interested in run-of-the-mill accidents and stabbings but Ernie made sure they did not miss the big ones.

My first ever Pat Roller story was about 71-year-old Tom Glasgow who won the Alice Cullen Charity cup for collecting £50 – a fair sum in those days – for an old folk's treat. The cup, which was donated by Alice Cullen, the Labour MP for the area, was competed for by pubs in Hutchesontown. Tom collected the money in the St Mungo Bar in Ballater Street which was one of the city's smallest pubs. I wonder if the cup still exists or if it disappeared when they ripped the heart out of the Sou' side.

Many of the stories covered in the column had a touch of humour to them. Such as the night I was sent to Castlemilk to interview the Gillen family after their 10-year-old son Pat had been rushed to hospital suffering from stomach pains after admitting to his mum that he had swallowed a sixpence.

Little Pat had started the episode by telling his mother that he had lost the coin and she was helping him to look for it when he admitted that he had swallowed it. Pat then took stomach pains and was taken to the Victoria Infirmary where an X-ray located the coin. He was allowed home with the tanner still inside him and told to allow nature to take its course.

The kids of Castlemilk obviously had a great affinity with the old sixpenny piece as I had already covered for the Roller column the story of six-year-old Caroline Adams who ended up with the coin in her tummy after she swallowed it while running to the ice cream van. Caroline was also taken to the Victoria Infirmary and given the same advice to let nature take its course.

I also had to see the funny side of life when I wore out my shoe leather in the Gorbals – before they flattened it – trying to find a Theresa Duffy. Gorbals had a high Irish population and the modern day equivalent of my task would be to be sent to East Pollokshields to find a Mohammed. I tracked down more than twenty Theresa Duffys, but none was the one I wanted.

However not all the stories in the column were lighthearted. I recall one night being sent to a house to follow up a fatal accident involving a young boy who had been killed crossing the road behind an ice cream van. Unfortunately I arrived before the police had been able to inform the family that the boy had died in the ambulance on the way to hospital. The boy's mother answered the door with another son. I asked if she had a photograph of the boy who had been knocked down. While she was talking to me she nodded towards her son, standing beside her, and said, "He says Tommy has gone to heaven, but the car that knocked him down was going very slowly, and Tommy will be alright."

It was only then that I realised the poor woman thought her son was still alive. I beat a hasty retreat.

Readers often phoned Pat Roller asking him to help some old

person who was perhaps living in poor conditions or to get someone's gas reconnected. He was looked upon as the readers' friend. One evening while I was on Roller duty we got a call from the father of two young boys, who had found a cat, trapped in an iron grating in Blythswood Street. The full power of the Daily Record immediately swung into action. We contacted the police, who sent a squad car to the scene but the helpful bobbies couldn't free the cat, who was called Tibby, for the purposes of the story. Then along came a helpful labourer who used a hammer and chisel to loosen the grating and Tibby darted off into a nearby tenement.

It was simple stories such as these which gave the column its character. In its heyday the Pat Roller column was the soul of the Daily Record. It occupied a prime position every day on Page 3 of the paper. Sadly in the early seventies, it was quietly dropped, and the space it once occupied was taken up by a different kind of Page 3 feature. It was felt that the Record had to discard its image of being a Glasgow daily and promote the fresher, more upbeat style of a truly Scottish national newspaper. No one would claim that the new approach did not work. The Record's circulation was just over 500,000 in those days and today it is 750,000. It's just a pity that a place could not have been found for Pat!

3. Flight 427

MY FIRST personal experience of a major disaster came in October 1965 when a BEA Vanguard crashed while trying to land in fog at London airport after a flight from Edinburgh's Turnhouse.

All thirty passengers, including an 18-month-old baby, and the six crew died when the turbo propped aircraft plummeted onto the runway at 140 mph while trying to land at its third attempt.

It was 1.25 am when Flight 427 to London crashed on Runway 28R at London Airport, now Heathrow. The flight was forty minutes late due to fog and I, along with many other Record reporters, was hauled from my bed in the early hours of the morning as the full extent of the disaster became known.

I was sent to Renfrew airport, the predecessor of the present Glasgow airport which was situated where the Dean Park housing estate now lies on the north side of the M8 Glasgow to Greenock motorway.

Air travel was a different world in the sixties compared to the present-day. Renfrew airport was only the size of the British Airway departure lounge at today's Glasgow airport and London had yet to be named Heathrow. The facilities at Renfrew were basic and obviously the number of people using air travel was much less than today.

My job was simply to wait until the airline authorities released the names of the victims who had been identified. I then relayed these to the Daily Record news desk in Glasgow who then sent out teams of reporters and photographers to gather personal details on the victims.

I was not alone at Renfrew. Every Scottish newspaper had a reporter staking out the airport. We gathered, first in the coffee lounge, then as the day wore on, in the bar, waiting to be called by an airport official who announced the names of the disaster victims to us as they were identified.

Our job was not difficult but the enormity of the disaster slowly sunk in each time the BEA spokesman appeared and took us to a quiet corner of the airport to read out further additions to the list of victims' names. Once we had the names we would rush to a telephone box and phone the news desk with the details. A similar operation was taking place at Turnhouse and London but the timings varied and in some cases names would be released at Renfrew before the authorities at the other airports got around to telling the press at their end.

I was one of the most junior members of the eighteen-strong Daily Record reporting team covering the disaster. The Record had reporters in Edinburgh, Dundee, Glasgow and London covering different aspects of the story and uncovering details of how individuals joined Flight 427 that night.

Stories were also coming to light of how others had escaped the tragedy. Some had changed flights, others had cancelled their travel plans at the last minute, so missing the fateful flight.

Fate decreed that Captain Norman Shackell and his five crew members should take over the flight. Less than twenty-four hours earlier Captain Shackell and his crew had flown to and from the holiday island of Majorca. They had been scheduled to be on a London-Dublin flight that evening but this flight was cancelled because of dense fog blanketing Dublin airport.

Instead Captain Shackell and his crew took over as relief crew on the London-Edinburgh route. The scheduled crew were fogbound on the Continent. Their flight north was uneventful, then Captain

Shackell flew south again, this time towards a fogbound London.

The Captain and his crew died as they made a third attempt to land. Relatives and friends had listened as the plane circled in the fog and heard the roar of its engines as it made several attempts to land. On its third attempt they watched horrified as it came through the shifting fog only to plummet onto the runway.

Today such a landing would be routine as most modern aircraft are equipped with automatic landing equipment which would have guided Flight 427 safely down, but in 1965 there was no such equipment and safety regulations required aircraft landing in poor conditions to have 400 yards visibility.

Fate appeared to decree that not only Captain and his crew should be on the tragic flight but also several of the passengers such as Edinburgh councillor, John Stewart who was travelling to London in connection with the forthcoming British Empire Games (they had yet to be renamed the Commonwealth Games).

Councillor Stewart should have been on the 4pm train to London with fellow councillors but was delayed on council business and caught Flight 427 instead.

Stewardess Janet Turnbull, who was only 22, was on stand-by duties the week of the crash to cover gaps, one of which, caused her to be on the fateful Flight 427. Another off-duty hostess 24-year-old Margaret Lindsay-Simpson had been spending the weekend with her parents in Arbroath and had intended to fly to London from Dyce Airport but could not get a direct flight and switched to the night flight from Turnhouse.

The list of last minute changes of plans which caused individuals to be on Flight 427 appears endless. Secretary Stella Millar worked in London and had been home visiting her parents. Twenty four year old Stella decided to have an extra day at home and that decision cost her life. News of the tragedy was broken to her parents by her boy friend who phoned the couple from London to say that the plane had crashed. . . and there were no survivors.

Many of the passengers were on the flight because of the cheap rate stand-by ticket of £5.4s (£5.20) which was available on late night flights to London. The four engine turbo propped 132 seater Vanguard flew at 19,000 feet on the hour long flight at a cruising speed of 400 mph. As the plane flew south many airports had been hit by seasonal fog and the weather at London airport was described as overcast with variable fog, but by the time the Edinburgh flight arrived above London the fog had closed in and landing became a major problem.

Waiting at the fog-shrouded airport to greet his wife, mother-in-law and baby son was London taxi driver, Douglas Rye.He watched from the airport apron as the Vanguard plunged onto the runway. His 18-month son Simon was the youngest victim. He told the Record at the time, "The plane was there one moment and then gone the next..."

The story had a haunting reminiscence of the Everly Brothers 1961 hit song, Ebony Eyes which recounted the fate of Flight 1203 when the announcement came over the loudspeaker... "Will all those having relatives and friends on Flight 1203 please report to the chapel across the street."

Just as many were on the plane by sheer chance, others who had intended to catch the flight changed their plans at the last minute and as a result lived. Among the fortunate was Provost William Smith of Newport who because he could not book a room in a London hotel cancelled his flight.

My role in the coverage of the tragedy was very mundane, but at the age of 22 it was my initial experience of a major disaster at first hand. The very act of taking down the names of people now dead who less than 24 hours before had been going about their normal lives was a sobering experience for a young man who had only been married six months and who took it for granted that a long life lay ahead.

Some of the senior reporters who were in charge of the coverage of the Flight 427 disaster have themselves passed away such as Jack Hart, who was the senior man for the Record in Dundee for many years and Alasdair Brown, who put all the information together, and wrote the Centre Page story of the tragedy.

It is one of the inevitable results of being a reporter that you encounter more tragedies and see more grief than most people, other than those in the caring or emergency services. The Record carried the story on the front and centre pages and while reading the archive material I spotted that in the evening when I returned home I would have had the choice of The Man from U.N.C.L.E on BBC or Danger Man on STV as my peak viewing choices. Channel Four and BBC 2 had yet to arrive.

Radio Luxembourg was the only independent radio station and the disc jockeys featured on it were Keith Fordyce, David Jacobs, Jimmy Young, Brian Matthews and Alan Freeman. Radio One had not yet arrived to steal them away. I mention these facts not only as a way of illustrating the era in which the disaster took place but also to illustrate what the young people who perished in the disaster have missed in the intervening years. Many would only now be in their middle years.

I covered other air crashes during my career but none on the scale of the Vanguard, although every premature death brought about by accident is no less tragic just because it is not one of many.

Almost three years later in April 1968 I was sent to the Mull of Kintyre when a Shackleton on a routine training flight from Ballykelly, Northern Ireland crashed into a hillside only 300 ft above sea level at Garvelt, ten miles from Campbeltown.

The Second World War bomber had been adapted by Coastal Command as a reconnaissance plane before the introduction of the Nimrod. Concerns had been expressed about their safety as in the previous five months four of the aging planes had crashed killing forty Royal Air Force men. They were due to be phased out.

On this occasion the entire crew of eleven perished and when we arrived, there was an eerie silence on the hillside as the police allowed us to inspect the wreckage which was scattered across the barren slopes. It was a strange feeling to walk among the debris and try to picture in your mind that only hours before a crew of young airmen had been conducting a routine training flight.

The hillside was known locally as Cemetery Hill, as several

planes had crashed on its barren slopes without any apparent cause, killing the crews. We went further up the hill and were shown the rusting remains of another aircraft which had crashed several years before.

Locals told us how they had heard the large plane circle for about half an hour in heavy mist and assumed it was preparing to land at the RAF base at Machrihanish, seventeen miles from where it came down.

The plane was being flown by Squadron Leader RCL Haggett, a 33 year old married man from Nottinghamshire, and the navigator was Flight Lieutenant GC Fisken, 26, from Berwickshire who had only married the year before.

I phoned my story over from Campbeltown and then had a pint in a local hostelry while the wire man used the mobile wire machine to send the photographs back to Glasgow – an early example of facsimile transmission (ie faxing). We then started the three hour drive back to Glasgow, arriving around 2am at the Daily Record in Hope Street, where my story was already on the front page.

Despite the bravado journalists covering such scenes often display, I can vouch for the fact that coming face to face with human tragedy has an inevitable impact. The reporting of the premature end of life brings home to you the reality that no one knows what tomorrow holds. It was not only the multiple deaths which have an effect. Newspapers in the sixties and early seventies reported in great detail every fatal accident and fire. Reporters were required to interview grieving relatives and unfortunately often intruded on personal grief.

Many of the fatalities I covered in those days still live with me. I will never forget being sent by the Daily Record news desk one Christmas Day to cover the story of a young mother who had been killed in a bus crash during the early hours of Christmas morning while working as a bus cleaner.

The family lived in a tenement flat in Clydebank and I can still remember clearly climbing the stairs and coming face to face with two toddlers playing on the landing with the toys Santa had brought them, unaware that their mother was dead.

I didn't have the heart, or the courage, to knock the door and ask for details and the usual photograph. Instead I asked neighbours and got enough detail about the family without troubling the immediate family. I returned to the office and I was asked by the person in charge of the news desk if I had spoken to the husband. Stupidly instead of saying he was not available I told the truth, and said I had not tried. I was then informed that just because it was Christmas Day that was no reason to 'do stories by half' and was sent back out to interview the husband.

I didn't even attempt to carry out the instruction but in an attempt to satisfy the news desk I tracked down distant relatives, and obtained a wedding photograph of the couple which thankfully satisfied my news desk. After my shift ended that evening I went to the Admiral Pub in Waterloo Street to cheer myself up. It was a silly thing to do as everyone knows alcohol is also a depressant and I went home with little feeling of festive cheer.

My daughter Lynn was only a few months old at the time and our families had joined Margaret and I to celebrate Christmas with the new member of the Conroy family. Sadly however my rejoinder to the greeting of a A Merry Christmas which greeted me as I walked through the door brought the family gathering to an end as relatives made a quick exit.

Thankfully media interest in individual tragedies has changed and there is no longer the same pressures on reporters to obtain photographs of every victim of a tragedy. It was one of the least attractive parts of the job. Although it is true that the media now focus in on certain cases which then become high profile, it is to be welcomed that grieving families no longer normally have to contend with journalists knocking on their doors.

4. Drinking on Duty

DRINKING ON DUTY is normally a sackable offence but not when you were on Pub Spy duties for the Sunday Mail. The Pub Spy column was published by the Mail throughout the seventies. It claimed to be the champion of the customers, highlighting public houses which were in need of a good clean up or where the customers were getting ripped off by high prices. With this remit you were despatched from the office to find a suitable pub in Glasgow, Lanarkshire, or Dunbartonshire. The District offices in Edinburgh, Dundee and Aberdeen covered their own areas for their local editions.

You were not given a pub to go to but were expected to find one yourself. This meant that your first question to the driver when you jumped into the editorial car was, "Do you know a grotty pub?"

During the seventies pubs in Glasgow had not yet been yuppified and many of the public houses, particularly those in the older parts of the city, left a lot to be desired. They were basically drinking dens, often with no toilet facilities for ladies, almost certainly no pub food, and soap was a stranger to the toilets.

Many were situated in tenements which were awaiting demolition and the pub was the only occupied part of the building. Indeed in some cases the entire tenement had been knocked down and only the pub was left standing as a square single-storey box.

In their defence it had to be said many of these haunts offered their clients drink at reasonable prices and they were frequented by regulars who were more interested in the pint and a chat than the decor or the state of the toilets.

Even the city centre establishments had not gone upmarket and there were still few lounges or theme bars where today young men and women go not so much to drink, as to be seen in the right place.

In August 1977 Pub Spy expressed horror at the prices charged by The Bank public house in Queen Street, Glasgow. We described it as "One of the dearest in the city centre." A pint of lager and lime (that was the popular drink in the seventies) cost 40p, while a bacardi and coke was 59p and a coke on its own 20p. These prices drew critical comments from the column. It is hard to imagine how the Pub Spy would react to the prices charged today.

Around the same period, City Limits in Union Street, Glasgow was described as a "modern bar" but also came in for criticism from Pub Spy for charging a "mighty 60p" for a gin and tonic and 50p for a vodka and orange.

Pub Spy, like the Pat Roller column in the Daily Record was written in the first person but was in fact written by numerous journalists. It appeared every week in the Sunday Mail with different premises featured in the various editions so the readers could identify with a hostelry in their own area. But it was a highly individual column. You were given the freedom to express your views as to how the pub was run, its cleanliness and prices. This meant that even if the premises did not come up to standard as far as toilets were concerned or the decor was not up to scratch but the staff were cheerful and friendly you could compliment the staff while criticising the surroundings.

Once a month there was also a Pub of the Month Award with readers being invited to write in to the paper and nominate their pub for the award. The pub chosen for this award would be presented with a mirror to hang on the wall and of course they received publicity in the paper praising their high standards. These mirrors can still be seen in a number of establishments around the country and must be becoming collectors' items by now.

One such winner was the Beechwood in Ardmay Crescent, Kings Park in the south of Glasgow which is frequented by many football supporters attending big football matches at Hampden. I remember the Beechwood gaining the Pub of the Month award because it was my local! But I had nothing to do with choosing it as humble Pub Spies did not get the 'good jobs' – we only got to cover the grotty pubs.

This meant that reporters doing a Pub Spy visited pubs which they would never normally have dreamt of dropping into for a quiet pint or a read of the newspapers. This meant that you often looked out of place and the pubs themselves were of the type that strangers appearing at the bar were a focus of attention. Most of the clientele were normally regulars from the immediate locality which meant that strangers attracted suspicious looks and sometimes downright hostility. Thankfully I was often mistaken for a policemen so few ever challenged me but the atmosphere during spying trips was rarely what you would describe as convivial.

Several times while on these undercover assignments I was accosted with the question, "Are you a copper?" But even more embarrassing was when the barman would lean over the bar and growl, "Are you Pub Spy?" On such occasions you tried to look innocent and made some joke, although after such approaches we didn't usually hang about for long in case we really had been 'spotted'.

Normally while out covering stories the editorial driver would stay in the car but when you were doing a Pub Spy you would ask the driver to come in with you as a witness. This meant that if an irate publican complained your story was factually incorrect, you had someone to back you up and corroborate the facts. Although you tried not to attract attention, anyone watching you closely would soon have spotted you taking a more than passing glance at the decor, visiting the toilets, watching what the bar staff were up to and buying an odd assortment of drinks in a short space of time. Reason for the latter was that it was not at that time a requirement for price lists to be displayed, and you had to buy a variety of drinks to establish what prices were being charged. You also took note of what other people were buying to try and cover as many drinks as possible. Reason for the short period of time was that normally the premises were such that you did not want to hang around too long.

This is not to suggest that Pub Spy was a short assignment. You would often have to visit several pubs before you would come across one worth writing about, and the longer the column ran the more difficult it became to find a fresh pub which had not been featured before. In some cases when a pub was particularly bad Pub Spy would pay a return visit to check if anything had improved since the first visit. Invariably nothing had changed and, to be honest, in many cases the customers would have been upset if they had.

A more frequent reason for the assignment not being concluded as quick as it might have been was that once you had a suitable pub under your belt you would go and have an enjoyable pint in more pleasant surroundings. Perhaps the worst pub I ever visited was the Oxford Tavern next to the Barras in London Road, Glasgow. It has since changed its name and been totally renovated but in those days it was something else.

For readers not acquainted with Glasgow, the Barras near Glasgow Cross is a market which only opens on Saturdays and Sundays where you can buy anything from a second hand simmet to a 'brand new' mountain bike. It is a Glasgow institution and when it's open the streets around are packed with shoppers looking for bargains.

It was a Saturday afternoon when I went to spy on the Oxford. It was busy with hawkers and stallholders standing at the bar. The centre of the floor was dominated by a rather large rag woman inspecting what she had in her bundle of rags. In her outstretched arms she was holding a rather large pair of knickers which she dropped on the pile of rags spread out on the floor at her feet before bending forward to rummage through the pile. To avoid this unseemly sight I turned in the other direction only to be confronted with a middle aged couple, both the worst for drink, seated against the wall engaged in what could only be described as heavy petting.

The performance behind the bar was not much better with the two barmen smoking and pouring fortified wine from the overflow trays on the gantry back into the bottles. If you asked for a half in the Oxford you were just as likely to get a glass of fortified wine as you were to get whisky.

The Blochairn Bar next to the fruit and fish market in Glasgow vied with the Oxford for the worst pub I ever visited. The Blochairn is mentioned elsewhere in the book as the Budgie bar as it is still known. I can remember that my visit as Pub Spy was equally short as my previous visits were while on crime background stories. There were no windows in the pub although it appeared that the owners were doing their best to allow some natural light in as there were several holes in the ceiling. Prices were reasonable. What else could they be, at 28p for a pint of heavy and 33p for a pint of Guinness? And to be fair the place was just about to be redeveloped in preparation for the arrival of the relocated fruit market.

Another less than salubrious public house I visited in my search for suitable subject matter was in the vicinity of Parkhead Cross. It was a busy pub but anyone trying to reach the gents toilet had to dodge flying darts as the dart players showed no sign of stopping to allow easy access. The toilets were often the worst element in the pubs visited, and on this occasion after I washed my hands I discovered there was no towel to dry them on so I braved the darts again and asked the barman if he had a towel to dry my hands. He threw me the cloth which he had been drying glasses with and asked for it back after I had finished!

The nearest I came to being discovered was when I called in at a pub in Cambuslang Road near where I now live. It is now called the Langford and is an entirely different establishment. I have enjoyed the live music in the lounge on several Saturday evenings in recent times but when I visited as Pub Spy it was an obvious contender for inclusion in the column. It was a Saturday morning around noon but no one had yet bothered to lift the chairs down from the tables. A visit to the toilets quickly established that they had not been cleaned from the previous evening, and the whole bar had an air of general decay. There were very few customers during our visit and our presence aroused suspicion. One of the regulars approached me and asked gruffly, "Are you Pub Spy?" Concerned for my continued well-being I denied it but after a short time he approached me again and demanded, "Are you sure your no Pub Spy?" Once again I denied it but quickly made my exit. When I wrote my piece I used the column to inform the gentleman who had approached me that he had indeed spotted Pub Spy. No doubt the air was blue when he read the article because the comments on the pub were far from complimentary.

There were a number of bars that were out of bounds as far as the Pub Spy was concerned. These were the pubs that we as journalists frequented. Pubs such as the Copy Cat and Off the Record, now closed, which were adjacent to the Record building at Anderston Quay in Glasgow. Or the Press Bar in Albion Street, more commonly known in the print trade as Tom's Bar which has served generations of printworkers from the Scottish Daily Express, Evening Citizen, Scottish Daily News, and now the Herald and Evening Times. To be fair none of these establishments would have been a candidate for Pub Spy!

Pub Spy was a popular column but it is doubtful with the new stricter approach to drink in the workplace and the higher awareness of the danger of alcoholism if a column such as Pub Spy could ever be repeated, but it was fun at the time!

5. Funeral Pyre

IT STARTED as a routine Monday morning but ended with me witnessing one of the worst fire disasters ever to hit Glasgow. I was sitting in temporarily as the third executive on the Daily Record news desk, part of the experiment of using senior reporters on a rota basis on the desk. The morning was following the usual pattern. Stories in the diary were allocated to reporters and calls were made to the district reporters to check what they had on in their areas.

My job, as number three on the desk, was to draw up the news schedule. This comprised of a list of the day's stories in order of importance. The news editor then presented this schedule to the mid day conference called by the editor to establish what was likely to fill next day's paper.

Around mid-morning the phones started to ring constantly. Readers were phoning in to tip us off that there was a big fire in James Watt Street near the City centre, less than a mile from our offices in Hope Street, Glasgow. A reporter and photographer were sent to check the story out, but the calls kept coming in and it became obvious that we were dealing with a serious incident. At the same time the reporter listening to the police radio told the news desk that the airwaves were humming with messages being passed between the police, fire and ambulance headquarters to the scene of the fire. Police reinforcements were being summoned to the scene and more fire engines were being called for. We checked with the Fire Brigade headquarters and were told that more units were on their way and that there were reports of people being trapped in the building.

Still more calls were coming in from the public, from callers who spoke of "screams coming from the building."It was obvious that what was happening in James Watt Street was indeed very serious and that a big story was unfolding. I was taken off desk duties and sent to James Watt Street to take charge of the story on the ground. Within a few minutes I was standing opposite the building, a former whisky bond, near the Clyde at the Broomielaw. Thick smoke was belching from the roof and sparks were flying into the air.

The first thing to strike me was the bars on the windows. A hush had descended over the onlookers who were mainly workers evacuated from adjoining buildings. Choked with emotion, they described how only a few minutes earlier they had heard the last screams fade away from those trapped inside. The only sound which could now be heard was the crackle of the flames.

The full horror of what had happened quickly became clear. Bystanders told us that more than twenty people worked in the building which was mainly occupied by an upholstery firm, and that few of the workers had escaped. We began to pick up hints that not only had the workers been trapped behind barred windows but that the fire escape exit had been locked. I contacted the office on our car radio and told them that we needed more reporters and photographers on the scene as we were dealing with a major disaster.

The Fire Brigade was trying to prevent the blaze from spreading further by hosing the building from turntable ladders and foam was being pumped into the basement to suffocate the flames. But the 100 firemen called to the blaze had been able to do little to save the lives of those imprisoned in the inferno. Firemen had tackled the steel bars with hacksaws to try to gain entry through the windows while others had used a sledgehammer to break the padlock on the fire escape door.

The police set up a mobile caravan unit in Broomielaw from which to direct operations and soon word spread through the city via radio news flashes of the terrible tragedy which had occurred. Relatives of those working for B Stern, the upholstery firm which owned the building and G Bryce the glassware firm which rented space in the premises began arriving to find out the fate of their loved ones. They were taken to the police caravan where the full extent of the tragedy was explained to them. Heartbroken, they were then taken by policemen and women to nearby Bethel Institute where they were comforted and given tea as they waited for the grim task of removing the bodies from the building to be completed.

A Rabbi, a relative of one of the victims, led them in singing the 23rd Psalm. During the day it was confirmed that twenty people had died in the blaze and two were still missing. Only three workers and a van driver delivering goods to the building had escaped. The death toll the following day was confirmed as twenty-two. It was the worst fire disaster to hit Glasgow since the Second World War, overtaking in human tragedy terms, the nineteen firemen who had died in the Cheapside fire in 1960.

All fatal incidents are tragedies but as the full story emerged about what happened that Monday morning, November 18, 1968 it soon became clear that we were dealing with a preventable disaster – a death toll caused, not only by human error, but also by deliberate acts of negligence. The authorities were reluctant to say too much on the record but it became clear as we spoke to police, fire, and ambulance personnel at the scene as well as the handful of survivors, that the rumours of victims being trapped behind locked fire exits were true.

Bailie James Anderson, the Convener of Glasgow Corporation's Fire Committee who visited the scene was moved to say, "These poor people were trapped like rats and they were only a step from safety."

The survivors described in harrowing detail how the blaze had started and the scenes they witnessed as their workmates screamed for help from behind the barred windows. Theirs were heartbreaking accounts. Sixteen year old storeboy, Gordon Paterson described how he had gone into the office to collect a pair of scissors and found clerkess, Mrs Elizabeth Price, trying to call the fire brigade. She could not get through because of incoming calls. Gordon ran next door to the offices of the National Union of Seamen to raise the alarm and when he returned found the building filling with smoke.

Gordon told newspaper reporters at the scene, "The fire went up like an explosion and everything lit up at once. Everything in the building was wooden – the stairs were wooden, the floors were wooden and the place was full of wooden picture frames."

The other storeboy who escaped, John Rodden had come downstairs with another boy to collect a picture frame when they spotted smoke. He told how the other boy had said, "let's go back up," before disappearing into the dense smoke just as the building erupted in flames. He was never seen alive again.

Van driver George Hendry had just driven into the loading bay when he smelled smoke then suddenly the entire building was alight. Mr Hendry related how he saw two men going up in the hoist and being engulfed by flames. One of the men had just said goodbye to his wife who had brought working shoes for him to wear. He had changed his footwear and gone back into the lift to return to work. His wife had to be restrained from running into the blazing building in a vain attempt to save her husband.

There were numerous eye witness accounts of trapped workers smashing windows and trying to wrench the bars free, all the time screaming for help.

Alex Goldberg, the Stern foreman, was spotted at the windows before disappearing into the smoke. Workers from nearby factories and whisky bonds had tried to get into the building but were driven back by the dense smoke and the blazing inferno.

Attempts had been made to reach the first floor windows but the ladder proved too short. The eyewitnesses then described how the faces disappeared from behind the bars and the cries for help died away. Among those who died was Mr Julius Stern, one of the brothers who owned the upholstery company and the building.

Press and television reporters along with camera men saturated the area. Reporters from all the papers staked out the police caravan to be given the names and addresses of the victims once they had been identified. This information was relayed back to the offices and reporters were then despatched to try and obtain what is known in the profession as a 'collect pic' and personal details of each victim.

This is one of the jobs which reporters hate most. A 'collect pic' is shorthand for a photograph of the person/victim which relatives give you from their family album, or in some cases from the mantlepiece. Understandably the relatives of the deceased are often too upset to talk to you and resent what they see as intrusion. To avoid upsetting the immediate family and intrude as little as possible, journalists often try to obtain such photographs and personal details from friends or neighbours.

However sometimes you cannot avoid approaching the immediate family and in the drive to give readers what they want, I along with other reporters have had the unpalatable job of knocking on the door of a bereaved family following a tragedy. Ironically this job is sometimes easier after a big disaster because people can more easily understand why the press is interested.

I was spared the unpleasant task on this particular occasion as my job was to make sure the we were covering all the angles which were coming to light at the scene and to keep the office informed of developments.

There were numerous individual tragedies. Amongst the victims was a mother and daughter, Mrs Mary Taylor and her fifteen year old daughter Betty. It later emerged that Betty had just celebrated her fifteenth birthday the day before the tragedy occurred and should not in fact have been working at all. She had been asked to return to work early because the factory was busy.

There were other tales of a young man who had struggled from his sick bed suffering from the flu in order to earn money for Christmas and several of the victims wives were pregnant.

Glasgow's firemaster George Cooper and Sir James Robertson the chief constable both visited the disaster scene along with Norman Buchan the Secretary of State at the Scottish Office who had flown up from London to see at first hand the full extent of the tragedy.

I returned to the Record office late in the afternoon to start writing my copy and collate the information from the other reporters. By this time darkness had fallen and the firemen had called a halt to the search for the bodies of two people still missing until first light the following day. The crowds had dispersed from the area and the only activity was a lone fire engine continuing to hose down the burnt out shell. My story described how the smoke from the burning building had risen like a "funeral pyre" over the city and recounted the anguish of those trapped behind those damned barred windows.

Fifteen Record reporters, as well as myself, had worked on the story as well as seven photographers. The next day alongside photographs of firemen fighting the blaze and distraught relatives at the scene we published photographs of eleven of the twenty victims who had been at that time identified.

Journalists cannot afford to become involved in the many human tragedies that they cover although sometimes you cannot avoid it. The James Watt Street fire was one of those occasions when you could not stand apart. It was obvious that there would have to be a full inquiry into the circumstances surrounding the blaze and at the Fatal Accident Inquiry which was held three month's later the public were horrified by the litany of errors and deliberate acts of negligence which led to twenty-two workers perishing that day.

The inquiry heard that the fire was probably caused by a discarded cigarette which ignited a large quantity of inflammable material stored on the mezzanine floor. After listening to all the evidence the jury unanimously found that some of the deaths were caused by the fact that the fire escape doors at the north end of the building leading to James Watt Street were all locked.

They had heard Mr Ewan Stewart QC, Solicitor General for Scotland state in his concluding speech that there were three glaring faults connected with twenty of the deaths. The first was that the fire escape doors were padlocked on the inside to the knowledge of Julius Stern. The second that the door at street level was padlocked on the outside to the knowledge of Julius Stern. The third was that the alarm hooters in the factory had been disconnected.

Mr Robert Reid QC who was appearing at the inquiry for HM Inspectorate of Factories launched a scathing attack on Julius Stern, the director of B Stern Ltd who died in the blaze. "He was mean to the point of parsimony, evasive and deceitful, putting off and deceiving where he could, untruthful, very security-minded, and very suspicious. He cared nothing for safety and was liable to throw it overboard if it cost him money."

The QC told the inquiry jury, "If you are looking for someone to blame you need look no further than Julius Stern." Mr Stern however was defended by Mr EJ Fraser Cook, solicitor for the family, who said, "If he had faults they were grievous faults and grievously has he answered them. He was not a lazy man and his workers found him a generous employer. Workers came to him for loans and some had been with him for many years."

Witnesses at the inquiry described how Mr Stern had been plagued by thefts and workers smoking and that the fire doors had been locked to prevent pilfering. The inquiry was told that after the firm had bought the premises in 1967 they had the automatic fire alarm system which was linked to the nearest fire station disconnected, because it was to cost £184 a year. The door leading directly from the first floor workshop on to the fire escape was kept locked and the key was kept in a pouch at the foreman's desk 20ft away.

The inquiry heard relatives of some of the victims say that the workers had complained to Mr Julius Stern that the key was missing and describe the factory as a 'death trap'. A police photographer witness described how when he was called to James Watt Street on the day of the fire he saw the bodies of fifteen of the victims huddled beside the factory's barred windows on the first floor.

In September a few weeks before the fire the Inspector of Factories instructed the company to reconnect the alarm system, but this was never done.

A month after the Fatal Accident Inquiry, in March, 1969 the surviving brother Mr Samuel Stern a co-director of AJ & S Stern Ltd was fined a total of £300 at Glasgow Sheriff Court when he admitted two charges arising from the fire. The company were also fined £300 on one charge. They had been charged with contravention of the Factories Act 1961 under which the maximum penalty was a fine of £300. Stern and the company admitted failing to ensure that the factory doors could be easily and immediately opened from the inside and also failing to test or examine the fire alarm in the three months between August 19 and November 18, 1968.

During the trial the court were told that Samuel Stern, who was the company's salesman and traveller, left the running of the factory to his brother Julius, but that he had known of the practice of locking the fire door and keeping the key in a pouch which was placed 20ft from the door.

The James Watt Street disaster was the fifth major fatal fire to occur in Glasgow during the sixties. The first was Cheapside when nineteen firemen lost their lives fighting the whisky bond blaze. Then in 1962 four died in a tenement fire in Main Street, Rutherglen. In 1966 seven members of one family died in an early morning fire in Cobinshaw Street, Shettleston, and in 1967 four children and a fireman perished in Cumberland Place, Gorbals.

I covered the Cobinshaw Street and Cumberland Place fires for the Record. These and other fires took place during the period in which Glasgow was rapidly earning the tag of 'tinderbox city' as the death toll in fires rose.

However I will never forget James Watt Street. Not only because of the numbers who died but because it need never have happened and the fines imposed did not relate to the anguish that had been caused.

The site still remains empty, the shell of the building having been demolished after the fire. There is nothing to tell passers-by of the tragedy which occurred there at 10.25am on Monday, November 18, 1968. It looks just like any other gap site in the city, waiting to be redeveloped. Perhaps when a new structure rises from the ashes someone will think to include a memorial to the twenty-two who so needlessly died.

6. The First Victim

IT WAS A BLACK NIGHT and the wind howled round the traditional red phone box which stood at the side of the A77 as it stretched across the Fenwick Moor. The gale force wind which I had to fight against to pull the door open was the arrival of Hurricane Low Q in the West of Scotland. Some ten miles to the north the citizens of Glasgow and surrounding areas were putting out their lights and preparing for a peaceful night's sleep unaware that Hurricane Low Q was heading towards them and would strike at 125 mph in the middle of the night with horrific consequences.

The Daily Record had received a call to say that a car had crashed into a bridge on a minor road leading off the Fenwick Road between Glasgow and Kilmarnock and that there had been a fatality. It was to turn out to be the first tragedy caused by the worst storm Central Scotland had experienced for forty years.

It was around midnight when I arrived at the scene of the accident on the Fenwick Moor which rises between Glasgow and Kilmarnock. A windswept place at the best of times, I had to struggle that night to stay on my feet against the force of the gale. Icy pellets of rain drove into me as if they had been fired out of a gun, and I wished I was back in the warm comfort of the Daily Record's Hope Street office.

Although we had been warned that someone had died in the

car crash on the Dunlop to Burnhouse road, we were not prepared for what we discovered when we arrived at the scene. A private car was lying some way from the road, by the side of a bridge, over the Lugton Water. The police activity, however, seemed to be along the river banks one hundred yards downstream. I soon discovered the reason why. The car, carrying the McNulty family, had struck the parapet of Laithgree Bridge and had toppled almost 40ft into the swollen waters of the river. Mr William McNulty and his wife Ellen had managed to struggle out of the car with their eight year old daughter Wilma, but their two year old son Patrick, had been thrown through the windscreen into the swollen river and swept away. Police were now searching the river for Patrick and pinpoints of torchlight could be seen in the black stormy night as police officers made their way along the banks. It was a grim story.

The local farmer and some farm workers were helping the police and they told me how Mr McNulty had arrived in a badly bruised state at nearby Laithgree Farm to raise the alarm. By the time I arrived, the family had been taken to Kilmarnock Royal Infirmary for treatment, while the police searched desperately for the missing toddler. Eventually they had to call off the search until daylight when a police sub aqua team began to scour the muddy waters. Little Patrick's body was not found until forty-eight hours after the crash, having drifted four miles downstream.

I phoned over my story from the roadside telephone box and by the time I returned to the office it was the early hours of the morning. The night news editor provided me with a taxi home to Tannochside, near Uddingston. Just before I left the office news came in of a tree crashing down on top of a prefab in Baillieston. I told the last few remaining reporters in the office that it had been wild out on the Fenwick Moor. During the eleven mile taxi ride home I could feel the car being bounced about the road and remarked to the driver that the high wind I had experienced earlier in the night must now be reaching Glasgow.

But stormy nights are quite common in the West of Scotland during the winter months and I did not give the weather conditions much thought. I slept soundly, undisturbed by the hurricane force winds battering our mid-terraced home, and it was not until I was lighting the coal fire the next morning, while my wife, Margaret, made some breakfast, that I heard the news over the radio that "twenty people had been killed in a storm which had hit Central Scotland in the early hours of the morning." I was stunned.

The scale of the disaster was hard to take in. Glasgow was worst hit. Of the twenty people killed, nine were in the city – not only because it was the largest area of population but also because of the poor condition of its housing stock. Many of the old tenements were badly in need of repair; indeed many should have been pulled down. The strongest gust of 125 mph was recorded at the weather station at Lowther Hill in Lanarkshire. Gusts of 117 mph were recorded on Tiree, 103 mph in Glasgow, 104 mph in Edinburgh and 110 mph on the Forth Road Bridge, but in the narrow funnels of Glasgow's streets, the strength would be even greater.

I was not due to start work again until the evening but I went into the office early to help out. The editorial floor was in turmoil. Reporters had been working since the early hours of the morning having been pulled out of their beds as news of the disaster became known.

I was dispatched to Partick which was one of the worst hit areas of the city. I knew the area well, not only because of my job as a reporter, but also because I had lived there until only a few weeks before in a room and kitchen tenement flat in Byron Street, Whiteinch. We had moved just before Christmas to our new house at Tannochside, Lanarkshire. The streets were strewn with tiles, chimney pots and guttering, which had been ripped from the buildings by the hurricane. Cars parked by the side of the roads had been damaged by flying debris and some had been blown over onto their sides.

The largest number of fatalities at a single address was at 555 Dumbarton Road in Partick, where four people were killed by a massive chimney which had crashed through the roof and penetrated down the entire depth of the building before shattering in the basement. Mown down in its path were Mrs Angela Best and her three year old daughter Angela. Mrs Best and her daughter had travelled to Glasgow from Swindon to attend the funeral of Mrs Best's mother who had died in a fire only forty-eight hours before the Great Storm struck.

Mrs Janet Gowran and her ten year old daughter were also killed as the huge piece of masonry plunged through the building. In scenes we are more accustomed to seeing on our television screens, it took rescuers twelve hours to recover the bodies from the debris.

There were many other tragedies, such as the three men who died when their dredger capsized in heavy seas off Princes Pier in Greenock; the Malaysian nurse who died while expecting her first child; and the married couple in Edinburgh who were killed when a chimney collapsed and fell through their ceiling.

Almost two thousand people were made homeless by the storm and three hundred homes were destroyed. Thousands of other homes were left exposed to the elements as a result of tiles being ripped from roofs. Those storm-damaged homes were to become a landmark in the city for many months as green tarpaulin sheets were stretched across the rooftops to give protection from wind and rain. More than 5,000 tarpaulins were flown into the city to provide emergency protection from the elements. Many of the homeless in Glasgow were taken to Foresthall Home and Hospital on the north side of the city whilst in Greenock, where four hundred people had to flee from their homes to seek safety, Civil Defence Halls were opened as emergency shelters.

In its wake the storm left severely damaged buildings. In Glasgow where there was the largest concentration of old tenements, fifty-two were officially declared dangerous buildings and there were almost 1,000 dangerous chimneys and more than 400 dangerous roofs. In Greenock 12,000 houses were damaged and in Renfrewshire 1,000 trees had been blown down, many blocking roads.

Those who could recall the war years said that the scenes resembled those following the Clydebank blitz. Shortly after 3am, when the storm struck, large areas of the urban west of Scotland were blacked out as power lines were blown down in the fierce gale. The storm reached its peak between 4am and 5am in the morning when debris was hurling down on the empty streets and Glasgow chief constable Sir James Robertson remarked, "If the gale had come during the day I dread to think what would have happened."

As it was, the toll in human terms was a heavy one. In addition to the 21 killed, the list of injured in Glasgow alone amounted to 146 seriously injured and a further 136 slightly injured. As the storm traced its path across southern and central Scotland, fatalities occurred in Dumfries, Cambuslang, Kirkintilloch, Bonhill, Greenock, Edinburgh and Glasgow and some of the media included, as I did, little Patrick McNulty's death on the Fenwick Moor among the storm victims.

Once the immediate shock of the disaster was over questions arose as to why no warning had been given. Weathermen pointed out that gale warnings had been given at 6pm on Sunday evening although it was thought then that the centre of the storm would pass over the remote island of St Kilda in the Atlantic. But the storm's course had been diverted eastwards towards the mainland. By midnight Hurricane Low Q, which was its official name, was centred over Benbecula and then in the next six hours swept across Central Scotland. It was the worst hurricane to hit Scotland since January 27 1927 when 127 mph winds created havoc killing 22 people, 11 of them in Glasgow.

For many months after the Great Storm it was a common sight to see workmen repairing roofs and tarpaulins flapping in the breeze as a grim reminder of that dreadful night. Sadly Hurricane Low Q brought further tragedy when several workmen were killed while working on the storm damage.

Lessons were learned from the storm. It was agreed that households should have received a storm warning and our television weather forecasts now regularly provide this service. The storm also hastened the demolition of many old tenement buildings which should have been demolished long before the disaster happened.

7. The Funny Side of Life

A REPORTER'S LIFE is all too often involved in tragedy of one kind or another. Interviewing the parents of a child killed in a road accident, speaking to relatives of a family who have perished in a fire, or reporting the murder of an innocent victim.

Thankfully however, there are some moments of light relief to prove that life is not just about tragedy. The saying, good news is no news, has a certain amount of truth in it but every now and then you have the opportunity to report on the lighter side of life.

One such opportunity came when I was working a Saturday shift on the Sunday Mail. The news desk asked me to check out a tip-off that there was a Ladyattendant looking after the Gents' loos in East Kilbride town centre. So what? you might say. Well, such an occurrence may not raise too many eyebrows in today's liberated society, but in the seventies it was unheard of for a woman to venture into a Gents' toilet, so off I went with a photographer to check out this highly unlikely story.

We located the toilets, which were attached to the main Plaza shopping centre in the town centre. They were the usual semi-detached design with the ladies adjoining the men's. We made a search of the male portion of the premises but could find no trace of an attendant female or otherwise. Our car was just about to drive away when I glanced back at the toilets and there, framed in the doorway of the gents, was a rather large lady.

I hurried over and enquired if she was the toilet attendant. "Yes," she replied, "I look after both toilets." She explained that there was an adjoining door which allowed her to pop back and forward between the gents and the ladies. I asked her how she liked the job and she said it was great – "the men are very helpful, they even hold the cubicle doors open for me."

"Could I have your name?" I asked.

"Mrs Peacock," she replied, as I tried to concentrate on what I was writing in my notebook, and stop myself bursting out laughing. When I returned to the office the news desk would not believe me and suggested, that the lady was "taking the piss out of you." They insisted that I checked the voters' roll to prove that a Mrs Peacock lived at the address I had been given. There it was in black and white, Mrs Peacock. The story was written up in a straight tongue-in-cheek manner and I'm sure many Sunday Mail readers had a quiet chuckle the next morning.

Most football fans, of my age group and older, will remember Scott Symon's departure from Rangers Football Club brought on by Celtic's success under Jock Stein. The Record sports desk were obviously covering the main story but the news desk asked me to get some reaction to Symon's removal from various football personalities. Hugh McMenemy, the then deputy news editor told me to contact Tommy Docherty who at that time was between managerial jobs. McMenemy said, "While your at it, ask him if he is interested in the job."

"But," I said, "Docherty's a Catholic."

Back came the reply, "That's not our problem. He's a good manager. Just because Rangers are bigots doesn't mean we have to pander to them."

I sat down in one of the cubicles reporters used for telephoning to prevent their conversation being drowned by the clacking of typewriters. Docherty was genuinely sorry to hear about Scott Symon's fate saying he had been a good manager for Rangers. I then took a deep breath and asked what must have been the silliest question of the year. "Would you be interested in the job?"

There was a long silence. Then the voice at the other end said, "Are you fucking joking!" And the line went dead.

Although new private flats have now been built nearby, there is still a large empty space where Hutchisontown E once stood in the Gorbals Hutchison E was a block of typical sixties council flats, flat roofed and constructed using concrete blocks. They were eventually demolished after a long campaign by the tenants against damp living conditions. Such was the extent of the problem that Glasgow District Council had to pay compensation to the families for ruined carpets, curtains and clothing.

Before the flats gained their reputation I was sent by the Sunday Mail to interview a family after we had received a phone call asking for a reporter to come out to see the conditions the family were living in. The photographer and I were shown into the couple's bedroom where wallpaper was hanging from the wall covered in fungus, and the windows dripped with condensation. The family had called out the Housing Department to see for themselves the damage caused by the condensation.

I asked, "What did they say caused it?"

"Heavy breathing" said the couple! Ah well...

"There's a monkey loose in Kings Park!" the caller to the news desk said. So off we went to check out the story. We soon tracked down a lady in Overwood Drive who had been bitten by the marauding beast when it climbed into her home through an open window. We were directed to the owners house in Aitkenhead Road where an elderly gentleman opened the door to us. Asked if his pet monkey had escaped, he said, "It bit me so I took out my gun and shot the damn thing," and then shut the door.

This left us in a quandary about what to do next. We contacted the news desk on the car radio and they told us to go back and see if we could get more details. This we did and got the usual reporter's welcome – a door slammed in our face. We retreated back to our car parked outside the gate, and were just preparing to drive off when the gentleman suddenly appeared and sat on the bonnet of the car. Our driver responded to this cheek by reversing – leaving our irate gentleman sitting on the road!

Two policemen then arrived on the scene and disappeared into the house, but soon reappeared, having obviously got a dusty response to their enquiries. We were chatting to them at the gateway when our monkey owner appeared out of his door, brandishing what appeared to be a rifle, and shouting at the top of his voice, "Briggs isn't the only one who has a gun." (This was a reference to Briggs, the Great Train Robber who had escaped from prison.) He disappeared back inside his house and we wrote a carefully worded story about the pet monkey that had escaped and then been destroyed.

The following day our 'dead monkey' was spotted larger than life on the loose in Castlemilk housing scheme just over a mile away from Kings Park. Police, fire brigade and RSPCA inspectors were called in to recapture the frightened animal which was being chased by a multitude of children. The monkey was finally caught, but not before it had led those pursuing it a merry dance. One photograph published at the time showed a policeman vainly trying to grab it as he fell flat on his face, arms outstretched and his cap flying off his head. Sadly it all proved to much for the poor beast, which died a few days after being recaptured.

Journalists have a reputation for enjoying a dram, but it was not every day that the news editor told you to go to the cashiers and draw £5 and "go and get pissed!" The amount of course reveals immediately that we are not talking about yesterday, but it was still a day to remember. The occasion was the introduction of the breathalyser laws. Fergie Miller, the Daily Record's news editor, decided that he wanted me to have a 'dry run' and explain to readers exactly what was involved. I was to demonstrate how a few 'half and halfs' turned the crystals green in the new test.

I arranged with Glasgow police to show me around their laboratory and explain exactly how motorists were tested. We arranged the visit to the lab for the afternoon to give me time to visit a public house, spend the fiver and be in the right condition to have a 'real life' test. I enjoyed my libation in the old Garrick Pub in Waterloo Street then went along to the Police HQ in St Andrew's Square near Glasgow Cross.

The police were very helpful, demonstrating how the tests were carried out and explaining how only one or two drinks could put a driver over the limit. The trouble began when I asked them to take a sample and test my blood so that I could explain to readers how much I had to drink and what it did to my alcohol level. The cops looked stunned, "We can't do that," they said. "You could charge us with assault!"

I explained that I thought that they had agreed to carry out the test on me and that my news editor had given me a fiver to have a drink and would be looking for his story.

"Not on your life," was the reply. So I had to wend my way back to the office and explain to an irate Fergie Miller that the cops had refused to co-operate. His description of me was almost enough to sober me up and I was sent packing home without writing a line.

The following morning I came into the office feeling slightly the worse for wear to be faced with a bright and breezy Fergie saying, "Forget yesterday, have another go. Get another fiver out the kitty and try again." The last thing I needed was another drinking session but orders were orders and had to be obeyed. So this time, learning from my mistakes, I arranged with a doctor who was friendly with the Daily Record to have a blood sample taken after I had a few drinks, then fixed up with the Lanarkshire Police to test the sample, and explain yet again the procedures used in breathalysing a motorist suspected of having a drink.

Off I went for the second time to the Garrick and, after a few drinks, went to see my friendly doctor. I was expecting him to take the blood sample by simply pricking my thumb but despite my protests he insisted on using a needle to take blood from my arm. It was not just the fact that I didn't fancy having a needle stuck in my arm which put me off the idea. I knew my doctor friend enjoyed a drink, and that as it was after lunchtime, the chances were he would not pass a breathalyser test himself. By the time he finally found my vein at the third attempt I had sobered up and thought I would pass the test!

I made my way out to the Hamilton HQ of Lanarkshire police where they tested my blood which showed me well over the limit, and once again explained the procedures which would be carried out when testing a motorist. Back at the office I wrote up the piece explaining step by step what the new test meant and what my alcohol level had shown after my lunchtime drink, then went off home to recover.

The following day on the way in to work I scanned the Record avidly to see the results of my two days of sacrifice but not a line was used! Obviously the editor did not share Fergie's enthusiasm for the story.

McGinty was an old heavy dray horse who gave kids cart rides round Kings Park on the South Side of Glasgow. When the time came for his carter, Jimmy to retire it was also time for McGinty to go off to some quiet pasture to finish his life munching grass under the shade of some leafy tree. At least that's how old Jimmy imagined it would happen, until to his horror he discovered soon after his retirement that McGinty was to be sold for the knacker's yard. Jimmy came to the Record and explained the fate which was facing McGinty and the paper immediately launched a Save McGinty campaign.

Reporters were put on the story to track down the whereabouts of the old horse in a race against time. McGinty was traced from dealer to dealer until the trail ended in Carlisle.

Jimmy was despatched with a reporter and photographer team to Carlisle while reporters in the office tried to track down the specific dealer in Carlisle who had finally bought the horse. The campaign to save the horse had gone on over several days with readers joining in the crusade to save McGinty. As youngsters many of them had enjoyed fun rides being pulled behind McGinty. But the sub editors in the office did not place the same faith in the reporters' ability to save McGinty as the public.

New technology had not arrived in newspapers and glue was still used to stick pieces of paper down. It was not long before glue pots began to appear around the editorial floor with 'McGinty' printed in large type over the labels.

Sadly they were to be proved correct. When McGinty's final destination was tracked down he had already been destroyed. This was several hours after the team had set off for Carlisle, but the news desk made what they believed would be a vain attempt to contact them on the office to car radio system. To everyone's surprise the car picked up our call and answered it. Our team had stopped at the Smuggler's Inn at Mount Vernon for a small refreshment before starting on the long haul down the A74 to Carlisle and as a result had only reached Hamilton when they heard our message.

The news desk told them the sad tale that it was too late to save McGinty and to return to the office. Prior to leaving they had been given advance expenses to cover an overnight stay in Carlisle and buy meals for what was expected to be at least a two day trip, but although they had only got as far as Hamilton they had spent the lot by the time they returned to the office. At least poor old McGinty had a decent wake!

My stint as the Labour Party's press officer in Scotland during the 1979 General Election campaign ended in disaster, and I'm not talking about the result, with a touch of farce thrown in for good measure.

The scene was Leith Town Hall where Jim Callaghan, the party leader and Prime Minister was addressing the last major rally of the campaign on the Saturday before polling day. The farce came at the beginning as I waited with Alf Young the Labour Party's research officer, in the North British Hotel, now the Balmoral, Edinburgh to accompany Callaghan and leading party figures down to the hall. It was decided at the last minute that the leader should delay his entrance until after the rally had started so that the television cameras could capture the rapturous welcome as he made his way through the auditorium.

"Great," we thought, until Alf, who had written the chairman's welcoming address, suddenly said, "God, I've included bits about Callaghan in the speech and I bet he will include them!" We jumped into Alf's car and raced down to the hall arriving just as the chairman rose to address the capacity crowd. Alf and I listened in embarrassed horror as 'Jim' was welcomed to the rally and congratulated on a great campaign and promised Scotland's vote. The chairman went on to congratulate the empty seat on showing tremendous leadership and forecast that after the election result was announced, 'he' would still be Prime Minister. All the while of course, the chair where Jim was supposed to be sitting remained empty! Jim Callaghan arrived almost twenty minutes later as the chairman's address came to an end and platform figures, who had been squirming in their chairs as the audience chuckled, had to prevent the chairman repeating his welcoming speech.

Everyone took it as good fun but what followed was anything but funny. Unknown to the organisers, the Troops Out movement had infiltrated the all-ticket meeting, and when the Prime Minister rose to speak began a highly organised series of disruptions. They had seated themselves separately around the hall and throughout Callaghan's speech they would rise individually in different parts of the audience to heckle and shout abuse. The hecklers refused to sit down and the stewards were forced to clamber along the rows of seats to eject them. No sooner had one been ejected than another would stand up and the entire scenario would start again.

But even this had its lighter moments. I had to remove my press officer hat and act as a temporary bouncer, hauling the culprits from their seats whenever they started their disruption. It was quite a trying and physical process because they would not go quietly and had to be forcibly removed. Jimmy Allison, then Labour's Scottish Organiser, stood in one of the aisles pinpointing the offenders until eventually I said to him, "How about you giving us a hand?"

"Sorry," said Jimmy, his arms folded, "I'm a pacifist."

The entire rally was wrecked. The Troops Outs demonstrators kept up their tactics throughout the meeting, saving the biggest disruption until the end when a young woman with a young child in her arms rose from her seat to hurl abuse. She was in the centre of a row and was surrounded by supporters who did not join in the heckling but sat quiet. They refused to budge and we had to clamber over them to reach the woman who was still holding her child as she screamed at the top of her voice.

I ended up taking the baby from her while others hauled her out. It was a field day for the cameramen and I had to remind my colleagues that I would be back at work in the Daily Record the next week and threatened them with Hell and Damnation if they carried a picture of me 'holding the baby'.

Callaghan's final rallying call was drowned out by the demonstrators. The TV news and the following day's papers were full of coverage of the Troops Out protest. I have sometimes wondered if they themselves had been infiltrated, for I could not see the sense in the Troops Out movement assisting a Conservative victory, but that is what they did.

8. Death on My Home Patch

THE FIRST HINT I had that a sex attacker was stalking Pollok and putting fear into women walking alone was while sitting on the top deck of a Glasgow Corporation Bus. I was on my way to Pollok with my wife Margaret to tell my parents that they were going to become grandparents. It was November 1967 and Margaret and I had been married for over two and a half years. Margaret had had three miscarriages and we were over the moon at the thought of a baby being on the way.

My ears had pricked up when I overheard several people discussing a number of sexual assaults on women in the area. My instincts as a Daily Record news reporter told me that there was a story and I eavesdropped on the conversation. However, all thoughts of any story went out of my head when I arrived at my parents' home in Southfield Crescent to be confronted with the sickening news that my father, Michael Conroy, had died late that morning. My dad had been ill for some time and had been operated on for stomach cancer a few months earlier in the Southern General Hospital. Since returning home he had grown weaker, but as many will realise when someone close to you is suffering, your mind often does not accept the obvious.

The communications which most of us now take for granted were not so commonplace thirty years ago. We were not on the phone and neither were my parents. We did not have a car which meant that the journey from Tannochside in Lanarkshire to Pollok took almost two hours and involved changing buses. The last time I had seen my father alive was a fleeting glimpse when we had visited a fortnight before. There had been no answer to the door but we had peeped through the bedroom window and saw Dad asleep. Unknown to Margaret and I as we made our way to Pollock, my family had tried to contact me through the Daily Record but I was on day off.

We were shocked by the news, but as relatives began to arrive Margaret helped to make them tea and sandwiches while I comforted my mother, Sadie Conroy. I also began, with my brothers, Michael and Bernard and sister, Maureen to make the funeral arrangements.

Later in the evening Margaret walked some of our older relatives to the bus stop in Braidcraft Road, only about a three minute walk away. On her way back she was followed by a young dark-haired man and became frightened. She began to run and could hear him chasing her, but she managed to reach the safety of the house.

She told my brother-in-law, Colin Young what had happened, and he went outside with her to see if there was any sign of the youth. There was indeed a youth standing across the road, but Margaret, who was still shaken, couldn't believe it was the same person. She assumed the guilty party would have run off, so she assured Colin that he was not the person who had pursued her.

At the time I was not told about this incident because Margaret did not want to upset me any further. Later, after the funeral, Margaret described what had happened and I then recalled the conversation I had overheard on the bus and wondered if there was any connection.

The previous month a 57-year-old woman, Mrs Josephine McAllister had been ravished and murdered. Her naked body was found on a quiet railway embankment in Craigton only two miles from Pollok. She had been strangled.

I told the news desk about the conversation I had overheard and about Margaret's close escape. They gave me the go-ahead to see what I could find out. I soon discovered that a woman had been assaulted in Levernside Road just round the corner from my parents' home and on the route Margaret would have taken to the bus stop. The assault had taken place outside the home of the Scanlan family whom I knew and they described to me what had happened and gave me a description of the attacker.

I tracked down half a dozen unsolved sexual assaults in Pollok and Crookston. The people I spoke to all gave me roughly the same description of the assailant which fitted the description issued by police hunting for the murderer of Mrs McAllister, and of the youth who had chased Margaret.

It seemed fairly obvious to me that there was one inidividual preying on women on the South Side of Glasgow. But when I approached Glasgow CID with this theory there was an eruption at the other end of the phone. Senior police officers phoned the news desk vociferously denying the possibility of such a scenario and accusing myself and the paper of inventing stories.

We were told that we were scaremongering and that such a article would cause needless panic among the female population in the district. I was warned by the CID to stop interviewing witnesses and the news desk was told that the police would withdraw all co-operation if we carried such a news item.

The result was I was pulled off the story and told to forget it. Three months later Mr James Brand and his wife Janet were murdered in their home in Montrave Path, Cardonald and a week later Samuel McCloy was charged with their murder. Within twenty-four hours he was also charged with the murder of Mrs Josephine McAllister and by the time he appeared at the High Court in Glasgow he had been further charged with the assault in Levernside Road.

I was put on the background to the case because of my earlier involvement in trying to establish that someone in the area was terrorising women. I had also attended the same school as the accused, Lourdes Secondary, and was familiar with the area where the crimes had taken place.

McCloy had been a regular at the Flamingo dance hall in Paisley

Road West only a few hundred yards from the home of the Brands, which was a regular haunt of my own before I was married. Later, during his trial it was revealed that he had been at the dance hall on the night the couple were murdered.

During my school days at Lourdes I had gone every Tuesday evening along with other fourth and fifth year pupils to the Flamingo where we would dance the Madison on the circular dance floor to the sound of Jack Anderson's big band and his Teanbeat rock group with its lead singer who went on to become a solo star under the name of Christian.

McCloy was only four years younger than myself and I was in the fourth year at Lourdes when he entered first year. Indeed many of my former schoolfriend's younger brothers and sisters knew McCloy. He came from a respectable family and my main task was to gather information explaining why a young man from such a background became a killer.

His mother had died two years earlier and his father the year before. McCloy's rampage of sexual assault and murder began shortly after he returned from a holiday on the Isle of Man, a favourite holiday destination for young people in the sixties.

McCloy lived with his sister in a flat in Paisley Road West near Bellahouston Park and his attacks all took place within a two mile radius of his home. His friends described him as a quiet person except when he had a drink when became 'a bit wild'. McCloy had not been particularly clever at school and could not find a job when he left. Instead, he helped in the family fruit shop in the Drumoyne area.

At his trial in June 1968 McCloy's counsel, Nicholas Fairbairn did not argue his client's innocence, but put forward a special defence of temporary insanity at the time of the offences. Certainly as I sat listening to the evidence during the trial at the Glasgow High Court I became convinced of the feasibility of Nicholas Fairbairn's defence. Prior to the assaults McCloy had always been drinking and apparently lost all control over his emotions. During their evidence, witnesses of his assault in Levernside Road described how McCloy had continued his attack on the woman even as householders shouted at him from their windows to stop.

Eventually he ran off, but only as far as Braidcraft Road less than fifty yards away. Those comforting the woman spotted him standing watching and one of them approached him. McCloy did not run off, but instead walked up Braidcraft Road for almost a mile chatting to the potential witness, who became convinced that he could not be talking to the assailant as no one who had just committed such an attack and been spotted, would stand waiting to be approached.

However it was McCloy, and he had carried out the attack. Sitting in the press benches listening to this evidence my mind went back to the night Margaret had been chased and how the youth had stood across the road even after she had come back out the house with my brother-in-law. It was this apparent disregard of the danger of being caught, which the psychiatrist called on his behalf used to argue that at the time of the offences McCloy was not sane and had lost all sense of reason and control.

The defence psychiatrist, Dr George Swinney told the court that although McCloy was fit to plead at his trial he was insane at the time of the offences. He told the court, "His reason and judgement were overwhelmed by his abnormal sex drive and I recommend that he be placed in the care of expert psychiatrists." The Crown produced other medical witnesses who gave evidence that McCloy was sane and fit to plead.

The first attack McCloy was charged with took place on August 20, 1967 when he was accused of attempting to ravish a young girl. The assault in Levernside Road took place on September 18, 1967 almost a month after the incident in Craigton Road but a month before the murder of Mrs Josephine McAllister. During the Levernside Road attack McCloy lost a ring with a blood red stone which the police found at the scene of the crime.

McCloy was questioned by police following the murder of Mrs McAllister. His alibi was that he was asleep in George Square, Glasgow at the time of her death. He fitted the description that they themselves had issued yet they did not take the matter any further. There appeared to be no attempt by police to link the murder investigation to the previous assaults which had taken place.

By the time of Mrs McAllister's murder the police had in their possession McCloy's ring but there was no indication that they made any attempt to establish whether or not it belonged to McCloy. By the time of Mrs McAllister's death, there were also a number of witnesses to various assaults who may have been able to identify McCloy. Yet McCloy, whose alibi was uncorroborated and who fitted the description issued by police, was never, to my knowledge, put in an identity parade.

It was not until the deaths of the elderly Brand couple in March 1968 that the police closed in on McCloy. Within a week the CID had arrested and charged him with the murder of 81-year-old James Brand and his 75-year-old wife Janet in their home which was in the shadow of Moss Heights and directly opposite Lourdes school.

The jury rejected McCloy's defence of temporary insanity and he was sentenced the life imprisonment although I understand that once in prison, he was transferred to Carstairs where the criminally mentally ill are treated.

9. Dance Hall Terror

STRATHCLYDE POLICE have over the past few years made a major assault on crime but I don't believe that Glasgow ever came closer to being controlled by organised crime than in the late sixties. Much of today's crime comes from the drug scene, and no doubt there are drug barons, but in the late sixties a handful of crooks controlled crime in Glasgow which included armed robberies and contract killings. Indeed there is no doubt that Glasgow crime barons hired out killers to the Krays in London.

It was common knowledge within the criminal fraternity that hit men from Glasgow would travel down on the overnight express from Central Station to do a job in London and then return the next day on a train, and be back in Glasgow before the body was found.

True, we still have the violent assaults and the murders, but most of today's assaults are the result of mindless violence caused by drugs or alcohol with the majority of murders being committed within families. During the sixties however, Glasgow was verging on being controlled by organised crime. Violence linked to protection rackets was rife.

Life was cheap among the criminals but there was a certain 'code' which meant that they did not cause any harm to those outside their fraternity. An innocent passer-by was safe. Harm was only done to those within the criminal community itself. The idea of mugging an old age pensioner was anathema. Indeed the toughest guy in the gang would normally have gone to protect an OAP from any assault. This is not aimed at defending what was done but to put the violence in the sixties into context. Drugs are what has changed criminality with drug- crazed people willing to do anything in order to obtain enough money for their next fix.

For three years I mixed with Glasgow's criminals and although it may be hard to understand I very often liked the people I met and very rarely felt threatened. They lived by a different code from me, but at least they had a code, and when they heard that my wife had given birth to a baby daughter gave me money for the baby's bank. The problem was I didn't know which bank it had come from in the first place.

Not all criminals however are violent. Safeblower Johnny Ramensky, who had changed his name to John Ramsay and was known as Gentle Johnny, was a case in point. Despite serving more than thirty years behind bars, Johnny Ramensky was completely non-violent. He belonged to a different generation of criminal as he was approaching retirement age.

I covered one of Gentle Johnny's last appearances in Glasgow's High Court while working for the Scottish Daily Mail in 1967. He was charged with breaking into the National Commercial Bank in Main Street, Rutherglen and blowing open a safe. He was also charged with assaulting a constable who heard the explosion and caught Ramensky as he tried to escape. The 62-year-old veteran criminal's haul was £109 cash along with £142 9s 6d foreign currency and £1 10s (£1.50) from an unlocked drawer. But Johnny Ramensky was more concerned about clearing himself of the assault charge than he was about being found guilty of bank robbery. He was proud of the fact that despite numerous arrests and escapes from prison he had never been charged with violence. At the end of the trial Ramensky was sentenced to four years for the safe-blowing but the jury found him Not Guilty of assaulting the constable, allowing Gentle Johnny to keep his reputation intact! Johnny Ramensky received a sympathetic press not only because of his non-violent nature but also because during the Second World War he had parachuted behind enemy lines to use his safeblowing skills to open Nazi safes.

The romance surrounding him was enhanced by his prowess in escaping from prison. Ramensky escaped from Peterhead three times in one year while serving a ten year sentence. After covering the two day trial the Daily Mail news desk asked me to interview Gentle Johnny's wife who lived in Eglinton Street, Glasgow near what is now the Bedford bingo hall on the south side of the city. I was given £1 from the wall safe in the news editor's room to give to the long-suffering Mrs Ramensky as a bribe to get the interview. Armed with this vast sum of money I climbed the stairs to the Ramensky home only to discover that the house was empty. Mrs Ramensky had plenty of experience of what happened after a trial and she had wisely made herself unavailable. The news desk insisted that I keep trying so I retreated to a local bar and settled down for the duration. Every half hour or so I would try the Ramensky home again to no avail. Eventually Tom Sheerin, the Glasgow news editor told me he was sending out another reporter to take over from me so that I could return to the office and write up the court story. Gordon Anderson eventually turned up and I handed into his safekeeping the £1 which was to buy the interview with Mrs Ramensky. I wrote up the story which was carried the next day under the headline, Gentle Johnny Back in Prison.

But the non-violence of Johnny Ramensky was the exception. Most of the criminals I came into contact with in Glasgow during this period were violent. I can recall one meeting I had with some relatively small time criminals while on a background story. They had decided that I was a 'good guy' and were becoming chummy.

To show their friendship they told me that in future they would tip me off on good stories, and then went on to ask me if I remembered the "guy who was found nailed to the floor". I said I did and my new-found friends said, "Well, it was us that did it. If we had known you then we could have phoned you, and you could have had the story before anyone else."

Such conversations sum up the mentality of the Glasgow criminal. There was not the slightest hint of remorse or understanding of the pain or cruelty they had afflicted on another person. As far as they were concerned they were offering to do me a good turn.

It was shortly after this encounter in the Garrick lounge bar in Waterloo Street that I decided crime reporting was not the career path for me. I felt I was getting too close to the criminals for comfort. Some of their children even called me Uncle Harry, and would bring in collections for Red Cross and other charities to the Daily Record building for me to distribute.

Following this chilling conversation I started to seek a different career path and thought of using a TUC correspondence course in Economics I had completed to find a job as an industrial or financial reporter. I was finally given the job of launching the Daily Record's new Money Page – You and Your Money. To start with I only worked part of the week covering finance and carried on as a crime reporter for the rest of the time.

During this hybrid period I helped cover the first two Bible John murders – that of Patricia Docker and Jemima McDonald in February 1968 and August 1969 respectively. I was not involved in the Helen Puttock murder which took place in October 1969 as by this time I was rarely covering hard news stories. Today Bible John would have been labelled a serial killer, and frankly the coverage would have been much more sensationalist, but at the time although the coverage of the killings grew in importance after the murders were linked, they did not attract the media attention and treatment that they would today.

Patricia Docker was a 25-year-old nursing auxiliary at Mearnskirk Hospital who had a four-year-old son but was separated from her husband and lived with her parents in Langside. She had been to the Thursday night dancing in the Barrowland and the following morning her naked body was found crumpled in the doorway of a lock-up garage in Carmichael Lane which runs between

Ledard Road and Overdale Street. She had been manually strangled. The police investigation was badly affected by the fact that for several weeks after the murder they had concentrated on the Majestic Ballroom in Hope Street, Glasgow where Patricia had said she was going. A witness claimed to have seen her in the dance hall, but later admitted that he had made up the story because he became entrapped by the glamour of being a key witness.

Detectives were also hampered by the fact that many potential witnesses were reluctant to come forward because at the time Thursday night dancing was known to be the evening when many married men and women took to the floor without their marriage partners and did not want to be found out. In dancing circles it was known in Glasgow colloquial terms as 'grab a granny night' and photographers often told stories of how when covering the murder they would appear with their camera to take a shot of couples on the dance floor and suddenly in the middle of a dance number the floor would empty. The majority of dancers, of both sexes, were supposed to be somewhere else and did not fancy the idea of their partner picking up the next day's papers and spotting them waltzing round a dance floor.

At the height of the Docker murder investigation the police had their normal mobile incident room housed in a caravan at the scene and soon after the discovery of Patricia's body I was sent out to check if there were any developments. I spotted a number of journalists crowded into the van and jumped to the conclusion that the CID must have called an impromptu press conference. I climbed inside the doorway and nodded to a few journalists I knew and stood at the back of the crowded caravan. I was surprised at how forthcoming the CID were and began to take notes, but when the detective started to ask the press questions I realised there was something strange going on. After all it's supposed to be us that ask questions.

Then I noticed that although there were a few photographers among the group they didn't have cameras. I whispered to the guy next to me, "What's going on?" He whispered back, "Were you not at the party?" "What party?" I asked "The one a few doors down from where the body was found. We were asked to come here to see if any of us saw anything." It dawned on me that I had gatecrashed the CID interviewing potential witnesses. The detective had recognised me as a reporter and assumed I was also at the party. I quietly withdrew without drawing attention to myself and did not go near the caravan for the rest of the day, but at least I had got some useful background information. I later learned that a Scottish Daily Express journalist had a party on the Saturday night Patricia was murdered which had carried on into the early hours of the morning. The police wanted to know if any of the journalists had seen anything suspicious as they were leaving.

The police investigation into the murder slowly wound down as the trail got cold. They had wasted several weeks on a false trail interviewing those who had been at the Majestic. Press interest in the story soon faded and it became just another unsolved murder.

Then eighteen months later the body of another young woman, Jemima McDonald, was found in a derelict building at 23 Mackeith Street, Bridgeton on August 16, 1969, only a few closes from her own home at No 15. Mima, a mother of three, had gone to the Barrowland on the Saturday and had not returned home. Her sister had started to worry about her and remembered hearing young children in the street talking about a body in an empty house. On the Monday morning she went to No 23 which was derelict and discovered her sister's partly clothed body in a bed recess. She had been strangled with her own tights. Once again CID officers descended on the Barrowland which was Mima's local dancehall. On this occasion other dancers recalled the 31-year-old woman leaving the dancehall in the company of an unknown man just after midnight and walking along Bain Street in the direction of her home.

At first no one linked the killing of Mima to the unsolved murder of Patricia Docker eighteen months before. Into the second week of their investigation the police let it be known that they believed the killings were the work of the same person.

Once again the police investigation drew a blank and less than three months later the serial killer struck again when 29-year-old Helen Puttock was strangled after having been seen home from the Barrowland by a man calling himself John. On this occasion the murder squad had a witness. Helen had gone to the dancing with her sister Jeannie who had accompanied her sister and a man who called himself John home in a taxi. Jeannie had also met a man at the dancing who called himself John and said he came from Castlemilk. The foursome had spent some time in the hall together and left together. Jeannie's partner said cheerio near Glasgow Cross to catch an all-night bus home, while Jeannie joined Helen and her John in a taxi home. Jeannie was dropped off at her house first, and Helen and John then drove off to 129 Earl Street, Scotstoun where Helen was staying with her parents. But the mother of two never reached home. Her body was found the next morning in the backcourt of a nearby house. She had been strangled with one of her own stockings.

Jeannie was able to give the police an excellent description of the man who had seen her sister home in the taxi. The murder immediately took on a higher profile than the previous two as it was immediately recognised that there was a killer on the loose, and that Helen Puttock was the third victim. But this time the police had a description of the man they were looking for. Evening Times reporter John Quinn gave the serial killer the tag of Bible John as Jeannie described to police how in the taxi home he had quoted from the Bible and had remarked while talking about the Barrowland, "My father says these places are dens of iniquity."

Detectives also discovered that around 2am that morning a man had got on the night service bus in Dumbarton Road and got off at the junction of Dumbarton Road and Gray Street. The police also appealed for 'Castlemilk John' to come forward to help them with any possible clues as to the identity of Bible John, but to this day no one has admitted to being 'Castlemilk John'. Once again the police investigation was hindered by the fact that many of those attending the Barrowland over-25s Thursday night dancing would not want it to be known that they were at the dancing that night.

Detective Supt Joe Beattie led the hunt but despite a massive investigation Bible John was never caught. The Bible John investigation saw the end of my crime reporting as I became a full time financial correspondent and my beat became the boardrooms of Edinburgh's New Town and the cocktail bars of the Caledonian Hotel and North British rather than some of the seedier bars in the East End of Glasgow. I followed with interest the latest events involving bodies being exhumed which were to solve the Bible John murders. But sadly I believe that this series of murders will become a successor to Jack the Ripper. Yes there will be suspects, but will anyone every be proven guilty? I doubt it.

10 Cheque Book Journalism

GRANDMOTHER Mrs Margaret Johnstone was killed when a bomb exploded beneath her feet in the MG Magnette sports car she was travelling in with her son-in-law Arthur Thompson. She was being given a lift to her home only a few hundred yards away in Hogganfield Street but as the car moved off from the Thompson family home at 176 Provanmill Road, Royston, Glasgow it was ripped apart by an explosion which rocked a passing bus.

The 61-year-old woman was killed instantly but Arthur Thompson escaped the main impact, although he was detained in Glasgow Royal Infirmary with severe leg injuries.

Glasgow CID quickly confirmed they were treating Mrs Johnstone's death as a murder inquiry. The police believed that the bomb had been intended for Arthur who had an interest in the Hanover Club, a casino in Glasgow's Frederick Lane. The entrance being in a lane meant that no matter which way a client left he had to walk down the lane before reaching the main thoroughfare. The crack in the newsrooms around Glasgow was that this was an incentive to customers not to walk out with too large an amount of winnings. Better to lose some on the tables than have it forcibly removed from you in the lane outside.

Within twenty-four hours detectives announced that two brothers Martin Welsh, 36, and George Welsh, 38, had been arrested and that they were searching for a third brother, Henry, 24. I was despatched by the Daily Record news desk to collect information on the Welsh family and called at an address in Provanmill. Fully expecting to have the door slammed in my face I was instead invited into the house. Standing in the centre of the living room floor I was in the middle of introducing myself and explaining what I was looking for when his family dropped the bombshell that Henry was in the house.

Henry came into the room and I told him the police would track him down and advised him to give himself up. It was all slightly unreal. Here I was standing in a council house living room, chatting to the man that the entire Glasgow police force was searching for.

Henry took my advice. First he phoned his solicitor then rang the Northern Division police headquarters in Midland Street, Cowcaddens and told them he was coming to the station.

I agreed to give him a lift down to the police station which was near the Scottish Television studios. Once again it was a strange feeling driving through the busy streets with a wanted man in the back of the car on his way to surrender himself to the police. We drew up on the opposite side of the street from the station, as we did not particularly want the police to know that the Daily Record had brought in the man they were looking for.

Innocently Henry asked if I was coming into the station with him, but I suggested that this would not be a wise move. He and his wife Bernadette disappeared through the side door of the station and we drove back to the office.

The three brothers were charged with the murder of Mrs Johnstone and the attempted murder of Arthur Thompson. They denied the charges and their solicitor, Laurence Dowdall, a top criminal lawyer, tendered a special defence of alibi on behalf of all three.

I was put on the background to collect personal details of the family's history and obtain photographs of the brothers in readiness for the High Court trial. The case had attracted a tremendous amount of news coverage and the media were clamouring for information about the Welsh brothers and Arthur Thompson. The bomb explosion had taken place in August 1966, three months after Arthur Thompson had been accused of culpable homicide in connection with the death of Patrick Welsh, the brother of George, Martin and Henry.

Patrick Welsh had died while he was a passenger in a van driven by James Goldie. It was alleged that the Mark 10 Jaguar driven by Arthur Thompson had deliberately collided with the van forcing it to mount the pavement and smash into a lamp standard, killing both occupants.

Arthur Thomson described himself later in his life as a retired businessman, but just exactly what kind of business was open to question. His home in Provanmill was like a fortress with video cameras filming visitors. Thomson had a 'colourful' background and was widely recognised as one of the leaders of organised crime in the West of Scotland. His son, who was involved in the drug trade, was murdered and on the day of his funeral, the bodies of two men suspected of involvement in his killing were found.

Arthur himself died of natural causes, the type of end he probably never expected. Everyone involved in the two cases lived around the Royston, Provanmill and Blackhill areas other than Martin Welsh who had moved outside Glasgow to Whitburn in West Lothian as part of the overspill programme.

There was intense rivalry between the newspapers in Glasgow at the time of Margaret Johnstone's murder. The Scottish Daily Express was at the top of the pile with a much larger editorial staff than any of its rivals. The Express had a reputation for being willing to spend money to get the big story whilst the Daily Record was the poor relation with a lower circulation and a reputation for not throwing money about.

The Welsh family informed me that the Express was willing to pay the brothers £100 each for exclusive interviews after the trial if they were found Not Guilty. I asked my news desk if I could offer a financial inducement to obtain the story and was told I could offer to pay the brothers a fiver each! I therefore knew that I could not compete financially against the Express but instead concentrated on building up a relationship with the immediate family who continued to speak to me.

I would do them small favours such as giving them a lift in the editorial car if they wanted to go to the shops or to a relative's home. This led to one farcical situation when I arrived at the home of one of the wives to be told that Arliss Rhind, a Scottish Daily Express reporter, was already in the house and that he was suggesting I was perhaps stringing them along. I stood on my dignity and said that I had better not come inside as I might cause trouble. I then quietly suggested to Bernadette not to say anything but to put on her coat and come outside and I would take her to the shops in the editorial car which was waiting. She did this and we drove off. But Arliss had spotted what I was up to and we then had a Keystone Cops style chase around a Glasgow housing scheme as we tried to shake off the Express car. All we were doing was going to the shops!

The family claimed not to have any photographs of Henry which meant that I had to trail round friends and drinking haunts trying to obtain a collect picture. The search took me to some strange places such as the 'Budgie' Bar in Blochairn which Henry frequented. The editorial driver came inside with me to give some support as I tried to engage several regulars in conversation about the Welsh brothers in general, and Henry in particular.

The barman, who looked like an all-in wrestler, soon made it clear that he did not welcome our presence and suggested that we leave. I continued talking to one of the customers but my driver decided that caution was the better option and told me that he would go and "put the heater on in the car". The barman then inquired if I was deaf and repeated his suggestion rather more forcibly that I should leave. I tried to reason with him but when he started walking round to my side of the bar I decided to retreat to the heat of the car outside.

Another bar I visited in my quest was the Glen Bar in Royston which Patrick Welsh had used. My welcome was friendlier but I still could not obtain a photograph. By the time the trial started in

Glasgow High Court in November I knew that the Express had 'tied up' two of the brothers if they were found Not Guilty, with the offer of £100 and an overnight stay in a Glasgow hotel. Despite my paltry offer of £5 Bernadette assured me that Henry would speak to me after the trial which kept the news desk reasonably happy.

Glasgow's High Court has been the scene of many eventful trials but few can have matched the events of that first week in November 1966. Arthur Thompson was found Not Guilty on the Wednesday on the charge of culpable homicide in connection with the death of Patrick Welsh and James Goldie. During his trial he agreed that he was part owner of the Hanover gambling club and that this meant that he had 'a number of enemies'. Shortly after leaving the dock he appeared as a witness in the trial of the three brothers.

He told the court that he had no enemies in the court and could think of no reason why the Welsh brothers would wish to harm him. Lord Migdale directed the jury to find George and Martin Not Guilty but the prosecution against Henry continued. He sat in the dock alone for an hour before the jury found the charge against him Not Proven. The three brothers were immediately surrounded by photographers and press men when they walked down the steps of the High Court building opposite the entrance to Glasgow Green, escorted by their solicitor.

To my horror all three were hustled into the waiting Express car. I grabbed Bernadette and asked her what had happened to our agreement that Henry would speak to me. Bernadette, who was not much more than five feet tall, marched up to the Express vehicle and hauled Henry out of the back seat. She told him in no uncertain terms he was coming with her. I immediately pushed them into our car and we shot off with Henry and Bernadette in the back seat. We arrived at the back entrance to the Daily Record in Cadogan Street to be confronted by an Express reporter who attempted to prevent Henry from entering the building and suggested that Henry should go with him to meet his two brothers who wanted to talk to him.

At this point I decided to take a hand in matters. I removed the reporter from the doorway and thrust him against the wall while forcibly pointing out that we were no longer outside the High Court and that his presence was undesirable. Meanwhile Henry was hurried upstairs to the editorial floor. His arrival caused some consternation. The paper wanted the story but I had to assure them that I had made no offers of money. Editorial executives were wary of being accused of 'cheque book journalism' but I assured them that no money had changed hands and then went to talk to Henry.

He told me, "Arthur Thompson may say he is a friend of ours but we are no friends of his." He wanted to make contact with his brothers as they had agreed while awaiting trial that they would all meet immediately after the verdict to discuss what to do next.

I phoned the Express and told them that Henry wanted to meet his brothers. Henry then had a telephone conversation with them. I then spoke to the reporters who were handling the story and it was agreed that I would take Henry with me to the Top Spot bar in Hope Street and they would bring their brothers along so that they could chat amongst themselves.

There was no sign of anyone when I arrived at the Top Spot with Henry, Bernadette and a photographer. Then an Express reporter turned up alone and tried to persuade Henry to accompany him to meet his brothers without me. I told him that was not the deal and Henry told the Express reporter to tell his brothers he was not leaving the pub and that he wanted to see them right away.

Eventually the two brothers arrived accompanied by a posse of Express journalists who once again tried to persuade Henry that he should join them. The discussion got rather heated with insults flying back and forth between myself and the Express team, particularly the reporter whom I had earlier used to support the back wall of the Daily Record. I was outnumbered and rang the Record for assistance. They sent another reporter who had obviously been dragged from another hostelry to come to my aid.

The only problem was that he soon fell asleep with his head on the table, leaving me to fend off the Express team still on my own. There were veiled suggestions from the other side that unless they had all three brothers there was no deal and I could not offer an alternative. The Welsh brothers were not too concerned about losing out on the cash but did want to take up the offer of overnight accommodation as they did not want to return to their own homes that night for whatever reason. I can't imagine what the couples in the crowded lounge who were having an evening out must have thought about it all.

At one point there were half a dozen Express reporters and photographers lined up against myself, a photographer and my sleeping companion. Voices were being raised and insults were hurled across the tables. It was suggested that all I was ever good for was doing the Television and Radio programmes (my first job as a journalist when I left the copy boys' desk) along with comments about my parentage. The quietest among us were the Welsh trio, who only hours earlier had been facing murder charges. Bernadette and Henry remained loyal to me but were worried in case the Express would not keep their deal with George and Martin about overnight accommodation. Eventually after 10pm when the lounge was about to close and I knew that the Express first edition was running I suggested that they go along with the Express as I could not offer them anything. I had at least delayed the Express and got my own interviews with all three brothers in the pub.

11. A Policeman's Son

THE COLD-BLOODED shooting down of three unarmed policemen in Shepherds Bush, London, in August 1966 sparked off one of the biggest manhunts in the history of British crime. Superlatives are too often used in tabloid journalism but on this occasion it was an accurate description to say that the nation was horrified by the murder of the unarmed police officers – Detective Sergeant Chris Head, Temporary Detective Constable David Wombell and Police Constable Geoffrey Fox.

All three were gunned down in Braybrook Street, London after they flagged down a car near Wormwood Scrubs prison in order to question the driver John Witney about the lack of a road fund licence. Within minutes all three were dead, shot by the occupants of the car they had stopped – John Witney, Harry Roberts and John Duddy. Detective Constable David Wombell was blasted as he stood beside the Standard Vanguard car and Detective Sergeant Head was shot in the back as he ran towards the police car. PC Fox was shot as he sat behind the driving wheel of the unmarked police car.

The gunmen escaped from the scene but almost immediately a nationwide search by armed police was underway to track them down. In the Daily Record newsroom in Glasgow we were appalled by the enormity of the crime but did not believe that we would be involved in the coverage as the murders happened in London. The shooting took place on Friday afternoon, August 12 and by Monday, August 15, the police had made their first arrest, John Witney, the owner of the car. The following day the police announced that they were looking for a Harry Roberts, aged 30, and John Duddy, 37. It was revealed that Duddy came from Glasgow.

We checked our cuttings files in the library but could find nothing on Duddy. He was also unknown to those of us who covered the Glasgow crime scene – but not for long. News filtered through to the news desk that Glasgow CID were searching for Duddy. Armed officers had raided houses in the City's East End and several pubs had also been visited by detectives. The Record began a parallel search. Duddy was an uncommon name and from our police contacts we learned that the wanted man had relations in the Calton district. Reporters were given the job of searching voters rolls looking for the name Duddy, while others tried to glean information from police contacts. Whenever we came across the surname Duddy in the voters roll a reporter was sent out to check if there was a connection with John Duddy. The difference between us and the police was that they were armed.

A warning had gone out to the public not to approach Roberts or Duddy as it was assumed they were still armed. The news desk didn't stop to think what might happen if we reached Duddy first! I could imagine the conversation going something like this, "Excuse me, I'm Harry Conroy from the Daily Record newspaper. Are you John Duddy that the police are looking for?" Reply, "Yes, would you like to come in and have a cup of tea!"

Most of the reporters involved in the search were in their early twenties and were full of the bravado which goes with youth. I was 23 but despite my cocky exterior my stomach was turning over as I entered the poorly lit closemouths in Calton and climbed the uneven stairs, stopping on each landing, to peer at the nameplates or the names scrawled in pencil on the whitewashed walls beside the doors, looking for the name Duddy.

I can remember going to one particular tenement flat near Glasgow Cross. Before knocking on the door I looked down the stairs, examining my escape route, wondering how I would make my getaway if I happened to strike it 'lucky' and come face to face with Duddy. A woman answered and peered round a half-open door. I asked her if she was Mrs Duddy and explained that I was from the Daily Record.

She asked me to wait and closed the door. A few seconds later she re-appeared and invited me in. I stepped into a large dimly-lit hall and came face to face with two large alsatians. Plucking up courage I enquired if she was related in any way to John Duddy, wondering what I was going to do if she said Yes. Thankfully she replied No and I made my way back down the stairs feeling rather weak at the knees. I returned to the Record office and was asked to check if there was a Duddy listed in Bain Street. I searched the voters roll but could not see any Duddy.

The following day, armed CID officers led by Chief Superintendent Tom Goodall arrested Duddy in a tenement in Stevenston Street, Glasgow. They had been led there by Duddy's brother Vincent. It transpired that the previous evening while we had been searching the area there had been a family conference at 8 Bain Street to decide what John should do. Indeed at one point John Duddy had been sipping a pint in a Gallowgate pub while armed police officers had been raiding several addresses. They arrived at the pub shortly after he had left. The family were concerned that if John Duddy was spotted on the streets he would be gunned down by police seeking vengeance for the cold blooded murder of the three officers. They believed he should give himself up, and Duddy was willing to go along with this decision, after he had spoken to his 74-year-old father.

But the elderly Mr Bernard Duddy who was on holiday in Ireland at the time had stayed on a few days extra. A bed was arranged for Duddy in the flat in Stevenston Street which was owned by someone who did not know him. Then the family decided that they could not wait until the father returned home and Vincent visited the Central Police headquarters less than a mile away. He led them to his brother on the understanding that no harm would come to him. Meanwhile the news desk remembered asking me to check the names in Bain Street. I was rollicked for missing the name, although I do not know what I would have done, or for that matter, what the family would have done if I had disturbed their conference.

It turned out that John Duddy was not armed. He had, along with Harry Roberts, buried the guns in London but he was a frightened and desperate man. Duddy had been in trouble with the police before for petty offences, none of which involved violence. He was married with four children. Roberts,the third wanted man, managed to elude the massive police search for 96 days, living rough in the countryside. He was finally cornered in a barn after the trial of Witney and Duddy has started. The trial was abandoned and a new trial was held at the Old Bailey in December.

My bloomer in missing the family's name in the voters roll did not mean the end of my involvement with the case. The popular newspapers' coverage of crime in the sixties included a tremendous amount of material which was published at the end of the trial. This was known as background reporting and entailed gathering facts about the accused's personal life and his family background, including photographs. You were deemed to have finally made your mark as a reporter in Glasgow when you were assigned to a background. The news desk treated it almost as if you were being awarded a privilege when they asked you to do a background.

You were expected to gather your material in your own time, either before you started work, or after you had finished. The information was not used until after the result of the trial and between the time of the person being arrested and the trial date you were expected to have prepared your story. There was intense competition among the Press to produce the best background and news desks read the rival papers' coverage with great care. Heaven help you if someone had a better angle or photograph. The Duddy case was my first ever background. I was not the main reporter on it – that privilege fell to Bill Robertson, the chief reporter. I was given the job of getting Bernard Duddy's story, John's father. This was of special interest because Mr Duddy senior was a former policeman and now his son was accused of being a cop killer.

Duddy's family knew that the press were after the story and were determined that we would not get it for nothing. Newspapers often paid money to those involved in major criminal trials but the Daily Record was usually reluctant to offer money – not from any ethical standpoint but purely from the economics of not paying out money unless you really had to. Prior to the trial, the family had made sure that no-one got near the elderly Mr Duddy. This meant that when the trial started we still did not have an interview with the father. Members of the family however, went to London to be present at the trial, and the news desk thought that this would provide an opportunity for us to reach the father. I was set the task of getting to Mr Duddy while Bill Robertson went down to cover the trial.

I tracked Mr Duddy down to the Elcho Bar in the Calton were he was a regular, and managed to introduce myself. I met him several times in the bar, and after a few drinks, would take him home in the editorial car. We would stop on the way home for a fish supper, and I would see him safely inside his ground floor flat in McAslin Street, Townhead, before saying goodnight.

I was after information but I also quickly got to like the old man, who had the Irish gift of the gab, and followed Celtic Football Club which gave us a common interest. Mr Duddy had been a policeman for three years and his beat had been the Gorbals. We would chat away sometimes about John, and the family's early days, but I was conscious that we were being closely watched by other regulars in the pub. Occasionally they would come across to join in our conversation but then would leave our company. Later I was told by one of the 'minders' that he had been instructed by the family to keep an eye on the old man and make sure the press did not get to him. He had spotted me, and had approached our table several times but had only overheard our conversation about Celtic and assumed everything was OK. Understandably he did not realise that part of a reporters' technique is to engage a person in general conversation, and come back to the 'main subject' from time to time, so as not to make the person conscious that they are being interviewed. In addition, I was aware that I was being watched and was careful not to talk about John Duddy when a third party was nearby. However, I was genuinely saddened, when I heard that Mr Duddy had been found seriously injured at the foot of a flight of stairs in a tenement block at 6 Alston Lane, Calton. He died in Killearn Hospital five hours later. He had sustained a skull fracture. The tragedy occurred almost at the exact same time as John Duddy was found guilty of murder, after a six day trial.

Although my job was to encourage Mr Duddy to talk about his son, I had enjoyed our chats and recognised him as an 'old gentleman'. But I did not realise the events that would flow from Mr Duddy's death. Shortly afterwards the satirical magazine Private Eye carried a story with the headline, Death on the Press. The story suggested that Mr Duddy had fallen to his death, because newspaper reporters had taken him for a drink earlier in the day, and that still suffering from the effects of the drink Mr Duddy had tripped and fallen down the stairway. Two reporters from other Scottish national newspapers were named as being regularly in Mr Duddy's company, insinuating that they had been with him on the day of his fall.

Shortly after this article appeared, I was invited to a meeting one evening in the Sans Souci bar in Glassford Street. Paul Foot, a former Daily Record reporter, and a nephew of Michael Foot, the former Labour Party Leader, was present along with James Latta, a Glasgow solicitor. Foot was a well known contributor to Private Eye and is now a national newspaper columnist. Latta was a criminal lawyer, who was later jailed for perverting the course of justice.

They explained that my name had been kept out of the Private Eye story, because I was a 'good guy', but that the other two reporters were now suing the Eye for damages. They wanted my assistance regarding information about the meetings the other reporters had with Mr Duddy. I told them that I wished they had named me, because I could have done with the money that the other reporters were bound to receive. I had nothing to do with Mr Duddy's death, and had not seen him on the day of the unfortunate accident. I also told them that I knew nothing about the other reporters' activities, but that even if I did, I would not be volunteering information to them. It was not a particularly pleasant meeting and showed a total lack of understanding on their part as to how reporters on background stories went about their business.

Background reporting was, and is, totally unlike covering a major news story, when the press arrive in hordes and hunt in packs. The entire ethos of a background story is to try and get an exclusive photograph, or interview, which the other papers know nothing about until it appears in your paper. You work on your own and avoid contact with other reporters. The truth was that I did not even know that those other reporters were working on the story. I left that meeting believing the matter was closed.

However a few days later as I left the Daily Record by the back door in Cadogan Street, I was confronted by several people whom I recognised from my visits to the Elcho Bar. They invited me to join them for a drink and I got the impression that I did not have much choice in the matter. They tried to persuade me that I should agree to give evidence against the Scottish Daily Express. Once again I explained that I knew nothing about the activities of other reporters, but they made it clear they were not happy with my attitude.

Worse was to follow. Shortly afterwards I was stopped in Wellington Street, having just left the Record, and asked to get into a car. I decided it was more of an order than a request, and obliged. I was taken to a house in Calton, where I was informed that "Jimmy Latta had said I was not willing to talk to him but that I might talk to them."

Once again I explained that even if I wanted to there was nothing I could say because I had no information on what other reporters did or did not do. It was explained to me, in the way that only a Glasgow hard man can, that there were no witnesses and I could be 'marked' if I didn't start talking. Put bluntly I was terrified, but I genuinely knew nothing. Eventually I was allowed to leave the flat, but for weeks afterwards I was waiting for another visit. Thankfully I was not approached again. Perhaps I convinced them of my ignorance.

Eventually Private Eye paid the other reporters damages. My involvement in the case was still not over. A Fatal Accident Inquiry was held into Mr Duddy's death and in the witness box his son Vincent claimed that some reporters and "a man call Conroy" had plied his father with drink. The FAI, however, was told that Mr Duddy had been drinking with friends after a funeral, and was found dying on the stair landing an hour later. Sheriff MG Gillies told the jury, "There is nothing to suggest that he was seen by reporters and the public houses are closed at that time." The jury returned a formal verdict.

John Duddy, along with his two accomplices, was sentenced to serve a minimum of thirty years imprisonment. He died in February, 1981 in Parkhurst Prison. Harry Roberts still languishes in jail.

12. The Press Baron

I HAD A DREAM. I woke up one night during the summer of 1973 with an idea for a chain of local newspapers in the suburbs surrounding Glasgow. Next morning, having forgotten all about my 'brainstorm', I was making my way to the Daily Record when the idea came back to me. I thought about it some more and decided to have a go.

The idea was to launch a series of local newspapers covering Pollok, Castlemilk, Easterhouse and Drumchapel. Despite having populations of around 20,000, none of these large housing schemes had a local newspaper. Each of my papers would carry local news but would have common feature pages and would carry common, as well as purely local, advertising. I decided that the first of the series should be launched in Pollok on the south side of Glasgow because that was where I had been brought up and I knew the area.

It is impossible to produce a paper from scratch single handedly, so I approached one of my best friends Ken Durie, a printer, who grew up with me in Southfield Crescent, Pollok. Ken was a lecturer in printing and would be able to look after the production side of the paper. I also approached Stewart McLaughlan, who worked alongside me in the Daily Record as the Political Correspondent. Stewart and I were great buddies and my idea was that Stewart would be in charge of the editorial while I handled the advertising and circulation side. Both Ken and Stewart agreed to give it a try.

We started with nothing but the concept. No money, no office, no staff, but we didn't let that put us off. We designed a dummy newspaper to show potential advertisers what we intended to produce. Stewart's brother-in-law, Bobby who owned a tarmacadam company agreed to allow us to work from his portacabin in Rutherglen. Everything was done on a shoestring. We could not afford to have the editorial properly typeset, so we used an electric typewriter with a 'golf head' which at least produced typefaces which looked better than a straightforward typewriter. We typed the stories on to sheets of paper which were cut to the width of our columns then pasted these down on lay-out boards. Ken did the paste-up and the headings which were produced using letraset. The newspapers were delivered by my wife Margaret, and Ken's wife, Helen.

Margaret and I had just had twin sons which meant that while she was driving around Pollok she not only had 2,000 copies of the Pollok News in the back of our estate car but also the tiny twins, and had to interrupt deliveries to feed the babies. Crazy, but she did it.

I chose to launch a newspaper in Pollok simply because I knew the area. I am a great believer that if you are going to launch an idea then you should do it in a business that you know, and also if possible in a market that you know.

I was born in Househillwood, a small council estate by postwar standards, and then moved to Hardridge Road, Corkerhill just outside the Pollok area. When I was about ten, the family moved to a three bedroomed, four in a block cottage flat in Pollok.

Pollok was made up of families who had been moved out of inner city slums such as Kinning Park, Gorbals and Pollokshaws. The population was working class with Old Pollok housing some clerical workers such as bank and insurance clerks, but in the main the wage earners were unskilled and tradesmen.

The sprawling housing estate, which to outsiders was known as Pollok, covered areas with their own loose identities such as Househillwood, Nitshill, Pollok, Crookston and Priesthill. In common with most other estates it had few amenities and struggled to find an identity. There were no public houses, no cinemas, no shopping centre, and no private housing. Most amenities were a busride away.

I grew up like most boys in the area playing football on a waste piece of ground, and riding on a bus to the pictures either to Govan, where there was the Lyceum or Plaza, or to Shawlands where there was the Embassy, Elephant and Waverley cinemas.

Pollution had yet to take a grip of our society and we were able to fish for minnows in the Levern and Brock burns which in the winter frequently overflowed. A big adventure for us in our youth was to trespass into the Pollok Estate where we would run off with the golf balls from golfers on the Haggs Castle and Pollok golf courses.

I lived in Pollok until 1965 when, at the age of 22, I got married to Margaret Campbell, and by the time the Pollok News was launched in 1973 I was living in upmarket Kings Park, some three miles, but a world away from the housing estate I had grown up in. I was, by this time, Financial Correspondent of the Daily Record so I approached my contacts in the financial world for advertising support which meant that our first edition carried adverts from institutions such as the National Savings Bank and the Clydesdale Bank.

Myself, Stewart and Ken each invested £50 to form a limited company, Suburban Graphics. Stewart and I did not want to tell the world, particularly our management, that we were launching a newspaper even although it was hardly a threat to the Daily Record. To avoid declaring ourselves openly, two accountants registered the company in their names with each of them holding one share which they immediately transferred to us once the company was registered.

The ploy did not work. I was tipped off by one of my contacts on the ninth floor where the directors hung out that a memo had been circulated with details of Suburban Graphics and the fact that Stewart and I were shareholders. No one ever approached us. Perhaps on reflection they decided we were indeed not a threat to them.

The first edition of Pollok News was launched on September 7, 1973. I took my sabbatical month's leave from the Daily Record during September so that I could work full time on the launch. More than twenty newsagents throughout Pollok agreed to take the paper which had a 3p cover price, with the newsagent taking 1p for every copy they sold. We printed 2000 copies of the first edition and our phone didn't stop ringing all day with newsagents asking for more copies. We sold out!

It was a great feeling to see your own paper lying on the newsagent's counter.It might not have been the most professional paper ever produced but it was all our own work.

The entire operation was a family affair. My wife Margaret and Ken's wife Helen delivered the papers. My father-in-law, the late Tom Campbell, a keen photographer, took the pictures and Margaret's Aunt Nettie kept the books and sent out the invoices to advertisers.

But it was hard work. We all had full-time jobs and the paper was put together on a Sunday and Monday evening. We would start putting an edition together around 1pm. on a Sunday and finish about 1am on the Monday morning. Then immediately after work on Monday night around 6pm. we would start again and finally finish putting the eight page paper together about 3am on Tuesday morning. Each night, after I had finished working for the Daily Record I would go with my father-in-law to youth evenings, football games and other community events.

Our circulation rose to 3,000 but it was difficult to attract advertising. We still could not afford proper typesetting, which meant that the paper looked amateur and at the same time Pollok, like all the other housing schemes at that time, did not have a shopping centre of its own. This meant that none of the large store groups had shops locally that they wanted to support by advertising.

It was ironic that our first splash was an exclusive story about plans for the £5 million Pollok shopping centre which is now in place. The first edition also included welcome messages from William Gray, the Lord Provost of Glasgow, and the two local MPs, James White and Bruce Millan, each of whom wrote a column for the paper on alternate weeks.

After six weeks Stewart decided that we were beating our heads against a brick wall and left Ken and I to soldier on alone. To assist the production we paid a compositor to type the stories up on our ready made strips of paper which allowed myself to gather the stories and hammer them out on a typewriter beforehand. This speeded up the operation and was working well. That is until Edward Heath's three day week hit us.

The miners had imposed an overtime ban which drastically reduced coal stocks and the Government, in a bid to conserve supplies, had brought in regulations which restricted the amount of electricity commercial firms could use to three days a week. Weekends were taboo. If we had obeyed these regulations the paper would have folded. We were by this time using the premises of freelance photographers Arthur Foster and George Wilkie. They allowed us to use their studio in Wellington Street, Glasgow on a Sunday.

The studio had heavy black curtains which cut out any light from the windows but more importantly acted like blackout curtains so that no-one outside would be aware that the premises were being used. However our 'typesetter' became suspicious when we drew the curtains in the middle of the afternoon and asked why we were doing this. We explained about the regulations and he gasped, "You mean this is illegal?"

We assured him that there was nothing to worry about, that we, as directors of the company, would take full responsibility. But he was not happy. I had never seen him work so fast. It took him less than half the normal time to complete his work and disappear. We never saw him again.

The three-day week also added to our production difficulties because the companies who produced our negatives and printed the papers were restricted in the time they had available to work and it was touch and go whether we would survive or not. It was also not a great economic climate for a fledgling paper to survive in.

Every edition was a battle for survival. On a Friday night I collected the electric typewriter with the golf ball head from a small printing firm in Govanhill which I returned first thing on Monday mornings. Photographs for the paper were always a problem despite the help of my father-in-law. From time to time photographers in the Daily Record would slip me a print of a picture the Record was not using.

This lead to one hilarious occasion when we used what was then known in the trade as a 'dolly bird picture' – not topless, I hasten to add. I was told that the picture was not being used in the Record and it would be okay to use it in the paper. From time to time I left copies lying around the Press Club in West Regent Street in Glasgow city centre, in the hope that one of the advertising agency people who used the Club would spot the paper and consider us. I did this with copies of the edition containing the 'dolly bird' photograph and then relaxed in a corner to enjoy a pint.

I was joined by Terry Meechan, the Record's publicity manager who picked up a copy of the Pollok News and began glancing through it. He remarked, "I see you're using Record photos now, Harry." I tried to pretend I didn't know what he was talking about, but he pointed to the offending photograph and said, "We're using that in our TV advertising campaign."

I quickly raced round the Club retrieving the papers I had left lying around while Terry sat chuckling quietly. My photographer friend had obviously assumed that, as the photograph had not been published in the paper, it had been dumped and was unaware that it had been chosen for wider display – on TV!

Every week we would collect the paper which was printed on two separate sheets which we would then have to fold and insert the centre pages. It was a tedious task but usually went smoothly enough except for one evening when a friend, Steve Jarvis, returned home with me from a farewell lunch for Hugh Cudlipp, the retiring boss of Mirror Group. It had been a riotous affair in the Central Hotel, Glasgow, attended by just about every journalist employed in the Daily Record and Sunday Mail.

Steve and I had arrived home by taxi complete with two bottles of champagne and found the family busy folding and inserting the pages. We volunteered our services and finished the job in record time. The following day, as usual, Margaret and Helen delivered the papers. Then the phones started ringing with calls from irate newsagents. Their customers were complaining about pages being upside down and in some cases missing. It appeared that Steve and I had not been quite up to the job.

Unknown to the populace of Glasgow, a desperate newspaper war was taking place in their midst. Another journalist, Joe Mulholland, had thought up the same idea as myself and had launched the West End News which circulated around the Partick, Kelvinside and Hyndland areas of the city.

At first neither of us were too concerned about each other until we realised that we both intended using the existing newspaper titles as launching pads for other titles around the city.

We each pretended to be doing better than we really were, although Joe's operation was more professional than ours. He had staff and the West End News was properly typeset. In addition the West End of Glasgow is a more prosperous area of Glasgow than Pollok, thus offering more potential advertisers.

After a few months it was mooted that perhaps we should join forces, so Ken and I paid a visit to Joe's patch and met him in Curlers, a Byres Road pub. The meeting got nowhere. I think Joe was up to the old fashioned businessman's trick of trying to learn more about his rivals.

Despite the difficulties we faced, mainly due to lack of resources, there was no doubt that we had identified a need for a local paper within the community. We covered the activities of numerous organisations and came in contact with local people such as William Smith and his family who founded the Hillwood Boys Club in Househillwood which ran eight football teams, and Mrs Mae Kirkwood who with the help of others formed the Priesthill Community Association. They, and many others, were struggling to create a community spirit in an area which had been neglected for many years.

Until the arrival of the Pollok News, their activities went largely unrecorded and unnoticed. The national newspapers only took note of the area when it was the scene of a crime or tragedy. There was little, or no, positive coverage.

However we could not afford to provide a community service. The Pollok News required financial support to allow us to improve the paper and attract advertising. Ken and I struggled on until the Spring of 1974 when we decided to pack it in. By this time we had an overdraft of around £500, and the circulation had dropped back from a peak of nearly 4,000 to just over 3,000 per issue.

Every week was a grind and there appeared to be no light at the end of the tunnel. After finishing my work at the Daily Record, I would go out with my father-in-law to take photographs of youth clubs, church meetings, and scouts. Then we would have the marathon Sunday and Monday sessions.

We could not see how we could radically improve the position. If we closed the paper and collected in the money owed to us then we would be able to pay off our overdraft at the bank and pay our bills. Not that there were a great many bills. Our printers always demanded their cash upfront.

On Good Friday, April 1974 we made the decision to close, and we went to see Wallace, the owner of Great Western Printers who at that time was printing the papers, to inform him that we would not be printing the paper that week.

Wallace, who owned a Bishopbriggs local paper, urged us not to close the paper. He offered to allow us six months credit on our printing bills to give us a chance to find our feet. We said no, as that it would only mean that in six months' time we would be in the same position we were in now but also owing six months printing costs.

Wallace then offered to take a stake in Suburban Graphics. He would buy a 50per cent shareholding in the paper, and immediately start typesetting the paper properly for us and the lady he paid to sell advertising in his Bishopbriggs paper would also sell advertising in the Pollok News.

Our resolve to close the paper began to waver and Wallace, noting this, said, "What about the other papers you were planning to produce?" Before we knew where we were we had committed ourselves to producing a second title – that weekend – the Shawlands and Pollokshields News. Again it was to be an eight page paper with four feature pages common to the Pollok News, but it meant that we had suddenly to produce twelve pages and find material in a new area.

It was bizarre. Instead of walking away without the burden of having to produce another edition of the Pollok News, we left the meeting faced with the task of producing two papers by Easter Monday. I can remember it was a brilliant Easter Weekend. Both Ken and I had young families but we didn't see much of them that holiday weekend as we slogged away. We consoled ourselves with the fact that as it was a holiday weekend we had the full day on Monday to produce instead of having to start at 6.30pm after work. Not that this meant we finished any earlier.

The first edition of the Shawlands and Pollokshields News appeared on Friday, April 20, and we sold almost 2000 copies. At the same time Joe Mulholland had obviously decided to declare war on us because the South Side News suddenly appeared on the counters. Joe had crossed over the river and was now competing with us on our own territory. This did not concern us as we now had some backing. We were attracting more advertising. Wallace was printing the paper on a Thursday so that it was available for sale earlier and because of the improved look of the paper sales of the Pollok News were increasing.

Meanwhile our accountant Michael Lorimer was drawing up the accounts for Suburban Graphics so that Wallace could become a partner. The deal was that he would pay us enough to wipe out our overdraft and he would take a 50 per cent interest in the company.

Everything appeared to be going smoothly. At the end of May I went to see Wallace and told him the share certificate and account details would be ready the following day. We arranged to meet so that I could hand over the share certificate and collect the cheque. Everything seemed to be set Green for Go. Life was certainly looking up.

Then disaster and tragedy struck. Early the next morning Ken rang me. Wallace had died of a heart attack during the night. I couldn't take it in. I had been chatting to Wallace around tea time the previous evening. He appeared fine. Poor Wallace, he was a nice man and had treated us very fairly.

It was the beginning of the end for Suburban Graphics. Wallace's partners were not interested in taking a share in the papers. They demanded immediate payment of the outstanding print bills and in future wanted paid upfront each week.

We were back to square one. We could not afford the typesetting and once again had to revert to using the golf ball typewriter head. We struggled on for a few weeks then the crunch came. I was going on holiday to the Isle of Man and Ken believed that we should call it a day. The paper folded the week before Margaret and I left to go on holiday.

Nine months hard graft had come to nothing. I returned from holiday to face the task of collecting the money owed to us by advertisers. We managed to collect enough to meet our bills and Suburban Graphics was put quietly to sleep and my dream of becoming a press baron, for the time being, had ended.

13. The Fall of the House of Fraser

I FIRST BEGAN to follow the life and times of the late Sir Hugh Fraser in 1969 when I became Financial Correspondent of the Daily Record. Sir Hugh had by this time been chairman of the House of Fraser for three years following the death of his father, Lord Fraser of Allander.

Sir Hugh's initial period at the helm continued the success story of his father who had started the business from a small drapers in Glasgow's Buchanan Street. Sir Hugh built on his father's success, expanding the store group and adding new companies to the family's industrial holding company Scottish and Universal Investment Ltd. He had all the trappings of a multi-millionaire – a beautiful wife in Patricia Bowie, a mansion and a string of horses which he kept on his farms in Stirlingshire. Sadly the business empire was to slip from his grasp and a series of broken relationships brought him grief in his personal life.

But in 1971 the Fall of the House of Fraser had not begun. The youthful Sir Hugh, who had a warm engaging smile, was able to tell shareholders at the Fraser Annual General meeting that their company was now the largest store group in the United Kingdom, having outstripped Debenhams. The Fraser group owned more than 100 stores with a turnover of £150 million and a staff of 27,000.

He confidently assured shareholders, "We will continue to

expand by filling in the blanks on the map."

The transformation from a small family business to a large public company had started in 1936 when Fraser and Son bought Arnotts. This was followed by the acquisition of a number of other family businesses. Then in 1959 the company, now known as the House of Fraser, shocked London's establishment by buying Harrods, the store where Royalty shopped. The price was £34 million. Although many in London resented the fact that a Scottish draper controlled the Knightsbridge store, Frasers had joined the big league.

Lord Fraser of Allander died in 1966 leaving behind a House of Fraser chain of sixty stores. He had also created in 1948, Scottish and Universal Investments, an industrial holding company whose interests included Outrams, the publishers of the Glasgow Herald and Evening Times, Whyte & Mackay whisky and a string of local newspapers.

Following his father's death Sir Hugh took over the reins of both companies but he renounced his father's title, saying that he wanted his father to be "the one and only Lord Fraser of Allander". Sir Hugh had married Patricia Bowie in 1962. They had three daughters, Patricia, Belinda and Caroline but the marriage lasted only nine years and ended in divorce in 1971. Patricia emigrated to Canada with her three daughters.

Despite this setback in his personal life Sir Hugh's business interests continued to expand and prosper. In August 1972 he interrupted a holiday in St Moritz to buy the giant AC Illum store in Copenhagen for £1 million and also added the Dalmore Whyte and Mackay whisky company to the SUITS portfolio in a £5 million takeover. Despite being entirely separate companies and both being quoted on the stock exchange, the two arms of the Fraser empire were very much intertwined with SUITS holding 25 per cent of the Fraser shares.

It was in 1973 that the first rumours began that the Fraser family dynasty might sell their heritage. Talks were held with British American Tobacco about a possible takeover, but nothing came of them. The rumours however continued that Sir Hugh was willing to divest himself of the House of Fraser and such was the size of his family's holdings that he held the fate of the group in his hands.

The name of Boots began to be linked with a possible bid for the company and I wrote a number of stories for the Daily Record on how the rumours were gaining strength pointing to the fact that the Fraser share price was rising in anticipation of a bid.

However it was a story which almost cut short my career as a financial journalist. By 1973 Sir Hugh and I were well acquainted. We had a friendly relationship which meant that he would invariably answer my calls, and I often phoned him at his Mugdock home to check out details of stories. As the Boots rumour gained strength I called Sir Hugh one evening at home to ask if there was any truth in the story. I did not expect him to confirm that Boots were about to launch a bid as this would have been against Stock Exchange rules, but there are ways of denying a story which allow a journalist to read between the lines and place his own interpretation on events.

Sir Hugh and I spoke for almost half an hour and he went into great detail on how there was no truth in the rumour. He volunteered the information that SUITS had recently sold 500,000 shares in House of Fraser which they certainly would not have done, he said, if a bid was in the offing. Such was the strength of his denial that he convinced me there was no bid looming and I in turn convinced my editor, Bernie Vickers.

Having briefed my editor on my interpretation of the position I left the office to attend two evening meetings and did not return home until almost 11pm. My wife Margaret was waiting anxiously to tell me to phone the office immediately as the editor was looking for me. The night news editor, Hugh McMenemy, told me I had better get myself into the office straight away. He explained that the Press Association had sent out a story over the wires about a £200 million plus bid for the House of Fraser by Boots, but the editor had put it on the spike because of my earlier assurances. The story had been confirmed and our rivals were all carrying it on their front pages!

Horrified, I grabbed a taxi and rushed into the office. Bernie

Vickers didn't speak to me. He didn't have to. His glare said it all. I quickly began to do a catch up and spoke to Sir Hugh at home even although it was after midnight. He was full of apologies for misleading me and explained that when I had been speaking to him representatives from Boots were actually in his home, and that he felt he had to put me off the scent. I told him he had succeeded in his aim but that he may have cost me my job. Sir Hugh explained that by selling the House of Fraser he would be able to concentrate on expanding SUITS and although he would remain on the Fraser board he would be putting his energies into SUITS.

I wrote the story up along these lines and put it across to Vickers who would normally have gone home around 10.30pm, but had stayed on because of Boots-Fraser story.

Within minutes Vickers summoned me across to the back bench in the centre of the editorial floor where he sat. He quietly informed me that he had two differing version of the takeover bid – one from Mirror City editor Bob Head, stating that Sir Hugh was to become the new chairman of the merged Boots and Fraser chain, and mine which said he would only be a non-executive director and would be concentrating on SUITS. "Which," he asked, "is true?" I swallowed hard and said that I stuck by my story.

"Alright, my boy," said Bernie. "I will use yours but it had better be right." Sir Hugh had told me that he was flying to London next morning and I was ordered to make sure I was on the same flight as him and to get a face-to-face interview on the takeover bid. I booked into the Excelsior Hotel at Glasgow airport and fell into bed around 2am, rising again at 6.30am to catch the first London flight.

I sat near Sir Hugh and grabbed hold of him as he left the aircraft at Heathrow. Looking rather sheepish he apologised again for having misled me and agreed to give me an interview in his Harrods office that afternoon. The meeting took place in the wood-panelled office which was his London base although the headquarters of the group continued to be firmly based in the Fraser store in Buchanan Street, Glasgow across from the original store.

Sir Hugh was in an expansive mood. He declared, "It might have been different if I had a son. I have three daughters, but if I had a son I would naturally have expected, or hoped, that he would have followed me into the business and succeeded me as chairman."

Sir Hugh at that time was 36 and had been involved in the House of Fraser since he left school at 17, when he had joined the company as a counter assistant earning £5 a week in the dress fabrics department. He was already a multi-millionaire and did not appear to need the £1 million plus which the sale of his personal shares in House of Fraser would bring him.

The interview made headlines at the time, but it is difficult to believe that the absence of a male heir to carry on the Fraser name was the real reason behind the proposed sale. Perhaps the truth was that the seeds of destruction had already been sown? The Boots takeover was eventually blocked by the Monopolies and Mergers Commission and under Sir Hugh's chairmanship both the House of Fraser and SUITS continued to grow, adding to the personal wealth of Sir Hugh.

But it was obvious his heart was no longer in the business. In July, 1974 SUITS sold 24 million Fraser shares to the American store group Carter Hawley for £28 million, giving the Americans a 20 per cent stake in Frasers. That same year Sir Hugh announced that he had joined the Scottish National Party following discussions with Winnie Ewing MP and party chairman William Wolfe. He told me, "I will be donating some of my personal wealth to party funds."

On the surface Sir Hugh still appeared to be on a continuous roller coaster to success. By 1976 the 146 stores in House of Fraser had a massive £400 million a year turnover with profits of £20 million. But, known to only a few friends, a timebomb was already ticking away. It was to lead eventually to Sir Hugh losing both his business empires.

Unknown to the business world or the public at large, Sir Hugh was an addicted gambler. This flaw in his character may have been hidden for some time, and indeed may never have been revealed had there not been a mistake in the SUITS accounts. SUITS had shown in their 1975 figures £4 million as 'cash at bankers', but when the following year's accounts were released it transpired that this money was in fact loaned to a property company, Amalgamated Caledonian Ltd, who had run into difficulties and the money had to be written off. Shareholders in SUITS were unaware of this costly error until the '76 accounts were issued. The accounts also revealed that Sir Hugh Fraser had sold more than 1,500,000 shares in the company before the loss was disclosed. He had sold most of these at 91p while once the disclosure was made the shares rapidly fell to 53p.

Allegations came thick and fast that the shares had been sold before the mistake was revealed in order to take advantage of the higher share price. A Stock Exchange investigation committee was set up to examine the sale of shares by Sir Hugh and other directors. Sir Hugh in his own defence told me, "Harry, I have nothing to hide. I did not give a thought to the loan. I sold the shares for personal reasons – one of them was to reduce overdrafts, and when I require money I look around at what assets I can realise."

Neither of us knew then that it was the beginning of the end of Sir Hugh's reign as a business tycoon. The following day I visited the SUITS registrar and asked to inspect the records of the buying and selling of shares. I pored over the columns of figures but could not trace Sir Hugh's dealings. Fortunately for me, that day I had a private lunch appointment at a firm of stockbrokers, Easton Goff. Leaving the lunch with an accountant I commented on the fact that I was trying to track down Sir Hugh's share dealings but could find no trace of them in the records. "Ask to see the directors' share register," he suggested.

I returned to the registrar's and followed his suggestion. At first the staff returned with the exact same volumes I had already examined. I insisted that it was the directors' register I wanted to see, explaining that it was a much smaller book. The clerkess disappeared into the back office and returned with a more senior member of staff. He asked me exactly what I wanted, although I knew full well that he knew exactly what I was after. I explained patiently adding that I did have the right to inspect the records.

Finally, with great reluctance, I was handed the small record book which was to be a goldmine of information for myself, and the Daily Record, but unfortunately a crippling blow to Sir Hugh.

The register showed that Sir Hugh was a regular dealer in SUITS shares, mostly as a seller. From January to June 1976 he had sold 1,333,500 for more than £1 million, and did not buy any back.

I broke the story in the Daily Record. The next day I decided to check on what Sir Hugh had been doing with his stake in the House of Fraser. Using my new-found knowledge of a directors' register, I soon obtained details of Sir Hugh's dealings in the store group shares. The House of Fraser register showed that from September 1975 until July 1976 Sir Hugh had sold 621,899 shares for more than half a million pounds. Sir Hugh obviously had a very large overdraft to clear!

The following week at the SUITS annual general meeting in the Merchants' Hall, Glasgow, Sir Hugh announced that he was standing down as managing director of SUITS although he would stay on as non-executive chairman. He told the angry shareholders that he had not known until May of that year that the loan to Amalgamated Caledonian had been wrongly classified in the accounts as cash at bankers. He explained that he had reported this to the directors in June but it was felt it would be 'misleading' to make the matter public at that time. The company's auditors Touche Ross accepted responsibility for not spotting the error and resigned. A Stock Exchange investigation committee were examining the affair and Sir Hugh told the shareholders it would be wrong to comment on his selling of shares as the committee was carrying out their investigation.

The committee did not report until the end of November and it proved to be a real Christmas Cracker. The report, a copy of which was sent to the Department of Trade, revealed that Sir Hugh bought and sold shares in SUITS according to his luck on the gambling tables. It stated that, "He admitted with natural reluctance that these were made to meet gambling losses," and added, "When asked why he bought back SUITS shares again in the latter half of October and in November and December 1975 he replied that during these months he had made gambling profits and had repurchased shares with the proceeds.

However at the start of 1976 Sir Hugh had another bad run at the roulette tables and continued to sell shares without any purchases. He explained that "he was having a run of gambling losses and having to meet increased quarterly bank interest payments." The Stock Exchange investigators checked with London casinos who confirmed that Sir Hugh had in fact made huge losses at the tables during this period.

A few days after the Stock Exchange findings were issued I met Sir Hugh in his Glasgow HQ. Pressure was building for him to quit the board of SUITS and during this interview he gave the first hint of what might lie ahead. He declared that he had given up gambling – a claim which unfortunately proved to be untrue. Commenting on his gambling habit he said wryly, "My only regret is that I was not the owner of the casino." But he added defiantly, "I would like to make it clear, and this is something that people forget, it was my own money I was gambling with. No one knows about the profits I made, but I was unlucky and my trouble was I did not know when to stop."

Despite his gambling-induced selling of shares Sir Hugh and his family trusts still held a massive 36 per cent stake in SUITS and he made it clear that if he was forced to quit the SUITS board these shares would be sold. He sounded a warning to those putting pressure on him to quit, "It would be my concern to whom I sold the shares, not the financial institutions."

Three months later in March 1977 Sir Hugh carried out his threat. He sold 7.5 million of his family's shares in SUITS to Lonrho for £7 million and stepped down as chairman of the company to make way for the controversial figure of 'Tiny' Rowland, the boss of Lonrho. Sir Hugh had been correct – the financial institutions were helpless in influencing who he sold the shares to but they showed their displeasure when Aleck Mackenzie, chairman of Scottish

Widows, a leading Scottish life insurance company, resigned from the SUITS board. Mr Mackenzie had joined the board at the time of the saga over the £4 million loan to a property company which was shown in the accounts as cash at bankers. He had joined to look after the interests of the financial institutions, but Sir Hugh, angry at the pressure being put on him to resign, had decided to put two fingers up to the City. The deal meant that Lonrho held a 24 per cent stake in the company while Sir Hugh and his family retained an 11 per cent holding, and Sir Hugh became deputy chairman.

The emergence of Lonrho on the scene was the beginning of a complex series of boardroom battles both within SUITS and the House of Fraser. Sir Hugh first opposed Lonrho in their bid to take over the House of Fraser which resulted in him being thrown off the SUITS board. He then switched sides and supported Lonrho which led to him being removed as chairman of the store group and finally quitting the board.

The continuous thread running through this sad series of events was Sir Hugh's continued gambling debts which led to him owing London casinos large amounts in IOUs making him vulnerable to pressure. At the time I asked Sir Hugh why Lonrho had stopped at a 24 per cent holding and had not made an all-out bid for SUITS. He told me, "They suggested 24 per cent. They wanted an investment in the company but did not want it to be too big."

It did not take Lonrho long to change their mind. A year later, in April 1978, they made a £40 million bid for the entire company supported by Sir Hugh and another fellow director James Gossman who had been a close friend of Sir Hugh's father. The three other non-Lonrho directors opposed the bid. The Labour Government referred the bid to the Monopolies and Mergers Commission. It became a long drawn out battle lasting for more than a year, details of which are described in the next chapter. Suffice to say here that Sir Hugh's inability to withstand pressure and make a firm decision was clearly illustrated in the SUITS takeover saga. He began the battle siding with Lonrho but switched sides later on as it became clear that Lonrho had the House of Fraser firmly in their sights. A takeover of SUITS would have given them a 29 per cent stake in the store group putting them in a strong position to make a successful bid for the store group.

By the middle of 1978 Sir Hugh's public image was fraying at the edges. In June he appeared at Glasgow Sheriff Court with several other SUITS directors charged with a number of breaches of the Companies Act relating to the £4 million loan which was 'lost' in the 1975 accounts. The trial lasted eight days and Sheriff J Irvine Smith issued a reserve judgement in July. Sir Hugh was fined £100 for failing to give a true and fair view of the affairs of SUITS in the balance sheet. He had already plead guilty to failing to notify SUITS within fourteen days of 60 shares transactions and was fined £500 on this charge. Several other directors were also fined on a number of charges. In his judgement the Sheriff said he was satisfied the misclassification had not been done wilfully, but he also said it was "difficult to resist" the conclusion that many questions had not been answered during the trial – and that many others had not been asked.

The trial ended on a farcical note when Sir Hugh reached into his inside jacket pocket and drew out his cheque book as he left the dock and made towards the Sheriff's bench to pay the fine. The clerk of court intercepted him to explain that he did not pay the Sheriff.

It was not only Sir Hugh's business life which lurched from one crisis to another but also his private life. In 1973 he married Aileen Ross, the daughter of a neighbouring Stirlingshire farmer and a champion showjumper in a romantic secret wedding on the Caribbean island of Mustique. It was a setting fit for a multi-millionaire tycoon but they separated in 1976 and finally divorced in 1982. Two years later Aileen was killed when her microlight aircraft crashed into the North Sea off Inverbervie.

Following his separation from Aileen Sir Hugh became friendly with 32-year-old Lynda Taylor but the relationship ended in tragedy when in 1979 she committed suicide in the garage of Sir Hugh's house at Cattermuir Lodge near Drymen.

I did not normally become involved in Sir Hugh's complex

love life as I had to have an ongoing relationship with him covering business affairs – news reporters normally covered the 'scandal' stories. But when the story broke about Aileen's death I was dragged in. The news desk had been trying desperately to track Sir Hugh down and I found out that he was due to visit the A C Illum store in Copenhagen the following day. I informed the news desk of his movements but warned them that he would not speak about Lynda's death.

The following morning when I came into the office a freak blizzard was blowing up. I was told that the editor wanted me to catch the late morning flight from Glasgow to Copenhagen. I was not prepared. Unlike the press men in the movies I did not carry my passport around with me. Indeed as events were to prove I didn't even possess a passport, and for the second time in my career my involvement with Sir Hugh was to put my job on the line.

An office car was despatched through the blizzard to my home in Kings Park about three miles away to collect my passport while I phoned home to ask Margaret to look it out and gather together some overnight things for me. A few minutes later Margaret phoned back to say she had found the passport but it was out of date! I was not the most popular man in the office when I passed on this piece of information to the editor. I was told I had better get myself a visitor's passport and catch that plane or else. A photographer took my passport photograph while Margaret searched out the necessary documents and sent them back in the car which had to plough through the six inches of snow that was grinding traffic to a halt back to the office at Anderston Quay to pick me up and take me to the passport office in West Nile Street.

This all had to be done against the clock as take-off time approached for the Copenhagen flight. But the blizzard saved my bacon. By the time I had managed to obtain a passport and drive to the airport I should have missed the flight. But because of the weather conditions the flight was delayed! Several newspapers had tracked down Sir Hugh to Copenhagen and I joined several reporters at the check-in desk, including Jack Webster of the Scottish Daily Express.

I knew that Sir Hugh was booked first class on a flight from Copenhagen to London that evening. I had a first class ticket for the same flight and in a spirit of camaraderie told Jack this as we waited at Glasgow Airport. He phoned his office and arranged for them to book him on the same flight, first class.

By the time we reached Copenhagen Jack and I decided that it was not worth our while travelling into the centre of the city as Sir Hugh would probably be on his way back to the airport. We were checking that Sir Hugh was still booked on the same flight when we spotted him racing up a stairway towards the departure lounge. He had switched flights at the last minute in an attempt to give us the slip. Jack and I gave chase and just as Sir Hugh reached the departure gates he turned and said, "Sorry, I'm late for my plane. I can't comment," before disappearing through the gates leaving us both dumbfounded.

We discovered he had switched to an Amsterdam flight, from where he would catch a connection to Glasgow. All we could do was phone our news desks and warn them to meet him at Glasgow airport as he came off the flight from Amsterdam. Jack and I then caught our plane to London and enjoyed the benefits of first class travel without having to worry about Sir Hugh. We both enjoyed the champagne and fillet steaks which were served up while Jack puffed a cigar – I didn't smoke. I was booked into the Piccadilly Hotel in London where I stayed overnight before catching a shuttle flight back to Glasgow next morning. The round trip cost the Daily Record almost £1,000 for nine words – over £100 a word!

Meanwhile in the world of big business Sir Hugh was becoming hopelessly entangled. He had begun by supporting Tiny Rowland when Lonrho made a bid for SUITS, then eleven months later, in March 1979, he made a U-turn and opposed the Lonrho takeover bid. Lonrho eventually took over SUITS and with it a substantial shareholding in the House of Fraser. Sir Hugh resigned from the SUITS board in May 1980, and in typical cavalier fashion Rowland replaced him with Hugh Fraser MP!

By then the battle lines were being drawn up as Lonrho lined themselves up for a bid for the store group. Sir Hugh Fraser, as chairman of the House of Fraser opposed this – at least to start with. Following their successful takeover of SUITS, Lonrho held 29 per cent of Fraser shares and in June 1980 began to flex their muscles. They demanded that the board's recommendation of a final dividend of 4p be increased by 2p. They also opposed the re-election of four directors and proposed four Lonrho nominees in their places.

I met Sir Hugh in his Buchanan Street office as he mobilised opposition to Lonrho. It was only a few weeks since he had resigned from the SUITS board and he described his relationship with Tiny Rowland as "ice cold". It was only a few days before the House of Fraser AGM and Sir Hugh was urging small shareholders to use their vote. He told me, "They are attempting to gain control of the House of Fraser. They are opposing four people who have spent a lifetime in the company." Sir Hugh declared, "The time for compromise is over. We must win." He argued that Lonrho would never get the 75 per cent support they required to overturn the directors on the dividend issue but pointed out that they only required to gain 51 per cent support on the question of directors and were starting with 29 per cent of the shares in their pocket. If they succeeded in their bid to have their nominees elected to the board Sir Hugh believed this would give them control of the company without the cost of a takeover.

Sir Hugh appeared to regret that his friendship with Tiny Rowland had come to an end. He told me, "We used to have dinner every two or three weeks. But he thought that once he had me as a friend, he had me as a yes-man and there would be no way I would do that." Of Tiny he said, "The man has done well but he has the style of a dictator." He mused, "I learned a lot from Mr Rowland. It is only a pity that it has finished the way it has."

A week later Sir Hugh enjoyed a personal triumph when Lonrho conceded defeat at the AGM and did not press their motions to a card vote. Sir Hugh's report to the packed meeting in the Merchants' Hall in George Square, Glasgow attracted loud applause. He was re-elected a director with only 100,000 votes cast against him compared to the 70-odd million in his favour. After the meeting Tiny Rowland claimed that given the chance he could double both the company's profits and their dividend. Sir Hugh retorted sharply, "He should double his own profits first." Sir Hugh had expressed the hope that if Lonrho failed in their bid they would depart from the House of Fraser scene. This was not to be and seven months later, in January 1981, he was to be personally involved in an amazing about turn which would finally end his reign at the head of the Fraser empire.

Six months later Sir Hugh and I met yet again in his Buchanan Street office. We spoke beneath an oil portrait of his father while he continually puffed cigarettes. The store group was heading for another confrontation with Lonrho who had forced an extraordinary general meeting of the company to overturn the board's decision to sell its London Oxford Street property of DH Evans for £29 million and lease it back. He expressed frank views on his relationship with Tiny Rowland, and Lonrho. For the first time he expressed regret over his decision to become involved with Lonrho when he sold them his SUITS shares. He said, "With hindsight it was a mistake to become involved with Mr Rowland. But he was very plausible. We had dinner very frequently, and were great friends. I should have looked round very carefully before doing what I did. He was very friendly as long as I could provide a useful service."

But Sir Hugh was confident that he could repeat his success of June 1980 when under his leadership the board had thwarted Lonrho's attempt to increase the final dividend by 2p. However he told me, "If I lose, then I will not be chairman of the House of Fraser." He was scathing in his criticism of Lonrho's tactics. "It is polite to call it harassment. It is sabotaging the company, the action he is taking. It is not in the interests of the company."

He sounded a defiant note when he remarked, "I have a good team. I am a draper and know the business better than Mr Rowland." On January 21 Sir Hugh led the board to another resounding victory over Lonrho when 71 million shares were cast in the board's favour against Lonrho's 51 million.

But after the meeting Tiny Rowland said darkly, "This is only the second round. It is really only the beginning and Sir Hugh knows it." Two days after the extraordinary general meeting victory, Sir Hugh made an amazing turnaround. He announced his support for Tiny Rowland following a meeting in the Marine Hotel, Troon, saying that Tiny reminded him of his father. That meeting had followed a letter from Lonrho to Sir Hugh concerning his gambling habits. A copy of the letter had been sent to the Fraser board prior to the EGM. The full contents of the letter were never revealed but it contained references to Sir Hugh's gambling activities. Following his *volte face* Sir Hugh described to me the events leading up to his decision to switch sides yet again! He revealed how he had been asked to resign as Chairman of House of Fraser because of his gambling habits.

The resignation call had been put to him by Lord Garmoyle of the merchant bankers Warburgs, advisers to the House of Fraser. Sir Hugh admitted to me that he still gambled despite his claim to have given up the habit more than a year previously. He was unrepentant, "Lots of business people go to casinos. I have gone to them. I built up a business taking risks."

Sir Hugh failed to realise that it was not his visits to casinos that was causing the problem but the IOUs which he owed to several gambling clubs in London. No one would have complained if Sir Hugh's visits to casinos were merely an innocent form of relaxation, but Sir Hugh was an addicted gambler. He built up huge losses as he played several roulette tables simultaneously. His losses were of such proportion they were putting his huge private wealth at serious risk. Sir Hugh had refused Lord Garmoyle's request. The next day came the telephone call from Tiny Rowland. He was calling from Paris and arranged to fly into Prestwick to meet Sir Hugh at the Troon hotel. Sir Hugh emerged from the meeting and posed for photographs for the Glasgow Herald, part of the SUITS stable. He announced his support for Tiny Rowland.

He told me, "We agreed to bury the hatchet. But I made it clear that I would be acting in the interests of all shareholders." It remained unclear what role the letter concerning his gambling habits had played in his sudden change of heart. But it later emerged that a private detective had followed Sir Hugh round the London casinos. Lonrho denied hiring the detective. They said that with the reconciliation of Sir Hugh and Tiny Rowland the letter had "no longer any relevance".

In August 1984, however a Department of Trade report by QC John Griffiths into Lonrho's dealings in House of Fraser shares revealed the extent of Sir Hugh's plight. The report cleared Lonrho of improper dealings to gain more influence over the store group but it threw more light on the pressure Sir Hugh had been under. The report revealed how a London gambling casino boss admitted passing photostats of bounced cheques from Sir Hugh to Lonrho and alleged that Sir Hugh sold shares in Scottish Universal Investments to Lonrho to clear gambling debts. The report also described how a Lonrho subsidiary had provided Sir Hugh with "a large financing loan".

The major financial institutions who held 30 per cent of the shares in the store group were incensed by Sir Hugh's sudden change of allegiance and a board meeting was called in London. It was to signal the end of the Fraser dynasty at the head of the House of Fraser. His fellow directors ousted him as chairman. Only the Lonrho directors supported him. Sir Hugh was replaced by Professor Roland Smith who had joined the board a year earlier to represent the major financial institutions who between them held 30 per cent of the shares in the company. Lonrho reacted immediately by announcing a £157 million takeover bid, and vowed, "If we win – and we will – Sir Hugh will be executive chairman of the House of Fraser."

Sir Hugh was now nothing more than a pawn in the battle for control of the group. Never again would his family control the company. After the board meeting at which he was removed as chairman, Sir Hugh declared that he no longer gambled. The declaration had an empty ring, following as it did several other similar claims which proved to be untrue. His consistency in gambling equalled his consistency in changing sides.

Sir Hugh flew to Scotland the next day and I was one of the

press waiting to meet him. He tried to put a brave face on his removal from office and brandished tape recordings which he replayed to us in the arrivals hall at the airport as fellow passengers jostled to get by. The tape recordings were of a meeting he had with Fraser directors.

However in an attempt to divert attention from his fall from power, Sir Hugh revealed that he had a new woman in his life. He told the reporters, "I just wish I had met her twenty years ago. We intend to marry when we are both free." He refused to name her but when I got back to the Daily Record office it only took a few phone calls to contacts close to Sir Hugh to discover that his latest flame was a 25-year-old schoolteacher, Annabell Finlay.

His new romance certainly diverted tabloid newspaper attention from his boardroom troubles at the House of Fraser. Sir Hugh convened a photocall at Rouken Glen, a park on the outskirts of Glasgow, to introduce his new girlfriend and posed for photographs with Annabell beside the pond in the park. But real life went on and Lonrho continued their battle for control of the store group. Sir Hugh was now little more than a bit player, throwing his personal and family trust shareholding behind Lonrho. But the Monopolies and Mergers Commission became involved in what was to be a long-running battle.

In February 1982 he resigned from the House of Fraser board although he still held 700,000 shares in the company and his family trust controlled 5 million. Despite his expensive and disastrous addiction to gambling he was still a wealthy man. In addition to his personal stake in the House of Fraser he owned three farms in Stirlingshire, the Winnock Hotel in Drymen, a small building company and a garage. He also had a string of twenty horses.

Having cut himself off from the House of Fraser Sir Hugh set about creating a third empire, having lost the first two – House of Fraser and Scottish Universal Investments. Allander Holdings was to be the vehicle for Sir Hugh's comeback.

The former tycoon had a vision of it becoming a second SUITS, with property, retail, manufacturing and investment divisions. Within months of resigning from the Fraser board he took over the site of the former Paisleys store in Jamaica Street, Glasgow, and opened a Sir Hugh store which was intended to be the flagship of his new chain of upmarket menswear shops. He described it as the "biggest gamble of his life" which for Sir Hugh was not the most apt description to use. Within fifteen months the Jamaica street store closed although other smaller shops which he had opened in places such as Ayr, Largs, Bearsden and Helensburgh continued to operate.

Sir Hugh spent the next two years acquiring a variety of small businesses ranging from a cosmetic business on the island of Coll in the Hebrides to knitwear factories in Aberdeen and Tillicoultry, and even a small newspaper in the West End of Glasgow. He also owned a majority stake in Air Charter which bought and sold small aircraft as well as chartering them.

The newspapers were still interested in Sir Hugh's activities and I arranged to have him photographed beside his fleet of small aircraft. I also foolishly agreed that I would fly with him in one of them to visit his Glen Gordon knitwear factory in Aberdeen.

The morning of the picture session was very blustery and I was hoping that Sir Hugh had forgotten my agreement to accompany him on the trip, but no such luck. After the photographs had been taken, and Sir Hugh was about to take off with BBC reporter Leslie Anderson accompanying him, he shouted, "Harry, you said you were coming with me." I had little choice but to clamber into the back of the tiny Piper Aztec and strap myself in beside Leslie. The take-off was bumpy to say the least, and my head collided with the roof of the plane several times. I am not particularly afraid of flying but I prefer large aircraft where there is something fairly solid between you and the elements. The flight north was hair raising. Not only were we being tossed about by the strong winds, but the pilot handed the controls over to Sir Hugh!

I couldn't believe it. I had driven with Sir Hugh several times in a sports saloon and was not too impressed by his attitude towards speed, so I didn't relish the thought of him throwing us around the sky. We reached the approach to Aberdeen Airport safely, and I could see through the swaying cockpit window the runway below us. For I minute I thought, "Don't tell me Sir Hugh is going to bring us in to land?" Then the pilot said he would take over the controls. Sir Hugh looked over his shoulder and asked, "Well, how did I do, boys?"

"Great," we replied, trying to disguise the relief in our voices. Sir Hugh showed us around his Aberdeen knitwear factory which made gloves and scarves to be sold in High Street chains such as Marks & Spencer and British Home Stores. After lunch we headed back to the airport for our flight south. Leslie had gone off to the BBC studios in Aberdeen, which left me alone with my thoughts in the back seat of the aircraft. The heater wasn't working, making me wonder unkindly what else was not working. It was pitch black as we flew south and I prayed fervently that we would manage to fly over the mountains I had seen on the journey north and not through them. We landed safely at Glasgow and such was my relief that I didn't notice what speed he drove when he gave me a lift into Glasgow. I was just relieved to be back home, alive.

Sir Hugh asked for my advice when he decided to make a move into newspapers. Despite the fact that he had once been chairman of a company which owned not only the Glasgow Herald and Eventing times as well as local papers such as the Hamilton Advertiser and the Airdrie & Coatbridge Advertiser, Sir Hugh had no understanding of newspapers. Not only was I a journalist, but I was also actively involved in the National Union of Journalists as an executive member and negotiated with companies throughout Scotland.

This led to Sir Hugh inviting me to lunch in the Fountain Restaurant at Charing Cross, Glasgow to discuss his intention to buy a small newspaper in Glasgow. He later called at my home in Kings Park to collect background documents on the industry, but like his other ventures it did not prove to be a success.

Once again Sir Hugh's love life did not run smoothly. Two years after he announced to the waiting press that Annabell was "the best thing that has ever happened to me", the romance fell apart. Two wedding dates had been postponed. The first, in August 1982, was to have been a full-blown society wedding at the Turnberry Hotel on the Ayrshire coast. It was cancelled because Sir Hugh's divorce from Aileen Ross had not been finalised. A second date was put off because of pressure of business.

Annabell, a divorcee, had been living at Sir Hugh's family home at Mugdock. She moved out in January 1983 saying tearfully that Sir Hugh had told her their romance was off. Sir Hugh told me, "Annabell is a sweet kid, but I don't want to make a third mistake."

My days of Sir Hugh-watching ended in September 1985 when I left the Daily Record to become General Secretary of the National Union of Journalists. By this time Sir Hugh rarely featured in the news. His attempt to build a third Fraser empire had failed. In the beginning I had followed his successes as he expanded his empire, and had interviewed him in the elegant wood-panelled offices in Buchanan Street and Knightsbridge. Later after his fall from power I had met him in his tiny Allander Holdings office at the end of a lane in Milngavie and in the dingy setting of the Sir Hugh store in Jamaica Street. It was sad to witness his fall from power. He was always a shy person who was rarely without a cigarette. He had genuine warmth and a lovely friendly smile. I liked him as a person and the addiction to gambling which brought about his downfall should be recognised as an illness. Sir Hugh did not have the cunning to match those he had to deal with in the world of big business, but that should not be counted as a great fault. Neither did he have the ruthless streak required to succeed in the jungle that is the City.

Sir Hugh Fraser was a very human person, who despite his great wealth, did not enjoy a great deal of personal happiness in his life. His family trusts helped a great number of needy and worthy causes in Scotland including assisting the National Trust to secure for the nation the island of Iona.

I was genuinely saddened when, sitting in my office in London in May 1987, I read of his death from cancer.

14. Get your Tanks off my Lawn

LONRHO SUDDENLY became a major figure on the Scottish financial scene overnight when, in March 1977, they bought 7.5 million shares in Scottish and Universal Investments from the Fraser family.

Lonrho paid Sir Hugh Fraser £7 million for the 24 per cent stake in the industrial holding companies whose portfolio included several leading Scottish companies such as Outrams, publishers of the Glasgow Herald and Evening Times, Scottish & Universal Newspapers, a chain of twenty local papers, and Whyte & Mackay the whisky company.

SUITS was not a high profile company within Scotland as it was seen, quite rightly, by most financial pundits, as the investment arm of the Fraser dynasty. But the arrival of Lonrho was soon to make SUITS a household name.

Among the company's many holdings was a 10 per cent stake in the House of Fraser, and it soon became clear that Lonrho had their eye on the department store chain, or more accurately Harrods!

Sir Hugh made the decision to divest himself of the SUITS shares shortly after relinquishing the position of managing director of SUITS following the embarrassing revelations in the media that he had sold more than one million shares in the company to clear gambling debts. Earlier ther had been the embarrassing episode when the company was forced to write off of a £4 million property loan which had appeared in the company's accounts as 'cash at bankers'.

Following the share deal with Lonrho Sir Hugh stepped down as chairman of the company to take up the deputy position while Tiny Rowland, boss of Lonrho, became chairman.

Lonrho's emergence as major shareholders in SUITS provoked an immediate reaction from the financial institutions who held shares in the company. Aleck Mackenzie, chairman of Scottish Widows, the leading Scottish life assurance company, resigned from the board and the firm's merchant bankers, Robert Fleming, also threatened to quit.

This was not a surprising reaction from the financial institutions who had had a prickly relationship with Lonrho for many years. In 1973, when Tiny Rowland was embroiled in a fight with City Establishment figures, Prime Minister Ted Heath had referred to actions by the company as "the unacceptable face of capitalism."

At first it was claimed that Lonrho were treating their 24 per cent stake in SUITS as an investment. But within a year, in April 1978, Lonrho made a £40 million bid for the company, initially with the support of Sir Hugh Fraser. The three independent directors of the company, led by Hugh Laughland, the managing director, opposed the offer.

It was the start of seven years of continuous in-fighting. First SUITS, then House of Fraser became a battleground as Lonrho fought to gain control of both companies.

I became personally embroiled in the battle following a phone call to my home in High Burnside by Bruce Fireman, a merchant banker with Charterhouse Japhet who were advising the independent SUITS directors in their opposition to Lonrho. Fireman asked me if I would be interested in writing a story if the SNP candidate in the Garscadden by-election were to call for the Lonrho bid to be referred to the Monopolies and Mergers Commission.

I said Yes, but putting on my political hat as a Labour Party activist, suggested that it would be a better story if the Labour candidate Donald Dewar made the call since Labour were in

Government at the time. Fireman immediately agreed and I approached Donald with the suggestion. Donald, as ever, was cautious and wanted to know the full facts, but I convinced him that it was crucial that control of such an important company should remain in Scotland. Fireman also had political contacts and was confident that if Roy Hattersley, the Prices Minister was approached then the bid would be referred.

Donald finally agreed to write to Hattersley asking for the referral and the Daily Record carried the exclusive story of the development. I speculated in my story that the Minister was likely to make the referral following an Office of Fair Trading Report. The bid was indeed referred to the Monopolies and Mergers Commission who took nine months to report, but by some strange logic did not block a Lonrho takeover on the grounds of public interest.

My personal feelings on the takeover were at the time, and remain so, that I am against Scottish companies being submerged and their headquarters and decision-making machinery being transferred out of Scotland, thus accelerating the process of turning Scotland into a branch factory economy.

This is a view with which many within Scotland's financial circles agree, although they are wary of being tagged with a Scottish Nationalist label. These feelings were to the fore in the Lonrho bid for SUITS. Added to these 'Tartan' sentiments was the view that Lonrho were trying to buy SUITS cheaply, particularly taking account of the company's substantial block of House of Fraser shares.

The Fraser shares were worth more than £18 million on the stock exchange, which meant that Lonrho was only paying £22 million for all the other SUITS assets which included whisky and publishing interests.

Lonrho's first offer for SUITS had been eleven of its own shares priced at 71p on the market for every six SUITS shares. This valued the SUITS shares at 130p. Following the clearance from the MMC, Lonrho made a new offer of one Lonrho share plus 100p for each SUITS share. They then increased this to one Lonrho share plus 115p, but still failed marginally to get over 50 per cent of acceptances.

Finally, in May 1979, they upped their offer to one Lonrho share plus 135p which valued each SUITS share at 214p, and this offer eventually won the battle for control of the Scottish company.

My role in the referral to the Monopolies and Mergers Commission became public when Fireman, foolishly as far as I am concerned, spoke to the Financial Weekly in London about the stout battle his bank had organised against Lonrho. In this interview he talked about the assistance received from a person they had nicknamed The Mole during the takeover battle. Fireman explained that The Mole was a Scottish financial journalist who had good political connections.

The Scottish media is not large and it did not take long for people to go through the names of Scottish financial journalists and pinpoint me. I was a member of the National Executive of the National Union of Journalists and known to have close contacts with the Labour Party in Scotland. The result was that I received a phone call from Murray Ritchie of the Glasgow Herald which of course was by this time owned by Lonrho, and asked about my activities during the takeover battle.

There was little point in denying it. The story was never carried, but of course Tiny Rowland knew all about it, and when I next called their Cheapside office in London both Paul Spicer and Rowland made not too unsubtle references to my political leanings.

This episode certainly did not endear me to Lonrho and the Daily Record, in its coverage of both the SUITS and House of Fraser stories, did not take a pro-Lonrho line, not because of my personal beliefs but because, as a Scottish newspaper, they opposed control of Scottish companies being removed from Scotland.

SUITS was now part of Tiny Rowland's substantial international conglomerate which he had created almost single-handedly since the beginning of the sixties. Tiny was born in India in 1917, to an English mother and a German father. After the First World War his family returned to Germany and stayed there until 1938 when they came to the United Kingdom. Tiny then changed his name by deed poll from Furhop to Rowland.

At the outbreak of the Second World War he was conscripted into the British Army, but because of his German parentage was not attached to a combat unit but instead to the Royal Army Medical Corps. He was involved in the Norwegian campaign, but because of his efforts to have his father released from internment he was discharged from the Army in 1942. He was then interned along with his father on the Isle of Man for a short time. On his release he worked as a porter at Paddington Station, London.

Following the War in 1948 he emigrated to Rhodesia, where he took up farming and bought a stake in a small goldmine. In 1961 he was approached by the Hon Angus Ogilvy, who was later to marry Princess Alexandra, to join forces with London and Rhodesian Mining and Land Company which was a small company with a turnover of £4 million a year. He agreed and in return for his mines he received a 26 per cent stake in London & Rhodesia Mining and Land Co which later became known as Lonrho.

Tiny transformed Lonrho into a international conglomerate with interests in forty-four countries, but the company always retained close ties with Africa and Tiny developed a personal relationship with a number of African leaders such as President Nyerere of Tanzania, Jomo Kenyatta of Kenya and President Sadat of Egypt.

In 1972 eight of his fellow directors tried to sack him because of his autocratic style of running the company. Details were revealed of how a director had received secret tax-free payments through the Cayman Islands. Rowland went to the English High Court in an attempt to prevent his own dismissal, but failed. The directors, however, made the mistake of delaying taking action until after an extraordinary general meeting of shareholders which had been called at Tiny Rowland's insistence. The small shareholders and the African interests combined together to defeat the move to sack Tiny and instead called on the eight directors to be removed. The vote in favour of Tiny was an overwhelming 29.5 million votes to 4.5 million.

Tiny brushed aside the personal attacks and continued to manage Lonrho in his highly individualistic style. He was therefore not frightened off by the reaction of the financial institutions to his ambitions in Scotland. He was well schooled in taking on the establishment and winning.

No one doubted during the battle for SUITS that the real goal was the House of Fraser, and with it Harrods. In October 1977 Lonrho had purchased a further 19 per cent stake in the store company from Carter Hawley, the American store group making them already with a 29 per cent holding, the largest single House of Fraser shareholder.

Shortly after their SUITS victory Lonrho began to exercise their muscle as the largest shareholder in the House of Fraser. In April 1980, they called on shareholders to reject the Fraser board's recommendation of a 4p final dividend and proposed instead that the dividend should be increase to 6p. They later added a further demand that the four directors up for re-election should be replaced by Lonrho nominees.

The financial institutions were well aware that Lonrho would soon make a bid for outright control of the store group, and had put in place Professor Roland Smith as deputy chairman of the company in August 1980. Lonrho opposed the appointment. They were highly critical of Professor Smith's fee of £50,000 a year for devoting two days a week to the store group and of his seventeen other directorships.

At the shareholders' meeting in the Merchants' Hall, Glasgow in June, Lonrho were defeated in their attempt to increase the dividend and to replace the outgoing directors with their nominees. But Tiny Rowland had no intention of giving up. The 2p dividend row was only the first shot in a relentless battle.

During the meeting Tiny Rowland sat silently on the platform as deputy chairman of the House of Fraser alongside the other directors, while Tory MP and grandee Edward Du Cann, a Lonrho director, spoke from the floor of the meeting on behalf of Lonrho. Mr Du Cann and Lonrho chairman, Lord Duncan Sandys were to become familiar figures in Glasgow along with Tiny Rowland as the fight for control of the House of Fraser intensified.

Accompanied by other directors of the international

conglomerate, they would fly into Glasgow on board Tiny's private executive jet and then dressed in the uniform of the City, dark pin-striped suits and black crombie overcoats complete with velvet collars, be whisked in large limousines to the latest confrontation.

The AGM attracted massive media publicity as did subsequent meetings. Financial journalists from the Fleet Street papers flew into Glasgow to witness the latest tussle. Invariably during the meetings Tiny would say nothing, allowing the silver tongue of Edward Du Cann to deliver the latest attack on the Fraser board. Then, as the shareholders dispersed immediately after the meetings ended, Tiny would descend from the platform to inform the waiting journalists of his verdict on the proceedings.

Despite the board's victory in the '2p divi' battle there was little respite for the store group. Within six months Lonrho used their near 30 per cent stake in the company to demand an extraordinary general meeting to oppose the board's decision to sell and lease back the DH Evans Oxford Street property in a £29 million deal.

Once again the Fraser board, backed by the financial institutions who had no love for Tiny Rowland or Lonrho, won the day at the EGM which was held in January 1981. However after the meeting Tiny Rowland made it clear that the fight was not over. He told reporters, "This is only the second round. It is really only the beginning and Sir Hugh knows it.

The fight began in earnest within a week of the EGM when Sir Hugh Fraser switched sides and allied himself with Lonrho after the dramatic meeting with Tiny Rowland at the Marine Hotel, Troon, described in the previous chapter. Following Sir Hugh's change of heart the directors removed him as chairman of the company and replaced him with Professor Roland Smith. Lonrho immediately announced they were making a £155 million outright bid for the House of Fraser.

Professor Smith was a tough cookie. He matched Tiny Rowland in size and in determination. He had been put on the Fraser board by the financial institutions, who between them held a 35 per cent stake in the company, to look after their interests and to fend off Lonrho.

I met him only a few days after his appointment on his first day at the company's head office in the Fraser Store in Buchanan Street, Glasgow. Our relationship did not get off to an auspicious start. I had arranged the appointment through the company's public relations advisers but when I arrived at the Fraser store I was kept hanging around and there was no sign of the new chairman actually meeting me. I returned to my office in Anderston Quay and phoned the House of Fraser's PR firm to advise them that "perhaps Professor Roland Smith does not realise that the Record is Scotland's largest selling newspaper and is sympathetic to the board's fight to keep it an independent Scottish company."

I made it clear that I did not appreciate being messed about and did not expect to be treated differently from the Fleet Street brigade. The message obviously got through because within a few minutes I received a call back informing me the chairman apologised for the misunderstanding and would see me as soon as I arrived back at the store!

We soon cleared the air when we met face-to-face and speaking with a broad Manchester accent he told me, "I am not a person to be pushed around. We want to see Lonrho off. The House of Fraser will remain a Scottish company."

The Monopolies and Mergers Commission intervened shortly after my meeting with Professor Smith but did not issue their report until the December of that year when they blocked Lonrho's takeover bid. Lonrho however were not going to be that easily put off. They continued to put pressure on the company.

In September 1982 they demanded another extraordinary general meeting – the third such meeting – to consider their proposal to hive off Harrods. Lonrho also said that following the MMC's decision they "would not wish in the present circumstances to renew the bid." Many City analysts believed that if they succeeded in getting Harrods hived off they would make a separate bid for the Knightsbridge store.

Pressure was brought to bear on Professor Smith who had proved to be a tough opponent and not easily bullied. Lonrho called on the shareholders to sack him. This proposal was withdrawn on the eve of the November 4 EGM but the meeting still produced a head-on clash between the two adversaries when Professor Smith told Tiny Rowland, "Get your tanks off my lawn."

Following the EGM the directors decided that it would not be in the best interests of the shareholders and the company's employees to de-merge Harrods.

Lonrho however did not obey the request to withdraw their tanks. Six months later in May 1983 yet another extraordinary general meeting was called to discuss the de-merger issue. Professor Smith and his board were recommending that Harrods remain within the company. The struggle became even more bitter and ended in the Court of Session in Edinburgh before Lord Mayfield when the Fraser board objected to proxy voting forms sent out by two Lonrho directors who were also directors of the House of Fraser. The judge refused to grant the board an interdict preventing the use of the proxy forms at the EGM due on May 6.

The non-Lonrho directors on the Fraser board made it clear that they would resign if they lost this particular battle. They feared that shareholders might be tempted by the prospect of holding shares in two companies – House of Fraser and Harrods – particularly as many believed that shortly after a de-merger a bid would be made for Harrods as an independent company which would boost the value of the shares and be financially attractive to shareholders.

Lonrho finally failed in their attempt to de-merge Harrods in July 1983 and shareholders were beginning to rebel at what they saw as the continual harassment of the company by Lonrho. The calling of extraordinary general meetings and the issuing of circulars to shareholders were not only taking up management time but also cost the company an estimated £3 million. In September 1984 the shareholders voted on a show of hands against the re-election of Tiny Rowland to the board and his re-election was not supported by the board although there was a call for a proxy vote.

In November 1984 the seven year battle for control of the House of Fraser came to an end when Lonrho announced the sale of their 29.9 per cent stake to Al-Fayad Investment and Trust for £138.3 million. Announcing their decision to get out Lonrho said, "We are fed up with the constant investigations by Government mandarins. We received £138 million – a handsome £72 million profit."

The Fraser board expressed their relief that the long-running saga was over – or so they thought. In March 1985 the Al-Fayed family made a £615 million takeover bid for the entire company backed by the board. It is believed the Fraser board supported the move because they feared renewed interest in the company by Lonrho who had re-appeared as shareholders with a 6.3 per cent stake.

Lonrho were still barred from making a bid by the Monopolies and Mergers Commission and had asked the Government to bring forward the report but the Al-Fayed deal had been concluded before the report was published and the bar was lifted!

Lonrho led by Tiny complained bitterly about the treatment they received at the hands of the Government which prevented them from launching an alternative bid. They also raised questions over the financial standing of the Al-Fayeds. The House of Fraser stores have since been hived off from Harrods, and now stand on their own with the Al-Fayeds keeping control.

Shortly after the Al-Fayed takeover of House of Fraser I gave up my position as Financial Correspondent with the Daily Record in September 1985 to become General Secretary of the National Union of Journalists. The last seven years of my journalistic career had been dominated by the Lonrho – House of Fraser battle. During this period I had attended every shareholders meeting and witnessed the jousting between Tiny Rowland and Professor Smith. I also had a number of verbal jousts myself with the Lonrho chairman and his trusted lieutenant Paul Spicer. Understandably they did not appreciate my involvement in the referral of their bid for SUITS to the MMC or the Daily Record's consistent support for the continued independence of the store group.

During this period I had many conversations with Tiny Rowland both face-to-face and over the telephone when he would deny that it was Mr Rowland speaking but would insist that it was "someone close to Mr Rowland." I can easily accept his description of himself as a 'revolutionary capitalist' and just about accept his claim to have always voted Labour which meant we had at least one thing in common!

I believe history has proved my stance correct during this episode. SUITS has since been dismembered, sold off in bits and pieces, leaving the individual pieces much weaker than the whole. The House of Fraser empire is now controlled from London and once again decision-making has gone south making the Scottish economy that little bit weaker.

15. There was a Crooked Man

HE WAS EVEN LARGER than I had recalled. His voice boomed even louder. But there was no mistaking Robert Maxwell. Flambouyant, loud, and a phoney. It was my first meeting with the man eyeball to eyeball. The year was 1981, and the reason for the meeting was his sacking of six members of the National Union of Journalists employed by Pergammon Press. My only previous encounters with him had been as a journalist, one of a pack, covering the launch of the Scottish Daily News.

In 1981 he was just beginning to expand beyond Pergammon, having taken over BPCC, taking advantage of the new Thatcherite atmosphere of business where anything went and success was counted only in profit terms. Troublesome workers were more easily put down.

He was establishing his credibility with British and international bankers while I was President of the National Union of Journalists, the highest lay position in the union. I was still employed by the Daily Record and Sunday Mail but they had given me a year's paid leave of absence to carry out my Presidential duties. Normally the NUJ's President mainly chaired union meetings and toured branches but I took a more active role in negotiations. It was therefore no surprise that the Pergammon NUJ chapel asked me to intervene in their dispute with Maxwell who had sacked them after they had gone on strike over a wage claim.

Maxwell was always a bully as well as a crook and a conman, and at the time I never for a moment imagined that a few short years later he would sit atop the Mirror Group Newspapers, and therefore be my employer as the Daily Record was part of MGN.

He claimed to be a socialist and a trade unionist, but his response when faced with an industrial dispute, whether official or otherwise, was to threaten to sack the workers involved, and he carried out the threat if he thought he could get away with it. Our dispute at Pergammon had been running for several months and there did not look to be any chance of a settlement as there was little economic pressure our six strikers could bring to bear on Maxwell.

During my first meeting with him he offered three jobs for our six members – one in London, one in Paris and one in Australia! None were at Oxford where our members lived and worked. It was an appalling offer but nevertheless I recommended to our members that they accept, as I believed we were powerless to extract a better deal. The chapel rejected the offer but asked that I continue to negotiate on their behalf. The dispute continued and the six strikers lobbied our delegation at the Blackpool TUC Congress in September. The union delegation which included General Secretary Ken Ashton agreed to seek the assistance of the National Graphical Association, then a powerful print union. During a reception the NGA gave during the Congress I lobbied Joe Wade, the then General Secretary. Joe eventually agreed to instruct his members at Pergammon not to cross our picket lines the following Monday. I then contacted Maxwell asking for another meeting through Sam Wright who at that time was acting as his Personnel Director and had been present at the earlier negotiations.

I asked Sam to convey to Maxwell the fact that the NGA had agreed to respect our picket lines. A meeting was arranged to take place immediately following the TUC, and we agreed the NGA should withhold their instruction to their members not to cross our picket lines until after our meeting had taken place. Maxwell, who always recognised strength, finally came to an agreement. It was not a straightforward settlement, and neither was it a particularly good one for the union or its members. Our six members were re-instated but he would not allow them back inside Pergammon headquarters at Headington. He was no doubt afraid the settlement might be seen as a victory. Instead the six strikers were banished to an office three miles away at Wheatley where no other Maxwell employee worked. They were not allowed to visit the main offices and their only contact with the company was through their supervisor. They were to be industrial lepers and Maxwell always harboured a grudge because he had been forced to take them back.

After the settlement he put his arm around my shoulders and boomed in that false English accent of his, "Well Mr President, you can tell your members that because of your persuasiveness I have agreed to give them their jobs back." My reply was, "You mean it had nothing to do with the NGA agreeing not to cross our picket lines?" After my year as President I returned to work at the Daily Record, and although I continued to be a member of the NUJ's National Executive, and an active trade unionist, I had no personal contact with Robert Maxwell for the next three years.

Then in 1984, disaster struck. Reed International renaged on a public assurance that they had given when the announced plans to float Mirror Group Newspapers. Sir Alex Jarrett assured everyone that it was their intention to sell to the widest possible number of shareholders to protect both the titles and workforce. I was always sceptical of these assurances as once shares are on the market they are vulnerable to any takeover.

Although no longer Father of of the NUJ chapel I was helping the Daily Record and Sunday Mail federated chapel, which represented all trade unions in the building at Glasgow's Anderston Quay in their campaign to secure the future of the Scottish titles. Reed had appointed Clive Thornton, who had previously been boss of the Abbey National Building Society, to oversee the flotation. Thornton was a well-meaning individual and no doubt a good enough administrator, but he was no match for the jungle of raw capitalism.

From the outset the trade union representatives at Anderston Quay did not believe that the Mirror Group could be floated on the stock market in a way which prevented a predator from launching a bid for the entire company . We believed that soon after the flotation a person, or company, would purchase shares to establish a major holding, then make an offer for the remaining shares. Newspapers attract people who enjoy the prestige and power, ownership of a national title gives them. What we did not foresee was that Reed would blatantly break their promise and sell to the worst possible individual buyer.

The federated chapel engaged Cooper and Lybrand to look into the possibility of the Scottish titles being sold off separately, a move that was opposed by our management, particularly by the deputy managing director Liam Kane. Unfortunately we allowed ourselves to be convinced that we should remain within the group after extracting promises of greater local management control over the Daily Record and Sunday Mail and greater representation on the management committee and trustees of the pension fund.

However rumours started to circulate that Robert Maxwell was interested in buying the group. Jarratt assured us that there was no truth in these and that Reed's intention was still to float the company. We were disturbed as the rumours gathered weight and demanded a meeting with Clive Thornton. I was a member of the federated chapel delegation led by Harry Templeton the Imperial Father (Convener) which flew to London to meet Thornton. At that time the federated chapel which represented all the unions at Anderston Quay was a well-organised powerful body.

We had an hour-long meeting with Thornton in his office at Holborn. He told us that he had advised Reed International not to give Maxwell any information about the company as this would prevent him from mounting a bid, then went on to inform us that Reed executives were at that very moment meeting Maxwell. I asked him if he really believed that Reed would not be passing on information to Maxwell about the company.

When he said Yes, I remarked that he must be naive. Thornton believed that it would be at least three weeks before Maxwell would be in a position to bid for MGN and urged us to use this time to organise a political campaign, aimed at the Labour Party, to prevent Maxwell from taking over the company. We agreed, and immediately after leaving his office Harry Templeton and I went downstairs to the Daily Record's London desk and decided to place a half page advert for publication in the next day's Daily Record, expressing the workforce's opposition to any Maxwell takeover. The advert stated,

"THE WORKFORCE OF THE SCOTTISH DAILY RECORD & SUNDAY MAIL LTD DO NOT WANT TO BE OWNED BY ROBERT MAXWELL.

MR MAXWELL IS CURRENTLY ATTEMPTING TO BUY THE PAPERS AS PART OF A BID FOR MIRROR GROUP NEWSPAPERS. MIRROR GROUP IS AT THE MOMENT OWNED BY REED INTERNATIONAL. LAST OCTOBER REED ANNOUNCED THAT THEY INTENDED TO SELL MIRROR GROUP THROUGH A STOCK EXCHANGE FLOTATION TO THE WIDEST POSSIBLE SPREAD OF INVESTORS. SIR ALEX JARRAT (REED CHAIRMAN) SAID IT WAS NOT IN THE BEST INTERESTS OF THE NEWSPAPERS TO BE SOLD TO AN INDIVIDUAL. HE SAID REED INTENDED TO PROTECT THE PAPERS' EDITORIAL INTEGRITY BY ENSURING A WIDE SPREAD OF OWNERSHIP. IT WAS THIS ASSURANCE WHICH PERSUADED SCOTTISH DAILY RECORD & SUNDAY MAIL WORKERS TO ABANDON A CAMPAIGN TO HAVE THE SCOTTISH OPERATION SOLD OFF SEPARATELY. NOW REED'S POSITION APPEARS TO HAVE CHANGED. NEGOTIATIONS HAVE BEEN TAKING PLACE BETWEEN THE REED BOARD AND MR MAXWELL.

SIR ALEX JARRAT HAD SO FAR REJECTED MR MAXWELL'S BID ONLY ON THE GROUNDS OF CASH AND CONDITIONS – APPARENTLY NOT BECAUSE IT CONTRADICTS PREVIOUS ASSURANCES.

THE SCOTTISH WORKFORCE BELIEVES THIS IS TOTALLY UNACCEPTABLE AND INTENDS TO MOUNT THE

STRONGEST POSSIBLE CAMPAIGN TO PREVENT OUR PAPERS
FALLING INTO THE HANDS OF MR MAXWELL."

We phoned the copy over to Glasgow and the advert appeared on page five. But unknown to us it was already too late. At midnight that night Reed announced that they had accepted Maxwell's bid and reneged on all their assurances. There can be few more callous sell-outs in newspaper history.

In the later editions of the Daily Record the story detailing Maxwell's takeover of the papers appeared on the front page, while inside the federated chapel's advert continued to appear. In a first act of defiance our members had refused to remove it. The delegation had been unable to catch the last flight back to Glasgow and had booked into a London hotel. I had gone to bed shortly before 1am not knowing that we had been betrayed and was wakened by a BBC Radio Scotland reporter wanting my reaction to Maxwell's takeover. At first I thought he was only talking about the rumours and told him it wasn't true as we had just spoken to Clive Thornton the previous evening. Then he read out the Press Association story and I realised the worst had happened.

After giving the reporter my reaction, even although it was not yet 7am, I phoned Clive Thornton on his private office number which he had given me the previous evening, with the intention of telling him not to resign and to stay in place for as long as he could so that he could supply us with as much information as possible about the takeover.

Robert Maxwell answered the phone! He boomed down the line that Thornton was no longer with the company. He asked me, "What's this bloody advert all about?" I told him that was the way the workforce felt and that we had a well-run company and he had a reputation of interfering in any company he had an interest in. He assured me that he had no intention of interfering and that we had a good 'manager' in Glasgow in Derek Webster, who was in fact our chairman and editorial director. I asked Maxwell to sell the Scottish company and told him that we knew of several interested parties who would gladly buy us.

He told me, "I don't sell companies. You had better remember who pays your wages." I replied, "Last night it was Reed International who paid our wages." The phone went dead.

The federated chapel made a last desperate bid to try to stop Maxwell from taking over the Scottish titles. We flew from London to Edinburgh to consult a QC to determine if we had any legal redress to prevent Reed International breeching their guarantees to us that the company would not be sold to a single individual. At Edinburgh airport we were met by an array of television cameras and press photographers as a result of our advert which had made our opposition to Maxwell very public.

Our first port of call was the Daily Record's Edinburgh branch office in George Street where a number of messages had been left asking me to phone people. One was from Tam Dalyell, the Labour MP for West Lothian. I thought to myself, "Well this is the support starting to come in." I phoned Tam and was dismayed when he told me that we were getting it all wrong. He informed me that once I got to know Robert Maxwell I would discover he was not such a bad guy. I told Tam that I already knew Mr Maxwell and that the last time I had met him had been over the sacking of six NUJ members. To my disbelief Tam continued to sing Maxwell's praises. I like Tam Dalyell but he carried this misconception of Maxwell right to the end. After Maxwell's death he wrote a laudatory piece in the Sunday Mail! I would love to ask him what he thinks now.

The legal advice we received was negative and the delegation returned to Glasgow to address a mass rally of the workers in the Apollo Theatre, Renfield Street. We had to tell our 1000 members packed into the hall that there were no legal steps we could take to prevent the takeover. There were calls from the floor for industrial action but the Fathers of the Chapel (shop stewards) advised against such action. We did not know at the time that Maxwell was already introducing his bully-boy style of industrial relations, having told our management to inform us that if we did not return to work immediately then we were sacked and the Daily Record would never be published in Scotland again.

Maxwell was a madman and I warned the workforce that what had happened was the worst possible situation. Nothing has happened since then to change my mind. Maxwell's reign of terror, for that is what it was, began immediately. Directors were called to monthly meetings in London and were forced to sit in the corridor outside his office for hours waiting to be called. He interfered in every small detail of the business. Journalists couldn't go abroad on assignments without his express say so, junior clerk vacancies could not be filled until he had given the go-ahead, his trusted lieutenants poured over Anderston Quay.

Nothing was too petty for Maxwell to interfere in whilst also controlling the major investment decisions regarding the plant. Prior to Maxwell's arrival on the scene we had been assured by Mirror Group Newspapers that much needed new printing presses would be installed at Anderston Quay. This had been one of the reasons behind us withdrawing our call for the Scottish company to be sold off separately. After Maxwell bought the company we wanted assurances that this investment would still be made. Allan Watson, the Secretary of the Scottish Graphical Branch of Sogat who represented the majority of the workforce at Anderston, made approaches to Maxwell and it was agreed that Allan and I should meet him privately to discuss his investment plans. We agreed we would meet him discreetly while he was in Glasgow in August 1984 to launch VV Grishin's *Selected Speeches and Writings*. Grishin was the Communist Party boss of Moscow and Maxwell's Pergammon Press had cornered the market in publishing the annals of leading Communists from the Eastern Block!

Allan and I were invited to attend the lunch in the City Chambers, Glasgow which was also to be attended by Mr VI Popov, the Soviet Union's Ambassador to the United Kingdom. Derek Webster and other directors of the Daily Record were also going to be present at the lunch but it was agreed that we would slip away quietly with Maxwell immediately afterwards. The opposite happened.

We were just starting the sweet course when Maxwell asked

everyone to excuse him as he had a meeting with Mr Watson and Mr Conroy.

The Lord Provost had made his private room available and the three of us left the other guests to go off and have our private chat! Maxwell always treated his executives shabbily, believing this would impress people, and showing his contempt for those who worked under him. He excluded Derek Webster from the meeting. Instead of being involved in discussion about the company for which he was responsible, Derek had to hang about outside in the corridor waiting for us to finish our deliberations. I'm sure it was because of such treatment that Derek Webster took early retirement. Maxwell gave us all the assurances we asked for. Three new printing presses would be ordered and installed at Anderston Quay.

The trouble was his word meant nothing. He really did open his mouth and let his belly rumble. Needless to say the presses never arrived. True, six years later in 1991, they almost got there when they were leased and left sitting in crates in an empty bus garage near Anderston Quay.

The MGN flotation document of April 1991 stated, "SDR is making a major capital investment in four new Koenig & Bauer Commander web offset colour printing presses to replace the existing plant which is now twenty years old. The new equipment is expected to be fully operational in 1994. It will allow SDR to produce newspapers with more pages and double the existing colour capacity. Together with its infrastructure, it is expected to cost approximately £83 million (of which £37 million has already been spent)."

The machines never got out of their crates. They had been leased and after Maxwell's death the banks who financed the deal claimed them. New presses were eventually installed by the management who took over from the Maxwell regime, and of course the titles are now printed at a custom-built plant in Cardonald. But none of this had anything to do with Maxwell's empty promises.

Before Maxwell's arrival the Scottish company had been allowed to operate with a fair degree of independence. Maxwell changed all that. The National Union of Journalists Daily Record and Sunday

Mail chapel put their annual wage claim in not long after he took over and I had become yet again the Father of Chapel. We suspected that he would not allow the management to negotiate freely. However our management insisted on carrying out the charade and assured us they had the power to negotiate. We took a detailed minute of every meeting to build up a case to prove that our management did not have this freedom.

Our negotiations began with Hugh Currie, the editorial Manager who made us the company's offer which we rejected. After several meetings with Currie we met Vic Horwood, the managing director of SDR & SM who had no more power to negotiate than Hugh Currie. Eventually we reached a stalemate and demanded a meeting with Maxwell who had made much of the success of the Scottish company and exhorted others in MGN to follow our example. This however did not prevent him from offering us the same percentage increase as the rest of the Group.

We met Maxwell along with Vic Horwood and Hugh Currie in London and after a lengthy meeting he assured us in front of the Scottish management that they had the power to put more money on the table and that we could continue our negotiations with them. We left the meeting satisfied and went downstairs to the Daily Record's London desk. Within ten minutes the phone rang. It was Hugh Currie. He asked if I had left the meeting believing they could negotiate with us and that there would be more money on the table. I replied Yes and he informed me that as soon as we had left the room they had been instructed not to increase the offer. Currie had always negotiated with us in good faith and was sickened by this two-faced approach.

We returned to Scotland and went through the charade of the management claiming they had the 'right to manage'. Some directors could not put up with being Maxwell's puppets. Liam Kane, the deputy managing director, left the company and Derek Webster took early retirement.

In September 1985 I left the Daily Record, which I had first joined as a rooky reporter in October 1964. I had won the election for General Secretary of the NUJ but it was not to be the end of my confrontations with Robert Maxwell. These were to continue almost right up to his death. Indeed I was pitched into meeting him on my very first day as General Secretary at the TUC Congress in Blackpool.

The NGA were on strike at the Mirror's plant in Holborn over the Sporting Life newspaper and the Sunday newspapers had all carried stories of Maxwell declaring that the Daily Mirror would never publish in Holborn again and that the printers were all sacked. Some people never change!

I knew the stories were a load of hogwash because Tony Dubbins the General Secretary of the NGA, (now merged with Sogat to form the Graphical Paper and Media Union), had contacted me to say that meetings had been arranged between him and Maxwell on the Sunday at the start of the TUC in Blackpool and it was agreed that I would make soothing noises about possible negotiations if approached by the media. Tony and Maxwell were ensconced in meetings all Sunday and from time to time I was asked to attend as obviously the journalists on the Sporting Life could be affected by the dispute or settlement. Eventually they hammered out a settlement and I was called up to the meeting to hear the details, which included Maxwell agreeing to sell the Sporting Life. But I was assured the NUJ members jobs would be safe.

Surprise, surprise! Maxwell never did get round to selling the paper. He asked us to keep the details confidential and make no statement to the media. I left the Imperial Hotel through the kitchens to avoid the press who were waiting at the bottom of the stairs in the foyer. Within ten minutes I received a call to say that I should get back to the Imperial as a Maxwell Public Relations Officer was making a full statement to the media. I hurried along Blackpool promenade and on entering the foyer I was faced with Paul Quaide the press officer standing on the stairs reading out a long statement to a mass of eager reporters and cameramen.

Maxwell had done it again. Only fifteen minutes earlier we had shaken hands and agreed to keep the deal confidential!

Understandably none of the workers trusted Maxwell and our

immediate concern was for our pensions. We had reached agreement with Thornton for better representation on the trustee board for all MGN employees but we also had better representation for the 1,000 employed at Anderston Quay. We decided that Harry Templeton who was still Imperial Father should be our trustee on the pension fund because he was known for his blunt honesty and would not be easily intimidated.

Maxwell did not want anyone among the trustees who would challenge him. He regarded the Pension Fund as belonging to him and told us so on several occasions. He tried to block Harry becoming a trustee and made it clear that unless a person was acceptable to him he would not be allowed to become a trustee. The Scottish Graphical Branch of Sogat and the NUJ decided to seek legal advice and after consulting with Glasgow solicitor George Moore, we were directed to an English barrister who specialised in Trust law.

Harry and I met the barrister in London and his advice was not encouraging. He explained that in reality the members of the pension fund had few rights and that basically the Pension Fund belonged to the company which meant in practical terms, Maxwell. Later events as we now know, were to prove how right he was.

Maxwell however, realised that although we might not have the law on our side, we were going to create a public furore and as he did not want any adverse publicity regarding pensions, he backed down. Harry became a trustee but quickly discovered he was almost always in a minority of one in his opposition to Maxwell's manipulation of the pension fund.

It is a pity that some of the highly paid directors and management people who were also trustees did not see where their duty lay instead of going along meekly with Maxwell.

In July 1986 I flew up to Edinburgh with my wife Margaret to meet Maxwell at the opening of the Commonwealth Games which he had 'rescued'! The arrangement had been that Allan Watson and I would meet him after the official opening ceremony. I was by this time accustomed to Maxwell's habit of keeping people waiting for an interminable time, and I had agreed to fly to Edinburgh only if we were definitely going to have a meeting and discuss the problems facing us. I was assured that there would be a meeting but I should have known better.

Maxwell passionately wanted to be accepted by the Establishment and with the Games being opened by Princess Anne, the nearest Allan Watson and I got to him all evening was watching the giant television screen as he glued himself to the Royal party.

His driving ambition in business was to outdo Rupert Murdoch and he told me several times that he would be "bigger than Murdoch". In terms of the MGN this meant the Daily Mirror outselling the Sun. The Record workforce had always been concerned that the London hierarchy might try to subsume the Daily Record into the Mirror so that the Mirror's sales would outstrip the Sun. Maxwell soon realised this and began to make moves to open the way for the Record to become a Daily Mirror edition.

At first he wanted to produce the Northern editions of the Mirror in Glasgow, then he switched to printing the Irish edition. More material from the Mirror in London was being used in the Daily Record and there was talk of a joint Mirror/Record masthead. Together these developments fuelled suspicions that the Record was being prepared for conversion to the Daily Mirror by the back door. There were fears that the print run of the Mirror would take precedence over the Record, which would suffer as a result and Record journalists would be asked to edit the Mirror's Irish edition which would begin to blur the distinction between the two titles.

The workforce were willing to take the extra work on as long as they received assurances that the Record edition changes and times would not suffer in consequence. These assurances were never satisfactorily given and eventually in 1986 the journalists went on strike at the same time as the Sogat printers. Maxwell's reaction, as always, was to sack the strikers. He settled with Sogat but they refused to cross the NUJ picket lines which meant that the papers stayed off the streets. Early on in the dispute he declared that he would "not talk to Conroy until the Clyde froze over." He also said that the NUJ were lions being led by donkeys.

Our chapel held firm with the support of Sogat. After three weeks, during which he sacked the NUJ members three times, Tony Dubbins and Brenda Dean, general secretary of Sogat intervened with Allan Watson. They were locked in negotiations with Maxwell for seven hours before he agreed to meet me face-to-face at 2am.

When I entered the room in Holborn he boomed, "Well Mr Conroy, we meet and the Clyde has not frozen over."

I replied, "It didn't concern me because since Maggie Thatcher de-industrialised Clydeside, the Clyde freezes over frequently." The talks went long into the night. The stumbling block was the management's insistence on the four-day shift week being abolished for journalists. I made it clear that I could not accept this especially for sub editors whose shifts are unsocial.

Eventually Maxwell and I went out into the corridor alone. He said he could not grant me the four-day week for sub editors immediately because of the opposition from his editors. I replied that this was unfortunate because I could not recommend a settlement without the four day week for at least the subs. He then said, "Look, I will re-introduce the four-day week in a month. Give me a month."

I accepted this and we shook hands on the deal. The understanding was that this part of the agreement could not be made public and Mike Smith, the union's national newspaper organiser, had to fly to Glasgow the following day to convince reluctant journalists to return to work with the four-shift week abolished. Understandably this was not popular, but I believed that after a month we would then 'negotiate' the four-day week for the sub editors.

Instead Maxwell reneged on the deal. Two months after the dispute ended I met him to try and enforce our 'gentlemen's agreement' but all I could extract from him was a nine-day fortnight for the subs. In twenty-two years of negotiations only two people have ever deliberately broken their word to me. Maxwell was one of them. The man had no honour. Despite this betrayal I could not call our members out on strike again. They and their families had suffered a great deal during the three week dispute, not only financially but mentally. Maxwell knew this and employed his usual bully boy tactics.

Maxwell's ego knew no bounds. He would insist on photographs of himself being used in the newspapers. Senior journalists were instructed to write stories on how he played an important role on the international stage. Even the Christmas cards he sent displayed his vanity. One showed his family in their graduation gowns outside Headington Hall, his spacious mansion outside Oxford which he rented from the council. Another featured his yacht with the caption, 'The most beautiful yacht in the world'. I didn't have to open it to know who it was from, but I was soon spared this annual embarrassment when he took me off his Christmas card list.

There was no danger however, of Maxwell being accused of playing Father Christmas. When he first took over the Mirror Group he sent all the staff a Royal Family souvenir book. This particular book had been issued with a sovereign coin held in its inside cover, and when the consignment of 1,000 books arrive at Anderston Quay, the management put a security guard on them in case someone tried to nick the coins. There were a few red faces when the books were opened and it was discovered that the space for the sovereign was empty! Maxwell had already nicked the sovereigns.

Another example of his boundless ego was when I met him at his Oxford headquarters with Mirror Group FOCs and while we drank our tea out of normal size cups he grasped in both hands a huge cup with the slogan "For a Very Important Person" emblazoned around its rim. In March 1987 he launched the ill-fated London Daily News.

The NUJ was concerned that we achieved a 'closed shop' on this title just as we had on all the other MGN titles, although since Maxwell's arrival his answer to any industrial action was to threaten the sack and to use the full might of the anti-union laws enacted by Thatcher.

Ironically Maxwell had involved us in his planning for the launch right from the start even before it became public. Mike Smith and I met him privately several times and after the launch became public we met him with his advisor Charles Wintour, a former editor of the

UK Press Gazette who was well known for his anti-NUJ views and was doing his best to prevent the union gaining a close shop.

Maxwell always boasted about being a trade unionist (he was a member of Apex, a union which mainly represented clerical workers) and claimed to insist that the people he employed join a trade union – although God help anyone who tried to organise an effective one! We finally met Maxwell with Charles Wintour and the newly appointed editor Magnus Linklater, who subsequenlty moved on to edit the Scotsman.

One of the reasons Wintour gave for not having a closed shop was that they wanted to produce a 'quality newspaper' and perhaps the best journalists available were not members of the union. I quickly pointed out that the Financial Times, Guardian and Mirror newspapers were all 100 per cent NUJ shops and Maxwell replied, "Mr General Secretary, you are pushing at an open door."

The paper crashed in the face of cut-throat competition from Associated Newspapers, the owners of London's existing evening paper, the Standard, and Maxwell's interference, when without any consultation he announced the new paper would be a twenty-four hour paper and not an evening paper.

On the day of the closure I went to Orbit House opposite the Mirror building to see Maxwell. Mike Smith, the union's national newspaper organiser, accompanied me. Maxwell disliked Mike, mainly because of the support he gave the Daily Record and Sunday Mail members during the strike and always referred to him as 'Brother Smith'. But we did not have a problem as he avoided seeing us. The nearest we got to him was listening to his helicopter take off from the rooftop.

There was no such thing as a good meeting with Maxwell as I realised I could not trust a word he said. However he employed around 700 NUJ members and as General Secretary I had to hide my personal feelings about him as much as possible. The union could only represent its members if we had a working relationship. But it was often difficult to hide your true feelings.

One particular meeting was more nauseating than most. It was the four hour session I had with him over the sacking of John Finlayson, the Father of the Daily Record and Sunday Mail chapel. John had been sacked for calling a union meeting during working hours without management's permission. He had not had the opportunity to defend himself as he had been advised rightly by the union not to attend a disciplinary hearing without Mike Smith, his union official present.

The Scottish management refused to delay the meeting to allow an official to be present and confirmed John's dismissal. We appealed to Maxwell and met him in his plush suite of office on the ninth floor of Maxwell House. Maxwell was supposed to act as some sort of independent arbitrator and come to a decision after hearing both sides of the argument. Endell Laird, editor-in-chief of the Daily Record, and Sunday Mail Personnel Director Kevin McMahon put the management's case while John and I put our side of the story. The meeting lasted for more than four hours. Maxwell loved playing God. We had to massage his ego and appeal to his sense of fair play and justice. There was no alternative to going through this charade because John's livelihood was at stake. It was not pleasant but at least it saved John's job, although Maxwell insisted that he be suspended without pay for three months.

Others sacked under the Maxwell regime were not so lucky, including the twenty-three NUJ members at Pergammon Press who were sacked for withdrawing their labour for twenty-four hours in June 1989. Before his death Maxwell sold the company to Elsevier, a Dutch concern, with the twenty-three memebers still sacked. I had several meetings with Maxwell over this dispute, during which he fulminated against these 'politically motivated' strikers and vowed they would never work for him again, especially their FOC, Jim Boumelha.

His first offer was £3,000 compensation to each of the sacked strikers. I told him that we wanted our members' jobs back and that in any case the financial compensation was not enough. The union rejected this offer. But a year later in June 1990 I recommended to our National Executive to settle the dispute, when he increased the offer to sums ranging from £4,000 to £10,000. There was still no offer of reinstatement, but I believed there was no way the union could win this dispute and sadly recommended that we accept the offer. The NEC rejected this by 10-8 and the dispute went on.

In the lead-up to this offer I met Maxwell with Norman Willis, the general secretary of the TUC, to finalise the compensation offer and to make one final attempt to get our members reinstated. The meeting took place in Maxwell's apartment on the tenth floor of Maxwell House. It was an ugly, opulent setting with mock Roman pillars, chaise-longes, and curtain fabrics in bright red with gold tassels. The meeting began with a conversation about the European newspaper Maxwell had launched and the TUC's contacts on the continent. This led to a discussion between Maxwell and Willis on their respective meetings with President Gorbachev, the Soviet leader. Maxwell boasted, "I had a forty minute meeting with President Gorbachev." I couldn't contain myself and said tongue in cheek, "I'm surprised you could spare him so much time." Maxwell raised his eyebrows and stared across the coffee table at me. He never did appreciate my sense of humour.

I was never to see him again. I lost the re-election for General Secretary of the NUJ in July 1990 and returned to Scotland in the September of that year to become Campaign Director of the Scottish Constitutional Convention. It was only as I was leaving the union's services that I discovered that my pension for the period I was employed with the Daily Record had not be transferred over to the NUJ Pension Scheme, despite my instructions for this to be done. The fault did not lie with MGN but with the administration of the NUJ scheme. I was in the process of transferring the lump sum into a personal pension scheme when Maxwell died.

I had been having a lunchtime drink with a friend from the Daily Record when the news came through that Maxwell was missing from his yacht and that a sea search was underway. No one I spoke to that day or since expressed any regret. In fact, almost immediately the jokes began to circulate. The reaction of the Record management team was to be expected. They issued a statement saying that "the workforce was stunned" and what a great friend Maxwell had been to the Scottish titles.

The truth was that the workforce celebrated the news. The public houses adjacent to the Record actually ran out of champagne as the celebrations continued into the night. Sick, some people might say. Un-Christian, others may remark, but I did not feel the slightest hint of sadness at the man's death. He brought misery to hundreds of workers at the Daily Record and Sunday Mail. He sacked them, he bullied them and he tried to take away their self respect. The reaction of the workers was no doubt partly brought about by relief that his reign of terror was over.

I was approached by the media for my reaction to his death. I told the truth. I said, "Mr Maxwell was no friend of the workers. He increased the profitability of the Scottish titles by brutal and unsavoury methods and I don't think anyone on the shopfloor will be mourning his death." I was informed that my reaction was not what others were saying and my reply to this was, "The difference is, I'm telling the truth. I don't work for the Daily Record and I don't expect to work for the Daily Record so I can afford to tell the truth."

This of course, was before news of the pension swindle broke, but immediately after his death I warned NUJ officials at the Record that it would not be long before the company was in trouble. I felt certain that Maxwell had been ripping off both the company and the pension funds. I had been warned as far back as 1985 by a senior management figure who had quit working for Maxwell because he could not take any more of his methods, that he was certain that money was flowing in and out of the pension funds. Maxwell controlled these at his whim and only a small coterie of handpicked people knew the full story. I never for a moment dreamt that it would be on such a large scale. He has brought misery to thousands of pensioners. Who can blame them for telling a few jokes. If you didn't laugh you would cry.

16. The Allison Street Shootings

I CAUGHT MY BREATH when, in the summer of 1994, book publisher Derek Rodger suggested that I act as his public relations consultant for a new book he was bringing out – Angels of Death.

The author, he explained, was Howard Wilson, a former policeman who was serving a minimum of twenty-five years for the murder of two former colleagues in Allison Street, Glasgow in December 1969.

He did not have to tell me any more. I had covered the story for the Daily Record almost a quarter of a century before. My mind immediately flashed back to the dark dreary December evening just after Christmas when I stood with other reporters outside the ground floor flat in Govanhill, Glasgow.

It seemed like another age, and it is. I had actually moved away from crime reporting to covering financial matters for the Record, but I was asked to go out on the story because of the enormity of the double murder.

The passage of time meant that Howard Wilson, the former policeman turned cop-killer, had faded from my mind, although occasionally when driving past the close in Allison Street I would remark to whoever was in the car, "that was where the two policemen were shot."

The story at the time was relatively easy to cover. We quickly established that two policemen, Detective Constable Angus McKenzie, 32, and Detective Constable Edward Barnett, 25, had been gunned down in the flat. We also learned that a senior police officer Detective Inspector Hyslop had been seriously wounded in Wilson's frenzied hail of bullets which came after Wilson and two others had been caught red-handed with the haul from a bank robbery in Linwood, Renfrewshire earlier that day.

Slowly as the evening went on, and we spoke to police officers trying to come to terms with the loss of two colleagues a picture emerged of the absolute mayhem which had taken place in the hallway of the small flat. We learned of how, after his three colleagues had fallen under the hail of bullets, one policeman had sheltered in the toilet while Wilson tried to force his way in to add him to his list of victims.

Wilson, and the other two bank robbers, who played no part in the killings, were arrested in the flat when officers from Craigie Street, police station, situated almost directly opposite, stormed in and overcame Wilson.

Six weeks later, in February, 1970, Wilson pled guilty in the High Court in Edinburgh to the murders and two bank robberies. He was sentenced to life imprisonment with the judge's recommendation being that he serve a minimum of twenty-five years.

All this information was coming to the surface of my memory as Derek Rodger explained that Howard Wilson's sentence was coming near to the twenty-five year mark and that while in prison Wilson had written a crime thriller which Derek's company, Argyll Publishing had agreed to take on. I had put together publicity campaigns for previous titles Derek had published which is why he had approached me. Derek suggested that I go with him to meet Howard Wilson in Saughton Prison, Edinburgh where Wilson was being held in the Pentland Wing, designed for long-term prisoners.

I readily saw the PR mileage in offering a paper the exclusive rights to Wilson's story. He had pled guilty so a great deal of detail had not come out at the trial. Even twenty-five years after the events I was confident the public would be interested to know why a former policemen should first turn bank robber and then muderer.

I warned Derek that Wilson had to be prepared to see headlines in the newspapers branding him as a cop-killer, and that I could not, as someone who had personally covered the story, do any kind of whitewash job. Derek Rodger came back to me to say that Howard Wilson understood the personal publicity he was likely to attract, but that if it helped the book he was willing to take the flak.

No newspaper would agree to pay convicted killer money for his story but any money we received would be shared between the publisher and myself as part of my fee for handling the publicity and would help to defray the publishing costs. Howard Wilson's hope was that the publicity would help the sales, which in turn would boost his royalty payments. The royalties would be held in a bank account until whenever Wilson was released. Wilson in 1994 was already 56 and fully expected to be in his sixties when released from prison which would make it difficult for him to earn any kind of a living. The Scottish Prison Service had agreed that the book, Angels of Death could be published and that I could visit Howard Wilson in prison for publicity purposes. So it was arranged that Derek Rodger and I would travel to Saughton Prison to meet Wilson.

On the journey through in Derek Rodger's car I was feeling slightly nervous and tense. I was not quite sure how I would cope coming face to face with the man who had killed two police officers. I was also unsure about how I would cope with hearing someone describe how they pulled the trigger which resulted in such carnage. I also found it difficult to imagine how Wilson could have survived such a lengthy sentence. I kept thinking about all the things I had done in the intervening years. My baby daughter, who was sixteen months when I first stood outside the close in Allison Street, was now married and about to start a career as an occupational therapist; three years after Howard Wilson had been sentenced my wife Margaret and I had the addition of twin boys to the family. They had grown up and were now young men. After spending another fifteen years at the Daily Record I had gone on to become General Secretary of the National Union of Journalists for five years, then for two years 1990-92 I had been been Campaign Director of the Scottish Constitutional Convention, and was now running my own public relations business as well as writing columns for the Herald and Evening Times. A lot of years, a lot of memories, a lot of water under the bridge.

But for Howard Wilson, a life spent behind bars.

Visiting a prison was not a new experience. I had visited Barlinnie Prison several times as a crime reporter, but that had been many years before. A prison warder escorted Derek and I to Pentland wing, through many doors which were unlocked and locked as we passed through them. Eventually we were shown into a ground floor recreation area which with two snooker tables could have been in any community centre, except for the bars which ran down the windows.

A warder went upstairs to Wilson's cell to tell him that we had arrived and brought him down. My first impression of the man I had written about twenty-five years previously was of someone stockily built, with a cheery face and receding hair. He shook my hand warmly, and offered us tea from the flask he had brought from his cell along with some biscuits. The other prisoners were on work duties and we had the room to ourselves. The arrangement was that we could visit Wilson until the end of the work period at 12 noon when we had to leave as the other inmates returned for their lunch. We could then return at 2pm and stay until the end of the next work period at 4pm.

While we sipped our tea I explained to Wilson the rules as I understood them. I would interview him about his life including why and how he robbed the banks, how he came to kill two police officers, and what life behind bars was like. He would see what I wrote, and once this had been agreed I would then offer it to newspapers for serialisation.

I warned him that other papers would pick the story up, and that there would be headlines branding him a cop-killer, and that he would have to be prepared for that. Wilson said that he fully understood but wanted to go ahead.

We began with his early life and Wilson described how he was born on February 21, 1938, and was still a babe when his father, a grocer to trade, joined the Royal Scots Fusiliers. Soon after, his father was killed early in the Second World War. He had not died engaged with the enemy but as a result of a shooting accident at a training establishement in Edinburgh. His father had been a gun instructor and a recruit had misfired. His mother remarried when he was eight or nine, and he had two brothers and a sister.

He felt that his mother, who was a dancing instructor, wanted the best for him to 'make up for' the loss of his natural father, and he was sent to fee-paying Glasgow Academy. The family went like many families at that time their annual holidays to Clyde resorts such as Ayr and Rothesay.

Wilson left school at age seventeen, having gained a Scottish Higher Leaving Certificate in English, History and French. He worked in insurance for a year before being called up for National Service in the Army. Wilson joined the RASC and after initial training at Aldershot he was sent to Dusseldorf where he worked as a clerk. He had been in the cadet force at school and was "familiar with weapons" which made it easier to adapt to Army life. He had also been a keen rugby player at school and was soon playing for both his company and divisional teams.

After completing his two years National Service the idea of going back to office work did not appeal to Wilson and with the encouragement of his mother he joined the Glasgow police force in, he said, "either 1958 or '59." After completing his training at Oxford Street he was sent to the Gorbals division on the south side of the city, working from the Lawmuir Street police station. Wilson spent eight years in the police force in what he described as a "very mundane job".

"Half of it was social work, cleaning up fights in pubs, and handling wife assaults. It was a very unglamorous job."

During his time in the force, he bought, along with a group of other police officers, a cabin cruiser moored at Balloch on Loch Lomond. It was while spending time down at the boat, a converted lifeboat, that he met his wife-to-be, Julie. They married in 1962 in the Church of Scotland in Polmadie Road on Glasgow's south side. The couple had two sons, born in 1964 and 1969 but Wilson explained to me that he did not wish to involve them in his story as they had their own lives to lead, while Julie, who divorced him, is now dead.

Fed up with what he described as the "drudgery and the shift work" of life in the police force Wilson quit in 1967. "I always had the ambition to be my own boss and run my own life," he explained.

Using the lump sum from his police pension Wilson bought The Orchard fruit and veg business at the corner of Cathcart Road and Stanmore Road in Mount Florida on the south side of Glasgow near Hampden football stadium.

Wilson enjoyed being his own boss and he enjoyed the shop work, but there was a nagging problem. His pension money had been enough to pay off the lease of the shop but he was not left with any capital. He had bought a second hand car and a second hand van to transport the fruit and veg from Glasgow's fruit market every morning. He was, he explained, "living out of the till," and although Julie got enough for housekeeping, the financial struggle became wearing.

"I used to worry that if something happened to me, my family would have nothing," explained Wilson. "If you start off with debt it is very hard to get out of it."

It was during this period that Wilson received an unexpected visit from a former colleage, John Sim, who had also left the police force, and was working as a mobile bread salesman.

"John asked me how I was getting on, and explained that he knew I had a shop in the area so had parked his van and dropped in to see me." During the conversation it became clear that both former policemen were short of cash. The talk turned to how it would be nice to get their hands on a bit of money and eventually turned to examining the means by which they could obtain money. The suggestions which flowed and had started off as little more than a joke became more serious, and Wilson invited Iain Donaldson, a petty thief he knew to join in their conversations. Donaldson suggested in a joking manner, a wages snatch. Wilson explained how he responded in a similarly jocular way, suggesting robbing a bank instead.

The 'make believe' conversation quickly began take on more meaning. When he next visited his bank with the shop's takings Wilson began to 'case out' the place. Sim and Donaldson both did similar checks on other banks.

"We started to think as criminals," Wilson admitted. "The lure of money and greed takes you over, and common sense goes out the window. It was down to greed – there is no other way to describe it."

John Donaldson came back with the suggestion that a bank at Williamwood in a leafy suburb on the outskirts of Glasgow was a suitable target. It was situated at the end of a row of shops and it had wooden double front doors which could be closed over.

All three accomplices visited the bank on separate occasions, and decided that this would be the bank they would rob. They began to plan the robbery. It was agreed that they would hit the bank at 3.30pm when it was due to close. Donaldson and Sim joined a gun club in Milngavie and bought a target Vostok pistol illegally. It was agreed that former policeman Sim would carry the gun while Donaldson and Wilson would be armed with ammonia sprays.

Donaldson visited a garage and took a car for a test drive. While driving the car he took a note of the number of the key. On the night before the robbery he stole the car using a replacement key he had purchased.

Dressed as businessmen wearing, soft hats, hornrim glasses and carrying briefcases the trio made their way to the Williamwood bank. First checking that no one was in the bank the three entered the premises. Closing the wooden doors behind them they pulled down the nylon masks they had rolled up underneath their hats.

"We all had prepared speeches," said Wilson, "but I just blurted out 'ammonia'." Not surprisingly the effect on the four bank staff was instant.

"One staff member just stood still with his eyes closed while another covered his face and eyes."

It was at this point in the interview that Howard Wilson expressed his first regret saying, "You don't realise that you are putting people under such stress or what you are setting in train." He described how he sprayed ammonia on the chest of a "tall member of staff" who walked out one of the offices. At this point the manager appeared saying, "We will not resist. Please don't hurt the staff."

Wilson told me, "I said no one intended to hurt anyone."

Despite this assurance one of the female staff members was obviously upset.

"I gave her some water, and told her 'No one is going to hurt you.' "

This action, and the fact that they were dressed in business style clothes, earned them the tag, 'League of Gentlemen' in the media following the robbery.

Meanwhile Sim and Donaldson were gathering in the cash and within five minutes they were making their getaway in the stolen car. They drove to Glasgow airport where they had earlier parked one of their own cars and drove to Wilson's house in Allison Street which was empty, Julie and the infant boys visiting relatives, and divided up the money.

Wilson then described how the following morning he carried on with his normal routine and went to the fruit market at between 4.30 and 5am. "At first I was horrified at the enormity of what we had done, then as the days go by you realise that you got away with it. Then you start to believe you are uncatchable, that you have carried out the perfect crime."

He added, "It is unfortunate that things went so smoothly. It was like taking sweeties out of a sweetie tin." The proceeds were split three ways. Wilson used his to pay off debts from the shop and after a few weeks purchased a fridge for the shop. He also began to think about saving towards buying a house.

His accomplices opened a garage as Donaldson was a motor mechanic but this business did not do too well, and John Sim once again appeared in Wilson's shop suggesting that they carry out a second robbery. Wilson at first told Sim he was not interested and to carry on without him. But then he thought about how he could use the money to help buy a house.

"The first robbery was motivated by need. The second by greed," admitted Wilson. The search began for a suitable branch and the trio finally decided on a branch near Linwood. Once again it had double doors which could be closed and there appeared to be four staff. It was decided to use a different plan for their second 'job' in the hope of putting the police off their scent, and come to the conclusion that the two robberies had been carried out by different gangs. On the second occasion it was agreed that they would arrange an appointment with the bank manager for 2.30pm on the false premise that they had a business proposition they were looking to finance. At the last minute they would phone to ask if it was possible to put the appointment back until 3.30pm, the bank's closing time.

They used the same method as before to steal a car, but wore disguises including false moustaches and glasses. During the robbery pillowcases instead of tape were used to blind the bank staff.

The three robbers went into the manager's room with Sim standing back saying, "After you" to the manager so that he entered the room last behind the unsuspecting manager and pulled out the gun. The staff were called into the manager's office individually except for one female who was bent over her desk working. Donaldson approached her and tapped her on the shoulder with his gun, saying, "Move."

"The girl must have thought it was a joke," recalled Wilson, "as she said 'don't be silly', and carried on working. Donaldson had to convince her he was not joking by jabbing her again with the pistol. Wilson then recounted a farcical scene which would have merited inclusion in a Carry-On film.

Donaldson had been sent to check that the main doors were closed but had not returned. Sim then went to find out what he was doing and reappeared with Donaldson and a woman with her child.

"It seems that the woman was knocking on the locked door when Ian went to check it," explained Wilson. "She was saying that she had arrived at the bank before closing time and demanding that she should be allowed in. When John Sim arrived he pulled her inside. She then informed him that she had a child outside and he had to open the door again to get the kid."

The arrival of the child added a further touch of farce to the entire proceedings as the youngster kept pulling the hoods off the bank staff who had been tied up with short pieces of rope. After collecting the cash from the bank the three once again drove to Glasgow airport to switch cars before driving back to Allison Street unaware of the terrible events which were about to unfold.

At this point in our interview I pressed Howard Wilson to explain how they had decided to carry a loaded gun and asked him if they intended to use it?

"The gun was intended to frighten, although at the time you do not think how this must traumatise people. The gun was loaded with live ammunition as this means that if you shoot at a wall the plaster crumbles, and people realise that it is loaded. A blank is no use for this purpose."

I pressed him again if they would have used the gun during the bank raids if they had come up against resistance, or police had arrived on the scene.

"We didn't intend to kill anyone with the gun. The plan was to use ammonia. As ex-police officers we knew that threatened with a gun a police officer's first consideration is the preservation of life. We had all agreed that the gun was not to be used to shoot anyone."

Arriving back at Allison Street the three made their way into the close leading to Wilson's flat with Donaldson bringing up the rear. By sheer coincidence, at that time, sitting in a police car opposite the house was was Inspector Hyslop. The three had agreed that if they saw a uniformed police officer they should ignore him and walk past.

"Ian Donaldson had been a criminal and he had an inbuilt instinct regarding the police. He made eye contact with Inspector

Hyslop, but instead of walking on into the close he turned back and caught Hyslop's eye a second time.

"Hyslop's watching, and Ian turned and caught his eye a third time," said Wilson.

Wilson described how he left the house to get some shopping. When he returned, he was confronted by plain clothes officers who said, "Can we see you?" and pushed past him into the house.

"The next thing I heard was one of the officers saying 'Jesus'. The suitcase we were carrying the money in was lying open with cash all over the floor."

Wilson then described his feelings as he realised that they had been caught red-handed and that his world was crashing down around him. "My mind was in a whirl, I was going frantic. All I can hear is Hyslop asking for the black box, and insisting that I hand it over. I didn't know anything about the black box. Donaldson must have grabbed it as he was leaving the bank."

At this point I could feel my mind beginning to race. I had to continue asking questions and taking down the notes accurately but what was being described to me was how two police officers died in a blaze of shots. A reporter is used to victims describing how they were assaulted, or advocates in a court room describe how a crime was alleged to have been committed, but I had never interviewed a murderer and had described to me the blow by blow account of the scene. I had to fight hard to maintain my concentration. I could sense a change in the atmosphere between Howard Wilson and I.

My questions were becoming shorter more clipped; his voice betrayed a certain strain as my questioning forced him to think of his terrible actions twenty-five years before.

Wilson then described how he went into the bedroom, with Hyslop following and spotted the wardrobe door lying open. "It was always kept closed," he explained because of our two young children. I thought perhaps the box had been put in there, and put my hands inside. I felt the gun. It was in a shoulder holster. Ian Sim must have taken it off and put it in wardrobe.

"I've got hold of the gun. I remember lifting it out. It was still in its holster but I pulled it out. I turned round with the gun in my hand and Hyslop started backing away. I felt a mixture of emotions. My world had crashed all around me. Logical thing was to hand the gun over but I pulled the trigger. I don't remember but I'm told the gun misfired."

Wilson's gun training both in the army and the police came into force. He reloaded the pistol and fired again hitting Inspector Hyslop in the mouth. Wilson explained that most of his recollections concerning the shootings are based on what he has been told by others. "I see everything in still pictures," he explained, "but after I hit him, Inspector Hyslop was lying across the hall against the skirting board. Two policemen came into the hall and got shot. I was shooting by instinct. Each person was hit in the head as I made eye contact. I don't know how many times I fired."

Wilson's next clear memory is of coming to under a pile of policemen.

He has been told that he had tried to force open the toilet door to shoot a policeman who had taken shelter inside, and had continued to pull the trigger of the empty pistol as he forced his hand around the side of the door. "I have been told that I kept pulling the trigger, and demanding another clip from John Sim who was standing petrified in the hall.

"It was an act of complete madness. It was completely illogical. I could have escaped out of the door. The gun that was supposed to only be used to frighten people had become a lethal weapon."

Reflecting on his dreadful deeds Wilson told me, "I can't explain it to myself. I was a happily married man with many business friends. When I came back to reality and realised what had happened I couldn't come to terms with it. But I knew it was me who had killed the officers. I realised that I would never see Julie and the kids again."

The next morning at the bar of Craigie Street police station Wilson told the officer. "It was me. I did the shooting."

Wilson was taken to Barlinnie where he spent Hogmanay in the cell that had previously been used for condemned prisoners. Recalling his feelings of his first night in prison lying on a mattress on the floor Wilson said, "A screw had a radio on, and I could hear Rolf Harris singing Two Little Boys. I never contemplated suicide. I realised what I had done. You realise that your wife and kids are outside. You can't come to terms with the fact that you have slaughtered two people. The enormity is too great."

Six weeks later, pleading guilty as charged, Wilson was sentenced to life, with a recommended minimum of twenty-five years. "I had been told while I was in Barlinnie waiting trial to expect a heavy sentence, but I couldn't grasp the enormity of twenty-five years."

After his sentence Wilson was taken to Peterhead where he was held for fourteen and a half years except for the time during 1972 he spent in the Inverness 'cages' which ended in a prison riot. For his part in this Wilson, along with Jimmy Boyle, Larry Winters and Billy McPherson, was given a six year sentence.

Since 1984 Wilson has been held in Saughton Prison. He started to write Angels of Death while still in Peterhead, and in 1984 it won the Koestler Award for artistic work by a prisoner.

After my interviews with Wilson the Today newspaper, which has since closed, serialised some of the material, and Wilson became news again for a short period. Not surprisingly the papers concentrated on Wilson's crimes rather than the content of the book, which is a pity as it is a very strong crime thriller. The book has achieved reasonable sales in the UK and a German publisher has translated it and plans to issue a German language edition in 1997.

I have seen Wilson several times in Saughton since my first visit. I like him. Nothing can ever erase the dreadful crime that he committed, and he realises that. He understands that for him to express sorrow to the families of the two dead policemen means nothing but he clearly regrets his actions which not only ended the life of two policemen, but ruined the lives of their close ones.

Wilson's release will be highly political. Relatives of the officers and serving police officers will no doubt express the view that he should never be allowed out, and the present political climate would point to the fact that this is how decisions to release prisoners such as Wilson are taken. I sincerely hope however that we take such decisions out of the political arena. Our justice system does not operate on the basis of revenge, otherwise why not allow the relatives of victims, or indeed the victims themselves pass the sentence?

The court decided that Wilson should serve a minimum of twenty-five years for his original crime. He has done this. Since his imprisonment he was sentenced to a further six years for his part in the Inverness cages riot. He has now almost served this in totality as well, despite his good behaviour since then.

Howard Wilson is not a danger to society. He has served the sentence imposed on him by the courts and he should now be released. The decision should not be coloured by imagined tabloid press headlines, or so called public opinion which is more accurately described as the personal opinions of those in charge of our popular newspapers.

17. Stop Press

FOR MOST OF MY entire journalistic career I led a Jekyll and Hyde existence. By day I was a financial journalist interviewing leading capitalists and by night I was an active trade unionist and Labour Party activist helping to organise journalists into an effective trade union force.

At the start of my work in newspapers in 1963, in common with most young Scottish journalists of the sixties era, my goal was to work in Fleet Street. However during this period my inbuilt feeling of the need to fight against social injustice came to the fore.

In common with most people, without realising it, my views on life were constructed during my early years. My upbringing had been in a home where money was not plentiful. My father was a ganger, that is a the foreman of group of building site labourers. Like my father himself, at that time most building labourers were Irish or of Irish extraction. He went on to become a caster in the Babcock and Wilcox foundry in Renfrew where in later years he became a storeman.

I was mainly brought up by my maternal grandmother Mrs Mullen, who was a strong Irish Nationalist, and in the evenings the radio would be switched to Radio Eirean to hear the Republic of Ireland national anthem, the Soldiers Song. Our family was Roman Catholic and my mother, Sadie, was a strong believer in the Catholic faith and I was brought up to go to Mass every Sunday. Indeed into my late teens I would go to many church services during the week.

This upbringing instilled in me a strong sense of right and wrong and of social justice. I am to this day a socialist. My political beliefs do not come from Marx but from the teachings of the Church. From my early schooldays I had an interest in politics and wrote compositions on Africa, socialism and the nuclear threat. At Lourdes Secondary School I can remember when I showed my compositions on the nuclear threat and Africa to my English teacher, Mr Murray, he warned me not to be so serious. But because my parents had never been politically active I had never channelled these views into any particular political party.

My involvement in trade union activity came about almost by accident and was certainly not a conscious decision on my part. It was 1967. I had just returned to the Daily Record as a general news reporter after a short stint with the Scottish Daily Mail. I had increased my wages by around £3 a week by first leaving the Daily Record to join the Daily Mail then returning to the Record. This was how journalists in those days increased their income.

I returned to the Record for an extra £1 a week making my weekly salary £27. I knew that this was £1 a week less than the top rate earned by my mate Bob Sutter but Bob was rated as the top Record reporter. I was quite content to be £1 behind Bob as he really was a good operator. (Bob is now an Assistant Editor at the Herald).

But when I arrived back at the Record the editorial floor was in turmoil. In the early hours of one morning, a inquisitive reporter had gone through the news editor's files and discovered that a newly recruited reporter was being paid £32 a week, breaking the psychologically important £30 barrier for the first time and well ahead of what any other reporter was earning.

Everyone, particularly some long service journalists, was up in arms. It was wrongly assumed that I had come back for the same money as the other recruit which, unfortunately was not the case. I was not too chuffed for I realised I had been conned. I had agreed my terms on the basis that £28 was the top rate.

Almost overnight the moribund National Union of Journalists Daily Record and Sunday Mail chapel sprang into life and crowded meetings were held on a daily basis in the conference room of the Hope Street building.

At first, having just returned to the paper, I didn't take an active part in the meetings. The chapel formulated demands for an immediate all round merit review. But as always, the best recruiting sergeant for any trade union is the bad – or stupid – employer and before long, I was as angry as everyone else at the way management were handling the situation.

The meetings culminated in a mandatory meeting in the Trade Union Centre in Carlton Place, Glasgow when the intention was to call an unofficial strike unless the management came up with a satisfactory offer. The Father of the Chapel, Bill Robertson, came to the meeting with an offer which he was recommending for acceptance. By this time several other younger reporters and myself were in full voice and we vehemently opposed the deal which was eventually accepted by a narrow majority.

Not long after this Bill Robertson gave up as FOC and the chapel turned for its new leadership to the Young Turks who been so vocal in the merit review dispute. James Cox, now of the BBC, was elected as FOC and I was elected his deputy.

During the sixties salaries were negotiated centrally at national level and the grass roots membership had little involvement in deciding their own wage rates. This changed when Mirror Group Newspapers, of which the Daily Record was part, negotiated an agreement with the members of the National Graphical Association Wire Room chapel in Manchester, giving them a £2000 a year minimum wage, much higher than the journalists.

Journalists might not be the raw material of which militant trade unionists are made but the one thing they are is elitist! The journalists in MGN's three centres – London, Manchester and Glasgow were in high dudgeon over the wire room deal, demanding their right to have house agreements. Management did not want to concede this, as they preferred to have one negotiation at national level, instead of negotiating with numerous chapels. Such local agreements were also against NUJ rules.

Eventually the battle was won. First in Manchester then in London, and Glasgow followed. James Cox and I negotiated a "mini house agreement" with no money element. James then left the Record for a educational visit to the United States and I became FOC.

The Daily Record and Sunday Mail chapel was by this time very active and we set ourselves the target of achieving a full blown house agreement with new rates of pay by the end of 1968.

A claim for a minimum annual salary of £1,750 was submitted, with additional service payments and a higher minimum for specialists. The management set their face against our claim which if we won would have given us by far the biggest rise ever. The chapel set a deadline of Christmas Day for a settlement and as the festive season approached I was in constant negotiation. Both sides, management and union were putting together an agreement virtually from scratch and every word was poured over.

By Christmas Eve we were almost at the end of the road. The management had offered a minimum of £1700 less than a £1 a week away from our claim on the minimum rate but the chapel would not budge. Eventually the chapel agreed to allow the Christmas Day deadline to pass as I pointed out that I would like to spend Christmas Day with my wife Margaret and four-month-old baby daughter Lynn. The members insisted however that we concluded the deal on Boxing Day. This we did when the management increased their offer to £1725 and I signed my first of many wage deals.

At the time I remember thinking, "Well, that's me done my stint as FOC, now I can get on with being a journalist again." I handed over the chapel leadership to the Record's political correspondent Stewart McLaughlan in 1969.

Not long afterwards I became the Daily Record's financial correspondent writing a weekly money page and later a property page. I still retained an interest in the union being a member of the chapel committee and attended meetings of the Glasgow branch. But journalism was my priority. Then in 1975 Stewart McLaughlan persuaded me to do another stint. I wasn't very keen because, by this time, I was responsible for both finance and property editorial within the paper. But we agreed in a meeting held at the bar of the Copy Cat pub between myself, Stewart and sports writer Ken Gallagher that I would do it for a year, before Stewart would again take over from me. That was the plan but things didn't quite work out like that.

It all started to go wrong, at least as far as my career in journalism was concerned, when it was suggested that I should take a look at what Reed International the parent company of the Daily Record and Sunday Mail had done with the newspapers' assets. A senior member of the Daily Record and Sunday Mail Ltd board of directors was upset that the company's main assets, ie their property, had been taken from them by the parent board. The Scottish board had protested to no avail and he believed that only trade union intervention could win this assets back.

At first I ignored the approach as I was involved in wage negotiations with the company. But a second approach was made asking if I intended doing anything about the situation. Rather reluctantly I agreed as I was only a part-time Father of Chapel, and my main concern was the wages and conditions of my members, not board politics or company assets.

By this time I had also become the Imperial Father of the Daily Record and Sunday Mail federated chapel (convener of shop stewards). Having agreed to take on the problem I began to organise a political and publicity campaign to have the assets returned to the Scottish company with the support of the federated chapel.

Our asset stripping campaign during 1976 had a high public profile and proved to be very successful. It gained all-party support and a TV documentary was made of the campaign. It was before the harsh brand of Thatcher politics had been introduced and our arguments carried moral weight.

Eventually Sir Alex Jarratt, chairman of Reed International and

Percy Roberts, boss of Mirror Group Papers agreed to meet myself and federated chapel officials at his headquarters in Green Park London. At this meeting Sir Alex agreed that the Scottish company should be given a 99-year lease on the Anderston Quay property. We had won an important victory. Shortly afterwards the building was returned to the full control of the Scottish company.

By this time my twelve month period of office was coming near to an end and I approached Stewart MacLaughlan to arrange the handover of the chapel leadership back to him. The reply was, "Aw, big man. I can't do it. I'm covering devolution." So it was that I agreed to carry on for another year and the die was cast.

In December 1976 I was elected to the National Executive Council of the NUJ and although I did give up as FOC after my second term I continued as imperial father and NEC member.

The federated chapel then started a campaign for equal pay for equal work to narrow the earning gap between Glasgow and London. This reflected the considerable anger within the workforce that although the Scottish titles were profitable and contributed more to the Mirror Group's profit figures than our London and Manchester counterparts, where the Mirror titles were produced, the wages paid to the 1,000 employees in Scotland were on average £7–8 a week lower than those paid in England.

We did not want, or expect, to receive the same wages as those in the South. London wages and practices would have crippled Anderston Quay financially but we believed that the gap was too wide.

The management, wisely from their point of view, did not wish to negotiate wages with the federated chapel, but we pressed them to discuss the principle and talks were eventually held with Vic Horwood, who had just taken over as managing director of the company.

During these talks Vic Horwoood refused to budge but we continued to put pressure on the company and brought in full-time print union officials, some of whom who were not too keen on our claim, or in the existence of a strong federated chapel. They felt an active federated chapel could weaken the sovereignty of the individual unions. What is it that someone said about "the workers united will never be defeated"?

The management could not deny the figures we produced, showing the gap between the wage rates. We had gone to London and canvassed the London FOCs who, at first, were reluctant to talk, but who, after a few whiskies, loosened up while we drank more slowly and took notes.

Because of management unwillingness to shift the federated chapel decided to take some form of industrial action. It had to be unofficial as the unions would never have countenanced backing a federated initiative. We struck on the idea of each of the eighteen chapels in the building having a one hour information meeting on the same day. Not very disruptive you might think but we added a little twist. The meetings were organised on a rolling basis. The first, I think it was the clerical, began around mid-day, followed by the journalists around 3pm. Then when we finished at 4pm the caseroom started their one hour meeting, followed by process, platemaking, machine room, despatch and finally transport about 1 o'clock in the morning. The meetings followed the flow of production through the building. The result was that the newspapers were very late in coming off the presses and then in being distributed as the van drivers were the last section to hold a meeting.

The company, and the unions, were seething but each chapel pointed out that they had only an hour's meeting which surely could hardly be described as disruptive? Both the management and the unions realised that the action had been co-ordinated and the production chapels were warned to behave, or else, by their full-time officials.

Management believed that the support they had received from the print unions to come down heavily on their chapels meant they had seen off our campaign and again refused to budge. We then planned a lightning unofficial strike for 11pm on a Saturday evening when we knew that management would not be able to contact officials to order us back to work.

The strike was successful and Sunday Mail production was halted. I was having a party at home that same evening and around midnight the calls started to come in – the company had pulled the shutters down and told us we were locked out until we gave guarantees to drop our campaign.

I was dumbfounded. I had never experienced such a situation before and quite honestly hadn't a clue what I was going to do next. I arranged to meet the FOC's at 8am the next morning. Anderston Quay was deserted when I arrived outside the building with only a handful of FOC's standing around outside the steel shutters which barred our entry into the building. Charlie Faulds the engineer's FOC was there puffing his pipe as usual. Po-faced, but with a twinkle in his eye, he said to me, "Fine mess you've got us into." Charlie didn't realise that I hadn't got a clue what our next step was to be but I bought time by arranging a federated chapel committee meeting in the Trade Union Centre in Carlton Place for later that morning, then disappeared to think what the hell I was going to do.

The unions in the newspaper industry were not known for taking united action and there were no ground rules or experience of fighting a dispute on a common front. We had to keep a 1,000 workforce united despite the fact that they were divided into seven different unions and eighteen chapels each with their own FOC.

At the meeting in the Trade Union Centre I took a gamble and suggested a mass meeting for the following day, a Monday, in a cinema in Renfield Street and hoped that none of the chapels would cave in and return to work before the mass meeting.

The media were naturally reporting the lock-out and when I arrived at the cinema next day they were asking to be allowed in to cover the meeting. I asked them to wait outside until I consulted with my fellow FOC's. The real reason was that we were not sure if anyone would turn up at the first ever mass meeting of the Daily Record and Sunday Mail workforce and we didn't want the photographers and camera men to show a half empty hall. However when we went inside, the stalls, and balcony were packed. There must have been around 800 workers in the hall.

The press came in and took shots of the packed rows before leaving to allow us to get on with our meeting. The atmosphere was electric and there was no sign of any crumbling. Local by-laws meant that you had to apply for permission to stage a march on the public highways but an NUJ member suggested to me in private that I inform the meeting I was going to walk down to Anderston Quay and invite the members to join me for a walk. No one could prevent us from walking and so it was that several hundred print workers strolled together through the city centre.

We headed – around 700 of us – down Union Street, Jamaica Street and along the Clyde walkway to the Record building beside the concrete structure of the Kingston Bridge. It was a strange feeling walking down the pavement of Union Street to realise that behind you there were 700 individuals strolling behind.

Several years later Liam Kane, who at the time was deputy managing director of the Daily Record and Sunday Mail told me that he looked out from the ninth floor window on the executive floor and saw us approaching along the walkway beside the Clyde and said, "What's that bastard up to now?!"

It was simple, I had informed the media that the workforce was walking down to Anderston Quay to present ourselves for work. Television viewers watching the evening news witnessed an entire workforce willing to work but being refused entry by an intransigent management. If anyone can, journalists should always be able to win the propaganda war in any industrial dispute with their bosses.

The lock-out lasted for a fortnight and was finally settled by the print unions General Secretaries at TUC level in London. The full history of that dispute cannot be recorded here, but the return to work formula narrowed the gap between us and London which was our aim and we returned to work as a united workforce despite attempts by some to divide us.

We received advice and assistance from many people but the Daily Record and Sunday Mail workforce owe a debt to the late Norman Buchan MP who turned up on the first Sunday to offer assistance and to Transport and General Workers officials Alex Kitson and Hugh Wyper who stood by us from start to finish.

At this stage I was also becoming more involved with my own union at national level. In 1980 was elected Vice President. And the Daily Record management gave me a year's sabbatical leave to carry out my duties as President during 1981-82.

The majority of people when asked what they most connect with trade unions immediately say, Strikes, and so far in this chapter I may have contributed to this attitude. But trade unions are involved in many other spheres which go unmentioned in the media. During my spell as a voluntary official of the NUJ – an activist – I was involved along with others in campaigns which not only benefited our own members but the community in general.

Two in particular stand out. The campaign to control the spread of free newspapers in Scotland and the opposition we mounted against the facsimile transmission of newspapers into Scotland from the south.

Free newspapers had swept uncontrolled through England taking away advertising from the traditional paid-for titles. They promised advertisers the prospect of delivering their advert into every house in an area. This on the face of it, is very attractive to advertisers because no one had yet cottoned on to the fact that you might pop such papers through letterboxes but you cannot force people to read them.

The result of the emergence of free newspapers was that many paid-for titles folded. Managements also converted paid-for titles into free newspapers with the inevitable consequence of reduced editorial. So what? you might say. Well I'm sure that with hindsight most people would agree that a free newspaper is not an alternative to a newspaper. They are designed primarily as a vehicle for carrying adverts, not news, and do not carry the editorial staff that any paid-for title would.

The first threat in Scotland came in Glasgow where the Thomson Organisation planned to launch the Clyde Post in 1982. This could have been the death knell of the Glasgow Evening Times which carries a large journalistic staff to cover politics, industry, local government as well as general news. The Clyde Post could have attracted the advertising from the Evening Times by offering cheaper rates as they would not have had the same overheads.

The NUJ along with the Scottish Graphical Branch of Sogat mounted a political and industrial campaign to prevent the Clyde Post being published. I worked closely with Alan Watson, the branch secretary of the SGB in this campaign.

For the next three years the two unions operated a policy of only reaching agreement with existing newspaper proprietors to allow them to launch a defensive free paper in their own area to protect their existing paid-for title from being attacked by an offensive free title aimed at taking the advertising from the existing paid-for title.

The joint union campaign was largely successful and Scottish local papers did not suffer at the hands of free newspapers the same way many English provincial titles did. The campaign saved not only many of our members jobs, it also retained for local communities the papers which have served them well for many years. We would not have opposed the setting up of a rival paid-for title which was offering the same news service to the local community.

The campaign against the facsimile transmission of entire national papers into Scotland was also motivated by the twin objects of protecting existing newspaper jobs and titles, and therefore a diversified truly Scottish press, as distinct from an English produced title with tartan on it. Once again it was a joint campaign between the NUJ and SGB and the first target was to prevent the Sun newspaper from faxing into the Kinning Park plant.

We were willing to reach a compromise if the management would agree to produce a number of live pages in Glasgow so that there would be some jobs and also the paper would offer at least a limited Scottish service to its readers. The management refused, although, when they finally did succeed in faxing into Glasgow they had to produce Scottish live pages to attract readers. We also acted to stop the Scottish Daily Express from faxing into Inverness. Once again we offered to negotiate a mixture of live pages and faxed pages but again the management refused and dropped their idea.

Our fear was that the Scottish indigenous press would be

overwhelmed by London titles offering only a Scottish edition of London newspapers with perhaps some Scottish sport but little else. This would have been damaging to a sense of a vibrant and active Scottish press, so important in a democratic society. We could only hold the line for so long in this fight and eventually the Sun, Sunday Times and News of the World broke through in the mid eighties on the back of the union-busting operation at Wapping. However our campaign bought the Scottish titles time and allowed them to strengthen their position in the market place.

My trade union career took me into many other newspapers and involved me in a number of industrial disputes but I can honestly say along with the vast majority of other trade union activists that I resolved more problems than ever I was involved in stopping presses.

Eventually my trade union involvement led to my being elected General Secretary of the National Union of Journalists in July 1985 and I said farewell to Scotland and journalism for the next five years. The years were a tumultuous period in the union's history.

18. Wapping

WHEN I TRAVELLED up from London to the TUC Congress in Blackpool on Sunday, September 1, 1985 I expected an eventful week. After all, the next day I was to take over officially as General Secretary of the National Union of Journalists, the largest journalist union in the world outside of China and the Soviet Union, a position I had never dreamt of holding. And, as if that was not enough, the Sunday newspapers were carrying headlines that Robert Maxwell would never print the Daily Mirror in London again.

The reason for the headlines was that the NGA print union members in the Mirror's Holborn plant in London were in dispute over the future ownership of the Sporting Life and Maxwell in his usual style had made his announcement to the world.

I knew that this was little more than Maxwell hype as in telephone conversations with Tony Dubbins general secretary of the National Graphical Association I was aware that private talks were due to take place in Blackpool over the weekend. Dubbins had asked that I temper anything I said about the dispute in public as I would be asked to act as a go-between in the talks. From my previous personal dealings with Maxwell I fully expected to be kept occupied as you never knew what he was going to say from one minute to the next. He would regularly contradict himself in the same sentence.

I was not to know that the oncoming week would see the start of my involvement in a dispute which would dominate the first fifteen months of my five years as general secretary. I am talking about the series of events that came to be known by the name of the new print plant that dominated them, Wapping.

This dispute attracted world wide attention when it finally began on Friday, January 24, 1986. News International sacked 5,500 printworkers employed at the Sun, News of the World, Times and Sunday Times for going on strike. Overnight the production of the titles transferred to Wapping in the East End of London.

The Mirror dispute was quickly settled at the start of the TUC congress after a series of meetings between myself, Tony Dubbins and Robert Maxwell. I had almost forgotten about it when near the end of the week a dummy newspaper which had been printed at Wapping arrived at Blackpool.

The production of such a dummy caused consternation among the print unions. There had been rumours about what was happening down at Wapping for many months. The unions had been trying to gain access to the plant which was in the process of being built but trade union officials and members were barred from entering the premises. Fears had already been expressed that Murdoch was building a newspaper plant which he would use to break any future strikes by print unions.

I had earlier passed on information to the NGA that a transport company called TNT had placed a large order for a fleet of trucks capable of carrying newspapers and that my informant believed it was for a contract with News International. This indicated that Murdoch was perhaps trying to circumvent the normal distribution channels which were highly unionised making it difficult to move newspapers produced during an official dispute.

Now we were faced with proof that Murdoch had machinery ready which could set and print newspapers. Myself and Mike Smith, the NUJ's national newspaper organiser attended a hastily convened meeting with SOGAT '82 and the NGA. It was the general consensus that officials of the print unions should meet FOCs (shop stewards) and urge them to take industrial action to force the company to allow them access to the plant at Wapping, and to negotiate agreements covering its use.

It is somewhat ironic that when Murdoch sacked the 5,500 printworkers he used, as an excuse, their propensity for going on strike. Yet when the unions urged the shop floor representatives to take action in September 1985 they declined, and instead called for talks with the company to establish the facts about Wapping.

The first meeting between ourselves and Murdoch took place three weeks after Congress in London's Inn on the Park hotel. Murdoch questioned my presence at the meeting as ten days before he had cleverly exempted the journalists when he issued six months notice to terminate the union agreements covering the production workers.

The NUJ members were a key factor in his carefully laid plans to de-unionise his newspaper operation. Hindsight coupled with the admission of EETPU leaders has confirmed what we suspected at the time. The leadership of the electricians' union was in cahoots with News Group and Times Newspapers to provide a substitute labour force to produce the four titles, but Murdoch did not have a shadow editorial workforce. He required his existing journalist workforce to go to Wapping and the introduction of direct input technology made this all the more important.

Looking over the table towards where I sat he said to me, "I would not have thought this concerned you."

I replied that although I realised the reason for the talks were supposed to concern the production workers in Gray's Inn Road where the Times and Sunday Times were printed, and Bouverie Street were the Sun and News of the World were printed, I believed the discussion might get round to Wapping as the two areas could not be separated. Murdoch merely nodded his head.

I was to be proved correct. The entire discussion that day centred around Wapping. Talks had already been underway between the print unions and News International but had not been getting very far, mainly because of the management's attitude.

Reading from a prepared statement Murdoch lambasted our

side of the table for the poor industrial relations record and the working practices which existed at Grays Inn Road and Bouverie Street. There was not much in what he said that I personally could disagree with. The trade union practices in and around Fleet Street bore no relationship to the trade unionism I believed in, or indeed was practised elsewhere in the country.

Fleet Street print union fathers of chapel did not work – they ran their departments, not the managers. I first learned this lesson when I attended a meeting of Mirror Group FOCs in the Metropole Hotel in London to discuss the Bullock Report which proposed works councils on which both management and unions would sit.

I was the only trade union representative from the Mirror Group's Scottish operation. The other 100 or so representatives came from Manchester and London. I was also the only trade unionist in the room to voice support for the setting up of a works council within Mirror Group. This puzzled me as I thought the majority of trade unionists would support having more say within the company they worked for. Following the meeting everything was made clear. The London and Manchester FOCs were against the idea of a works council because they did not fancy the idea of sitting around a table with management and sharing their power.

Once he had got his gripes off his chest Murdoch then expanded on his plans to publish the London Post which had first been mentioned in March. He issued us with an ultimatum. Reach agreement on manning and other conditions for the new 24 hour paper by Christmas or he would press ahead with the project using non-union labour.

The entire proceedings were a sham. Murdoch never intended to publish the London Post. It was a smokescreen to give him time to prepare the machinery and workforce already inside Wapping to produce his existing four titles. He also needed to bide his time waiting for Wapping to be ready before provoking a strike among the 5,500 workers who presently produced the four titles.

When I was told that March 17, St Patrick's Day was earmarked for the launch of the London Post, I enquired if it was being produced by leprechauns? It was certainly not going to be produced by journalists. The NUJ represented at that time 32,000 journalists throughout the United Kingdom and Ireland. Whenever a new title was being planned we inevitably received calls from journalists being interviewed for positions on the new paper asking for information. We did not receive a single call about the London Post, because there was no recruitment.

A folklore has grown up around Wapping. In newspaper management mythology it is portrayed as a dispute over the introduction of new technology. Nothing could be further from the truth. Wapping was a union busting exercise, nothing more, nothing less.

Certainly the print production unions had prevented the introduction of single keying by journalists for perhaps as long as a decade. They did so to protect the jobs of the compositors who reset the words keyed in by the editorial, and to a lesser extent, advertising departments which meant that newspapers were produced by outmoded and expensive methods.

The single key issue however had just been settled between the unions following a bitter inter-union demarcation dispute which had resulted in 160 print workers at the Wolverhampton Express and Star losing their jobs.

This dispute had been at its height when I took over as General Secretary at the beginning of September and I had made it my priority to reach a settlement with the NGA. We had achieved this with the help of the TUC who appointed Lord McCarthy to chair talks between ourselves and the NGA. Although this agreement only covered the provincial newspapers in England and Wales the principles it was based on were used to present a joint claim by the NUJ and NGA to allow direct input by journalists working on the proposed London Post.

Bill O'Neill, who was Murdoch's right hand man as far as Wapping was concerned, dismissed the proposals out of hand. This type of management attitude towards the negotiations was continued throughout what was supposed to be the negotiating period. I met

O'Neill along with Charles Wilson, the editorial director of the London Post at the end of October. I knew Charles Wilson well from his days as editor of the Glasgow Evening Times when I was the NUJ's national executive member for national newspapers outside of London. Charles was a hard man which had earned him the tag of Charles 'Gorbals Boy' Wilson. Although we had crossed swords many times over the negotiating table during his spell at Albion Street where the Evening Times was published alongside the Herald, he and I got on fairly well and enjoyed a bit of banter.

It was at this meeting when O'Neill told me that the London Post was going to be launched on March 17 that I asked Charles if the paper was going to be produced by leprechauns. During the meeting O'Neill told me that the company had not yet prepared a draft agreement for journalists who would work for the new title, although draft proposals had been prepared for the other print unions and would be presented to SOGAT and the NGA the following day.

This was all part of News International's ploy to steer away from a fight with the NUJ. They wanted to keep the NUJ in a different position from the other print unions. Their game plan was to pick a fight with the production unions in order that they could sack their members. It boiled down to the fact that with the connivance of the EETPU they had an alternative workforce in place at Wapping for everyone but the journalists.

The company maintained this tactic all through the dispute until the picket lines had been withdrawn and they then turned their attention to de-unionising the editorial floor.

The proposals which the company made to SOGAT and the NGA were devastating. They included the cliché, Management's Right to Manage. Dictate might be a more accurate description. In-house trade union organisation such as chapels would not be allowed. Anyone who withdrew their labour would be sacked and the agreements would be legally binding.

During November talks between SOGAT, NGA, AEUW and the company got nowhere. I will not mention the EETPU in this regard as it has been publicly acknowledged by that union's then general secretary, Eric Hammond, that his union were in cahoots throughout Wapping with the company, a fact Dubbins, Deans and myself all believed throughout the dispute.

On December 9, we were all called to Congress House for a meeting with Norman Willis, general secretary of the TUC to discuss a common approach. By this date I had still only been general secretary of a national union for three months and I found it strange entering the TUC headquarters with television cameras recording my entrance and a horde of industrial correspondents from national newspapers door-stepping the meeting. It was a scene I had witnessed on News at Ten many times, but had never imagined that I would be one of the participants.

I had been at Congress many times during my career as a trade unionist but I had never before been into the general secretary's inner sanctum. This was also a strange experience. Prior to being elected general secretary of the NUJ in July I had been a lay member of the union's executive, and my full time employment was as financial correspondent for the Daily Record. The other GS's present had all been full-time trade union officials for a number of years before being elected to their respective union's chief executive. My world had changed rapidly in the space of six months.

We were greeted by Norman Willis who was accompanied by Ken Graham, his deputy, and John Monks who was effectively number three in the TUC hierarchy. I had met Willis once before when he had attended a meeting of the NUJ's executive to discuss our opposition to the Press Council. I was not impressed then, and I was not impressed at this meeting. Both Graham and Monks were much more able, particularly Monks. Do not misunderstand me Norman Willis was a very likeable person, but he was not cut out for the cut-throat, sometimes nasty and underhand business which being at the top of any organisation involves.

One episode during the December 9 meeting summed this up. The meeting was held, like all the others which followed after, in an ante-room off of the general secretary's office. We all sat round a rectangular table normally with a couple of bottles of white wine on the table. Willis, Hammond and myself were alone round the table as Dean and Dubbins were involved in a side meeting with Graham and Monks. I cannot recall where Jack Whyman of the AEU was at the time.

Willis, a folk song fan, sat facing Hammond and I across the table. He leant forward and explained how he had written a little song. To my amazement he then asked if we would like to hear it. I was taken aback as I had thought that we could have spent the time more usefully. After all, one of the purposes of the meeting was to put Hammond and his union under some pressure, not to serenade him with ditties. Willis duly sang his song and Hammond told him he thought it was very good, and while reaching into his briefcase sitting on the floor beside him, asked Willis if he could sing it again.

Willis agreed and as Hammond produced a small tape-recorder, began another rendition. I sat silently picturing in my mind Hammond reporting back to his executive about the meeting and asking them if they would like to hear how he was put under pressure and then playing the tape of the TUC General Secretary singing a ditty. Worse still, the chances are he played it for News International executives at one of their many clandestine meetings.

It was agreed at the meeting that we would jointly reject Murdoch's proposals and tell him that we were ready to negotiate flexible agreements designed to avoid disputes. We asked for an urgent meeting with Murdoch which took place the next day.

At the meeting Murdoch refused to budge and was supported in taking this stance by the fact that Tom Rice, the National Secretary of the EETPU who arrived late, announced that his union was not opposed to a legally binding agreement and recognised the management's right to manage. The EETPU's position had already been released to the press and there is no doubt that Murdoch knew about it. The following day the four unions registered a complaint against the EETPU.

The pace was hotting up. On December 19 we were summoned once again to the TUC and Willis, under Rule 11, issued the following instruction.

1 No union (AUEW, EETPU, NGA, NUJ and SOGAT)
should enter into an agreement or arrangement with News
International covering all or part of the operations or
groups of employees at Wapping except with the agreement
of the other unions concerned; and
2 It is imperative and urgent that the five unions seek to
agree a common approach to the proposals from News
International.

We met Bill O'Neill the following day, December 20, to try to
persuade him to withdraw the legally binding no-strike clause. It has
to be said that by this time it was all a bit make-believe. I think
everyone knew that News International had no intention of reaching
a settlement, no matter what the unions offered.

Realising this position the production unions decided to try
and take the initiative and amended their claim for their members
working in Grays Inn Road and Bouverie Street, claiming a guarantee
of employment for their members and that they should be offered
jobs at Wapping if any work was transferred there. The company
continued in their strategy to try and keep the NUJ apart from the
other workers. Murdoch, when he returned from a ski-ing holiday
over the Christmas and New Year period, announced that he was
prepared to continue talking to the NUJ and the EETPU about the
London Post.

On January 8 I addressed a meeting of the Times and Sunday
Times to inform them that I would consider any offer from the
company "in consultation with the other unions and the TUC".
This was within the TUC directive and within the terms of Rule 11.
However I also told those present that I thought the London Post
was "a sham" and that the company was planning to switch some or
all of the titles to Wapping.

True to their divide and rule strategy the company, or to be
more accurate, their subsidiaries Times Newspapers Ltd, and News
Group Newspapers gave the 5,500 members of SOGAT, NGA, AUE,
and EETPU six months notice of the termination all union
agreements. Only the NUJ contracts were exempt.

Readers may wonder, why if the EETPU were collaborating with Murdoch they were included in this move. The reason is simple, the Fleet Street members of the EETPU were a fiercely independent group and were not under the sway of Hammond or Rice. Throughout the dispute the EETPU members employed by both companies were paid for doing nothing. They were never allowed to go to Wapping, simply because they represented trade unionism. Their union betrayed them.

The company then began to step up the pressure to provoke the strike which their solicitors Farrer & Company had advised them they required to allow them to sack their 5,500 workers. On January 12 the Sunday Times announced that the following week they would print a section of the paper at Wapping. Despite requests from Norman Willis to Eric Hammond to stop his members in Wapping from producing the sections, the print run went ahead and was part of the January 19 edition. The clock was now ticking for the showdown that Murdoch wanted. He was throwing down the gauntlet to the 5,500 workers, enticing them into a dispute so that like a spider he could smother them in his web and then discard them.

What was to follow is one of the saddest tales in British industrial history. Workers were goaded into withdrawing their labour by the blatant breach of existing agreements so that they could be sacked. The company followed the advice of Farrer & Co, to ensure that they had no legal responsibility towards their existing workforce as under British law if you withdraw your labour you are in breach of contract.

Both SOGAT and the NGA had held strike ballots and the results announced on Wednesday, January 22 showed a large majority in each union supporting strike action – in the case of SOGAT 3,534 for to 752 against with the NGA returning a 843–117 vote in favour of industrial action. On the same day a joint Sun and News of the World NUJ chapel meeting had agreed not to go to Wapping without an agreement.

It had been tough getting the decision through. Mike Smith

and I had been given a hard time at a meeting of the two chapels earlier in the month in St Bride's Institute, a traditional trade union meeting place off Fleet Street.

The members of neither chapel had, with some reason, no great love for the printers, for often the vice-like grip of the printers had led to papers needlessly being stopped and the production chapels were guilty of treating journalists with some contempt.

However I had a duty, as general secretary, to uphold the official position of the union which was that no agreement would be reached with the company without the blessing of the other unions and the TUC. I should say that I agreed with this approach as I recognised that News International's game plan was to bust trade union organisation within the company. This meant that they would play ball with the journalists only as long as they needed to, but there was no prospect of the editorial departments in the four titles being allowed to be an oasis of trade union organisation in a non-union plant.

Those who were not unionised would soon have recognised the benefits of being in a union as NUJ members gained better job protection, conditions and salaries as a result of trade union negotiations, while their individual conditions would have lagged behind. This would inevitably have led to the other departments seeking trade union recognition. I was certain that Murdoch saw News International's future as being union-free.

Journalists at the Sun and News of the World did not accept that this was the company's intention and even if it was, they naively believed that they had the collective power on their own to protect their position as an NUJ chapel. It had been the long-held belief by many journalists, that once the editorial staff had the single key stroke, removing the compositors from the production process, they would inherit the trade union power traditionally wielded by newspaper caserooms which resulted in compositors often earning more than journalists.

This inferior position in earnings rankled with journalists who believed that as they created the papers they should be the highest earners. I had often explained to members that it was not the hands on the keys which gave compositors the industrial muscle but trade union discipline and the ability to take their hands off the keys all at the same time. This power came through the closed shop which meant that in England and Wales all compositors were members of the NGA and in Scotland the Scottish Graphical Branch of SOGAT.

In Fleet Street and in Manchester and Glasgow the NUJ also enjoyed the closed shop but there was not the same discipline among members. Journalists by the very nature of their breed are fiercely independent souls which makes organising them into a collective unit, to say the least, a difficult task.

After a lively debate we had succeeded in getting the two chapels to agree that they should not go to Wapping without an agreement covering new technology, ie direct input/single stroke. We had pointed out to them that they had always sought a financial reward for embracing this new technology.

Having succeeded in achieving this position, two days later SOGAT and the NGA called their members out on strike, immediately throwing the NUJ into the crisis. The company played it very cleverly.

They attacked our weakest link, the Sun chapel. The production strike had already started when around 6pm Kelvin MacKenzie walked on to the editorial floor and began the strangest 'negotiations' ever. He told the 100 or so journalists still on the floor that they had to go to Wapping. Their union house agreement would remain unaltered and there would be no redundancies but during his first address, if that is how it can be described, he made no monetary offer.

On his third visit to the chapel floor he offered the journalists a rise of £2000 a head and a guarantee that the existing house agreement would remain in place for twelve months. I was waiting in another office while MacKenzie made the last of his appearances and then Malcolm Withers, the paper's financial correspondent and FOC, ushered Mike Smith and myself into the room. It was obvious from the start that it was going to be a hostile meeting.

People were hurling questions, insults and statements from all directions. No one really wanted to listen. They kept referring to their own dispute two years previously when production workers had walked through their picket lines – so why should they support the print unions now? They tried to justify their position by saying we had not kept the chapel informed. If it was true the chapel were not kept informed of the developments it was not down to the union. We had several meetings with Withers and committee members as the negotiations had progressed to keep them up to date.

Both Mike and I did our best to calm the meeting and explain why even if only from their own self-interest, they should present a united front to Murdoch. I warned them that the only reason the company was offering them £2,000 to go to Wapping was because they needed journalists to see them through the dispute, but that if the company was allowed to defeat the print workers then the company would de-recognise the NUJ and they would be left unprotected.

This message went unheeded. They believed that somehow they would be able to protect themselves where the might of the production workers had failed. They voted overwhelmingly to take the money and go to Wapping the next day for training. The editorial room quickly emptied after the meeting. Only a handful of journalists approached us afterwards to say that they would obey the union's instruction – the instruction which the chapel had agreed with only two days previously – and not go to Wapping.

Among those who remained loyal was Eric Butler, a 60-year-old sports sub who was eventually to take the message of the dispute around the UK and to Australia addressing meetings. Ollie Duke, a member of the Socialist Worker Party, was also among the first refusniks as the journalists who did not go to Wapping came to be called. Malcolm Withers, the FOC, who was also a Labour Party parliamentary candidate did go despite claiming that he would not. But he did eventually join the dispute several months later.

Television cameras were waiting on the steps outside Bouverie Street and when I watched the pictures later, I realised that I sounded dejected, and gave the appearance of someone who had been defeated. I vowed after that never to allow my feelings to show on TV when being interviewed.

It gives me no pleasure to say it, but most of my prophecies came true. Once the pickets were removed a year later, when the strike ended, the company moved quickly to start demolishing the house agreement. There is no trade union recognition in the Sun today. Only a few will have any real say in the level of wages paid to them.

Having succeeded in persuading the Sun journalists to move to Wapping and operate single stroke without an agreement covering basic conditions such as health and safety, the management next tackled the News of the World journalists on the Saturday. We had been trying to arrange a meeting with the News of the World chapel but a phone call to my office in Acorn House told me that they had agreed to go to Wapping after a meeting on the editorial floor.

It was a pretty bleak situation but no matter what you thought of Murdoch's actions in sacking 5,500 of his employees, you had to admit that they had planned it very carefully. They did not give the NUJ the opportunity to exercise the old truism, Unity is Strength. They picked off the NUJ chapels one by one. They did not approach the Sunday Times chapel on Saturday January 25 at the same time as the News of the World because they knew that the Sunday Times journalists would be a harder nut to crack.

The Sun journalists having been successfully bribed, Charles Wilson, editor of the Times, addressed his staff on the paper's editorial floor in Grays Inn Road, only a mile up the road from the union's headquarters. Wilson told the Times staff that the Sun journalists had voted to work at Wapping and urged them to follow suit. The same offer of a £2000-a-year increase was made. The journalists were told that if they did not agree to go to Wapping they would be in breach of contract and face the sack.

This time around, it was not such an easy ride for the company. The Times journalists were proud of their paper, resented being bullied and realised that they were being bounced into the move by the management. The Times chapel made no decision on the Friday night, agreeing instead to meet the following day to start a debate which turned into a seventeen hour marathon. The meetings began at 2pm on Saturday afternoon in the ballroom of the Royal National Hotel in Bloomsbury, London. The chapel committee led by their FOC, Greg Neale supported the union's position but we realised that it would be a difficult job getting the rank and file chapel members' support. After all, Murdoch had already sacked 5,500 printworkers. What was to stop him sacking a couple of hundred journalists.

The difference we knew was that he needed the journalists and that as long as they maintained a united front they could stop the Wapping bulldozer.

Mike Smith was again at the meeting as was Jake Ecclestone, my deputy general secretary, who had been a sub editor at the Times and had been FOC in 1980 when the journalists had gone on strike for more money.

The management, realising that the Times journalists were a tougher nut to crack, had put together a new technology agreement for the move to Wapping which they had presented to Greg Neale the previous evening. Once again News International management were demonstrating how flexible they were prepared to be in order to get the journalists to move.

Once again the chapel were angry and many took their anger out on the union. They did not like what was happening to them. They did not want to go to Wapping but many of them were afraid. Most realised within themselves that they would in the end decide to go to Wapping but did not want anyone to point out the harsh truth that the correct decision was not to go.

Cliff Longley, the paper's religious affairs correspondent, was perhaps the best example of how individuals behaved. At one stage in the long proceedings which spread over two days he said, "I'm damned if I'm going," but when the decision time came Cliff was able to argue the opposite and became an advocate for going behind the barbed wire.

During the meeting Jake Ecclestone whispered to me, "Cliff always argues with his conscience and wins." Cliff actually became the Times NUJ FOC inside Wapping and during the year-long dispute I had many meetings with him in the Entrecote restaurant near Russell Square when he would justify working behind the wire.

Faced with an obvious wrong being done to them the Times chapel members made the same mistake as many trade unionists before them. They assumed that if they were being wronged then the law would support them. In a vain attempt to find an escape route from their dilemma the chapel sought legal advice. I tried to persuade them that they were wasting their time and money but we were assured by several chapel members that they had been advised by 'legal friends' that they could seek an injunction against the company for breaching their house agreement.

English law, or Scots law for that matter, is not designed to protect workers' rights. If anything, it leans in the opposite direction. However in order to keep the chapel onside with the union and also to play for time, I agreed that the union would put money towards taking counsel's opinion.

The chapel meeting adjourned and a QC was contacted. Of course to contact a QC you have to go through a solicitor and when you meet a senior QC he is accompanied by a junior QC. So it was that the chapel committee met with a senior QC and his junior along with a solicitor in one of the hotel bedrooms.

If my memory is correct the consultation which lasted for around an hour cost in the region of £3,000 and at the end of it the advice to the chapel was similar to what various union officials had explained earlier.

The chapel meeting reconvened around 9pm and went on to almost midnight. The meeting ended after passing a motion deploring the management's tactics but saying that they would be willing to go to Wapping if certain conditions were met, including negotiations on health and safety, and deletion of the management statement saying that they had to operate the direct input technology "without any reservation whatsoever".

It was agreed that they would reconvene the next evening, which of course meant that journalists who were due to work a day shift the following day would be able to go to Wapping and then attend the meeting. Sadly this is what happened, and when the chapel met again at 6pm on Sunday, January 26, in the Marlborough Crest Hotel in Bloomsbury, a good number of those attending had already indicated that they had made their minds up, having gone to Wapping earlier in the day.

During this meeting the management tried to sway the decision in their favour by sending a message that they would delete the words "without any reservation whatsoever", a wording which by its very presence in the original document betrayed what the future management style of the company would be.

They also stated that the safeguards on the use of the new technology would meet EC standards. Mike Smith, the union's national newspaper officer who had previously been responsible for our new technology policy piped up, "There are no EC standards." This interjection at least brought a momentary smile to the lips of some of those attending.

I had tried to find a way out of the situation in a telephone call from the hotel lobby to Norman Willis at his home. Speaking in subdued tones to avoid journalists from other newspapers overhearing my part of the conversation I asked if there was any way the TUC could relax the directive.

Willis was sympathetic and said that when the Printing Industry Committee met the following day they would consider if there was any way the NUJ could be allowed to negotiate separately. I vainly hoped that this message would be enough to gain us another day. But it was not to be.

By a show of hands the chapel meeting voted to go to Wapping. Greg Neale their FOC told them that he had made a personal decision not to go to Wapping and was resigning as their Father of Chapel.

It was an emotional end to the meeting and many chapel members, who were acting out of fear for their jobs, were in tears. I felt drained. Three out of the four NUJ chapels had now decided to go behind the wire. It was not a pretty picture.

The Sunday Times chapel was next in line for the Murdoch propaganda machine with editor Andrew Neil addressing around 150 journalists in the Mount Pleasant Hotel. This was probably the first time that most of the Sunday Times journalists had ever been in the hotel, despite the fact that it was situated less than half a mile away from their Grays Inn Road offices. The Mount Pleasant was for many years the hotel which the NUJ used to accommodate out of London lay members who were attending meetings at Acorn House. I had first experienced the delights of the "Mount Unpleasant" when I joined the NEC in 1976. I had been asked by the union's finance staff where I normally stayed while on Daily Record business in London and had mentioned the Strand Palace, Imperial and the Russell hotels only to be informed that all were out of the union's league, and was booked into the Mount Pleasant which was a converted working man's hostel with hotel rooms which resembled cells in size and decor.

It was in these less than salubrious surroundings in the basement of the hotel that the Sunday Times journalists gathered to hear Andrew Neil appeal to them to transfer to Wapping. After Neil left, Mike Smith and myself addressed the chapel. In Linda Melvern's book *The End of the Street* my speech was described as "long and boring". The chapel eventually voted by 68-60 to go to Wapping, and according to Melvern Kim Fletcher, the FOC of the chapel believed that if I and other NUJ officials had not spoken at the meeting the motion would have been carried.

I find this hard to believe and hardly credible. Whether I bored the chapel or not did not change the harsh reality of life. The company had sacked 5,500 printworkers. The company was breaking the union agreement with the chapel. The company was making it clear that if you did not go to Wapping you were likely to be sacked.

The truth is that individuals were frightened of losing what were in anyone's terms highly paid jobs. That is why 68 people voted to go, not because they were bored by a speech. They may not have liked my message that as members of a trade union which was a member of the TUC we were bound by the TUC directive. Not a happy message, but the harsh reality nevertheless.

Despite this vote around thirty Sunday Times journalists turned up at their normal place of work in Grays Inn Road the next morning, refusing to go to Wapping. This band quickly became known as the refuseniks and held out for almost a week before the majority, worn down by management pressure, decided to go to Wapping.

The decision by the majority of the Sunday Times chapel meant that the NUJ was enjoined in the battle proper. We were no longer merely abiding by TUC directives or offering the production unions solidarity. We now had our own members, the refuseniks who had refused to cross the picket lines at Wapping, to defend and represent.

The twenty or so original refuseniks, who were all suspended, included Ian Blunt, Eric Butler, Ollie Duke and Mike Topp of the Sun, the entire labour staff of the Times, Don Macintyre, David Felton and Barrie Clement, as well as FOC Greg Neale of the Sunday Times. At the Times Paul Routledge the paper's South East Asia man refused to file copy to Wapping from Singapore and was suspended. On the Sunday Times we had Harry Coen, Robin Mead, Don Berry, Martin Huckerby and FOC Kim Fletcher.

However even the enormity of the Wapping dispute faded into insignificance when I received a call during the first week of February from my wife Maargaret to warn me that my mother, Sadie was unwell. Margaret told me that she thought I should travel home to see mum. My family still lived in Glasgow as we had yet to find a home in the London area.

I immediately travelled to Glasgow. My mum was still not on the phone despite several attempts by myself to persuade her to have one. This meant there was no way I could contact her direct. When we arrived at the family home in Pollok, an aunt told me that she had been taken to the Southern General Hospital. We found mum surrounded by my brothers and sister wearing an oxygen mask.

She took the mask off to say simply, "You've come up." Mum was obviously struggling for breath and could only say a few words at a time. She had always been a heavy smoker and I could pinpoint the start of her decline into bad health when she became unwell while on holiday with us in Scarborough in 1982. She had never fully recovered and suffered chest complaints on an increasingly regular basis.

The next day when we visited her she appeared to be slightly better and was sitting up in bed although she still had the oxygen mask on. She was quite cheery and gave me her usual warning about being careful and not to get myself in any trouble. Mum was always concerned about my involvement in trade union marches and picket lines. I think she thought I was some kind of revolutionary.

After visiting hour in the evening Margaret and I had returned to our home in Kings Park. The phone call from my sister came at around 1.30am to say that mum had died. She was 72. I was devastated. It was because of her Christianity that I had been drawn to socialism and to become a trade unionist. She had no craving for worldly goods and was always willing to help anyone.

At her funeral in St Conval's Chapel, Pollok I was comforted by the wreaths which the Daily Record and Sunday Mail NUJ chapel and the Glasgow Herald chapel had sent as well as one from the union itself. The chapels had also sent representatives to share our grief and Ray McGuigan, the union's President had flown to Glasgow from his home in Dublin. She was a good mum and may God Bless her.

On my return to London, I had to quickly pick up the pieces of the Wapping dispute as well as deal with the many other calls made upon me as general secretary of the union. We were not only up against the full might of News International but also the anti-trade union laws passed by the Thatcher government and a police presence around Wapping which was never neutral.

During the dispute we had several discussions with Neil Kinnock, Leader of the Labour Party in his office at the Commons. The first such meeting took place shortly after the dispute began. We wanted to brief Kinnock and also ensure that the Labour Party did not co-operate with journalists from the Sunday Times, the Times, Sun and News of the World. I asked Kinnock not to invite any

journalists from these four titles to Labour Party press conferences
or to issue them with press releases.

Kinnock, to be fair, was sympathetic, but understandably he
was not giving us any firm commitments. After all we were talking
about very influential titles and Kinnock did not want to declare a
war against them. The Sunday Times was the highest selling quality
Sunday, the News of the World was the highest selling Sunday tabloid,
and the Sun was the highest selling popular daily.

After a little while I decided to take the bull by the horns. I
reminded Kinnock that the staff in his press office were all members
of the NUJ and that if he did not instruct them not to co-operate
with the News International titles, I would issue an instruction to
them as NUJ members.

Kinnock's face turned beetroot. He exploded and started a
tirade about how badly my members treated the Labour Party in the
Tory press and asked why did I not do something about that rather
than attack the Labour Party. I made some soothing remarks and
the meeting ended on a calm note. No commitment was given at
the meeting but the Labour Party did not invite News International
journalists to their press conferences and took them off their mailing
lists.

On February 10, SOGAT were fined £25,000 and their assets
sequestrated for action they had taken against the distribution of the
News International titles and on March 4 the courts ordered all the
seizure of all SOGAT officials' cars.

The picketing at Wapping and the company's Glasgow plant
in Kinning Park was causing the company concern. Already journalists
who had gone to Wapping under duress were finding working behind
barbed wire an unpleasant experience and were, in increasing
numbers, finding other jobs.

Our decision to make Brenda Dean our spokesperson on
television was also helping us win the propaganda war. Brenda was
the acceptable face of trade unionism. It was difficult for the
management to portray her as a union baron.

The first sign of a shift in the company's attitude came when we met them on Friday, April 4 at the Mayfair Hotel in Berkeley Street. The venue was kept secret as neither side wished to be doorstepped by the media. My own NEC was meeting that day and I had attended it in the morning. Around the table were more than twenty journalists including Giles Smith, who was the ITN's industrial correspondent. He along with others pressed me to reveal where I was meeting the company but I refused. Giles made an eloquent speech about my responsibility to press freedom and that as general secretary of the NUJ I should not be withholding information from my own members. He threatened to have a car waiting outside Acorn House to follow me when I left.

I replied that my first responsibility in the dispute was to help secure a settlement for the NUJ members currently suspended for not crossing the Wapping picket lines. It was not my job to provide journalists with a story and that the company had warned that if the venue became public they would cancel the meeting. I added that he was welcome to have a car sitting outside as I intended to travel by tube.

However despite the company's coyness about the location of the negotiations I had received a tip that Murdoch had arranged to be interviewed that evening by Channel Four News which suggested that they were up to something. I passed this information on to the other General Secretaries before we sat down round the table.

Murdoch was not present and Bruce Matthews was leading for the company's side. We were going round in circles and Mike Smith and I, sitting at the end of the table, played noughts and crosses on hotel notepaper as both sides slagged each other.

However after an adjournment we decided to confront the management with the fact that we knew Murdoch was being interviewed on television that evening. Matthews at this point said the company had an offer to make.

There then followed a brilliant propaganda coup. Matthews unveiled a proposal to give to the unions the back end of the Grays Inn Building along with printing presses and typesetting equipment. I scribbled a note to Mike Smith saying, "clever bastards."

There were several conditions attached to the offer including that we could not print titles which were in direct competition to the News International titles. Murdoch thought he had stolen a march on us. He believed we would be tied up at a secret venue in a private room negotiating with his team while he was appearing on TV announcing to the world his offer of a printing plant to the unions.

However we had made arrangements for Brenda Dean to go to the Channel Four studios so that she could reply to any Murdoch statement. However there was no doubt that to the general public the company's offer would appear generous. After all it would provide at least some of the sacked printworkers with alternative jobs. News International claimed that the offer was worth more than £50 million. Although we were all sceptical it had to be seriously looked at. Our side had also put forward proposals at the meeting regarding recognition and employment but the company paid scant attention to them.

There followed a series of meetings with the company while in the public arena we organised a rally in Trafalgar Square on Sunday, April 20. Despite pouring rain this was attended by a crowd of 7,000. I can remember standing on the platform watching Brenda Dean address the crowd huddled under umbrellas. I was soaked and the rain was dripping down the back of my neck, yet there was Brenda standing without a hair out of place. I don't know how she did it.

At a meeting on April 16 the company had increased their offer by adding £15 million to make ex-gratia payments to those who did not secure employment at Grays Inn Road. Once again there were no real negotiations or, for that matter, discussion on our proposals regarding employment and recognition at Wapping.

We asked Unity Trust bank to examine the practicality of us taking over Grays Inn Road and producing a Labour movement paper on the presses. Their report back made gloomy reading. They estimated the value of the building at only £1 million and said that it would take nine months to do a proper feasibility study. Meanwhile Frank Barlow, chief executive of the Financial Times who had been asked for his views said that the production of a Labour movement paper would only provide around 300 jobs and half of these would be for journalists.

News International had given us until the end of May to decide on their offer and secret negotiations were set up for the Bank Holiday weekend on the Sunday and Monday, May 25/26 in the Sheraton Skyline hotel near Heathrow. These talks were very hush-hush and only those attending on the union side knew that they were taking place.

On the Saturday I was in Glasgow to address a demonstration outside of the News International plant at Kinning Park. We were to speak from the top of an open deck bus outside the factory and Labour MP Donald Dewar who was the shadow secretary of state for Scotland was our guest speaker. Donald of course was unaware of the talks that were to take place the following day and I felt it only right to warn him to temper his remarks as further negotiations were about to take place and I expected the company to make a new offer.

Murdoch was not present at the first set of talks on the Sunday. He was flying in on Concorde to take over the talks the following day if it looked like progress could be made. Bruce Matthews led for the company on the Sunday. Brenda Dean told the company representatives that their offer of the rear part of the Grays Inn Road building was only worth £1 million and the company agreed that they would pass over the front part to the unions which would raise the value to £5 million. We tried to bring the talks round to the £15 million compensation but Matthews was not willing to talk about this in the absence of Murdoch.

The proceedings reached what I believed was a farcical situation when Bruce Matthews and his cronies told us that the BBC's Heart of the Matter programme was covering the dispute that evening, and they wanted an adjournment so that we could all watch the programme.

I thought it was ludicrous that here we were trying to resolve a dispute in which 5,500 printworkers had been sacked, and the management wanted to watch themselves on television. I made my views known that I had not joined them on a Bank Holiday weekend to watch TV. I adjourned to the hotel bar with Mike Smith and we were joined by Tony Dubbins and Alf Parish the NGA's National Secretary.

The talks resumed after the programme but got nowhere. The following day Murdoch joined in and Norman Willis joined our side. Progress then started to be made, at least on the compensation side. Murdoch at first offered three weeks money for every year of service and there would be a minimum of £2000 for each employee. We estimated that this offer was worth a total of £30 million.

Later in the afternoon Murdoch increased the offer to four weeks bringing the cost to the company up to £50 million and said that this was his "final offer". There was no recognition of the unions within Wapping and no jobs. The position of the journalists who had refused to cross the picket lines would be "determined by the editors".

SOGAT, NGA and the AEU put this offer to their members but they rejected it and the dispute continued. At the NUJ we were intensifying our efforts to convince our 600 members still working in Wapping and Kinning Park not to cross picket lines. I was attempting to walk a tightrope. On the one hand I wished to give every support I could to the other print unions but I also wished to keep the NUJ intact. The journalists inside Wapping were still our members. I did not wish to alienate them.

A sizeable portion of our executive wished the union to simply issue an instruction to the members in Wapping to withdraw their labour. I realised that once we took this action we would be faced with demands for a ballot which we would lose. If we did not hold a ballot we would certainly be taken to court either by the company or our own members. This would have led to sequestration, bringing with it all the problems that this entailed, without any benefit, as our members would have continued to work in Wapping. In addition once we had issued such an instruction and it was ignored, or held a ballot and lost, we would have to walk away from the dispute unable to offer any practical support to either the sacked printworkers or indeed our own refuseniks.

Walking the tightrope became a regular feature of national executive meetings which invariably had a motion calling for an instruction to be issued. Ray McGuigan, the union's lay President agreed with my strategy and together we would marshal our troops on the NEC to win the vote. It was always a tight decision with our side coming out on top by one or two votes.

I had to look forward to the union's position after the dispute. Unlike the other unions we had members inside Wapping and I tried to keep lines of communications open. Fleet Street was traditionally one of the NUJ's well-organised areas and I did not want to create an area of non-unionism. To this end I continued to talk to the FOCs in Wapping including Cliff Longley of the Times and Malcolm Withers of the Sun. The latter eventually joined the dispute during the summer. Cliff was convinced that the NUJ could still deal with News International. He spoke of holding the "high moral ground" and believed that our House Agreement with the company would remain intact. I tried to explain that if the print unions were defeated and the pickets withdrawn then it would only be a matter of time before the company turned its attention to the NUJ chapels. I tried to explain that the company was going through the motions as they still needed the journalists and could not afford an official dispute with the NUJ in which the members took action.

Sadly Longley never listened and he became one of the victims of the aftermath of the Wapping dispute when he was made redundant by the company.

I also met Charles Wilson, editor of the Times, a couple of times during the dispute. On each occasion we met over breakfast in the Waldorf Hotel. Having known each other from our Glasgow days we had a large number of mutual acquaintances, even friends. The meetings would remain quite friendly until we broached the dispute. Then the temperature would rise rapidly with Charles telling me that the unions were finished and my warning him that the pendulum would swing back some day and we would have long memories. Our meetings would finish with Charles offering me a lift in his car back to the office, and my replying that I wouldn't be "seen dead" in his car. All good knockabout stuff. On a personal basis Charles and I remain on friendly terms as we both have a sense of humour.

Meanwhile we continued to attempt to get our members on the right side of the wire. By the end of May when I addressed the NGA's biennial meeting in the Winter Gardens at Blackpool I was able to tell the delegates attending that eighty of our members had obeyed our instruction and that another thirty had got jobs outside Wapping.

For a brief period of twenty-four hours in June it looked as if the Sun journalists would go into dispute with the management when they voted to reject a 3.5 per cent wage offer. Murdoch's response to this threat was to immediately up the offer to 10 per cent.

The exodus of journalists from Wapping gathered pace throughout the summer with the proposed launch of the Independent which attracted twenty journalists from the Times and by July the number who had left the four titles had risen to 150.

At the start of the dispute the refuseniks had been suspended as the management tried to avoid a confrontation with the journalists who had agreed to continue working. But faced with looming industrial tribunal cases from printworkers News International sacked the refuseniks.

The Sunday Times chapel agreed to ballot on industrial action following the management's decision to sack six of their refuseniks. The chapel put the matter into dispute and the management agreed to go through the motions of the dispute procedure so that they could claim they were honouring the current house agreement.

This meant that I had to come face to face with Andrew Neil, the editor. The meeting was held in the Tower Hotel and the only "victory" I won was forcing Neil to tell the Farrer solicitor sitting next to him to leave the room as the House Agreement clause did not allow for legal representation.

Everyone knew we were only going through the motions in

the dispute procedure and the management refused to budge on the sackings which led to a ballot for industrial action. The union produced a Special Bulletin aimed at the Sunday Times members urging them to vote Yes in support of their own colleagues. We failed to persuade the Sunday Times members and with the Times chapel having rejected a similar move earlier in the summer our last opportunity of convincing the journalists behind the wire to act was gone.

It was not surprising that the votes were lost as many of the journalists sympathetic to the union and their sacked colleagues had already left Wapping to take up other employment. The flight of journalists was however causing the four papers some concern.

On September 17 News International made a second final offer which increased the compensation to be paid to the sacked workers but did not offer anything on recognition or jobs. The company demanded a reply by October 8. The offer to the sacked workforce gave four weeks earnings with a ceiling of £205 for each year of service. The offer was rejected by the majority of the membership of all three unions and the dispute carried on with marches taking place every Saturday night at Wapping.

On Saturday, January 24, 1987, a large demonstration was mounted to mark the first anniversary of the sackings. I was among those asked to address the gathering in a small park adjacent to Wellclose Square directly opposite the road leading to the Wapping plant. It was estimated by some that there was a crowd of some 30,000 on the march. Certainly I had never addressed such a large gathering before. I had only started my speech from the platform when I became aware of a stirring at the back of the crowd and those at the front began surging forward, as if pushed from the back.

I was not aware of what was causing this movement until I saw people beginning to scatter as mounted police forced their way through. It was the start of what has become known as the Wapping riot. This is an unfair description. Use of the term "riot" suggests an unruly crowd. I saw no reason for the police mounted charge. It was unprovoked. Police began spraying people with red dye and officers in riot gear were clubbing people indiscriminately. Home Secretary Douglas Hurd later denied in Parliament that the police had sprayed demonstrators with red dye, suggesting instead that a pot of red paint had been thrown by one of the crowd. Not true. I witnessed the spray, the clubbing and the cavalry charge by the mounted police.

Such scenes in other countries would have been condemned but instead police statements that they only used the necessary force to curb violence from demonstrators were initially accepted by the media as being accurate.

At first the Metropolitan Police claimed that only forty demonstrators had been injured while 160 police had suffered violent attacks. Later they had to admit to 300 members of the public being injured. Legal observers at the march were among those clubbed by some police officers.

What happened that night at Wapping had nothing to do with democracy. It was a yet another example of how the police had been used as a force to intimidate, bully and assault those whom the Government saw as the "enemy within". In this country we like to pretend that we live in a democracy where State violence against individuals is not allowed. Such pretence makes life easier to get on with but blinkers can be dangerous if you do not remove them quickly enough.

Only a few days before the demonstration Murdoch had returned to the High Court issuing writs against the NGA and SOGAT claiming damages for costs of security and transporting his staff into Fortress Wapping. Following the January 24 episode he threatened to go back to court on the basis that the unions had acted in contempt of court in not meeting and holding to the previous High Court decisions in regard to picketing.

Faced with the possibility of being again sequestrated the SOGAT executive met on February 5, 1987 and decided to end the dispute and accept the offer made in September. The NGA, AEU and ourselves followed suit. The Wapping dispute was at an end with little justice for the 5,500 sacked workers or the NUJ refuseniks.

A police investigation was eventually set up to look into the behaviour of members of the police on the night of January 24. The NUJ refused to co-operate with it because we did not believe that it would be impartial. Neither did we believe that it would lead anywhere. We were proved to be correct. It took two years for charges to be brought against a number of police officers but the charges were thrown out by the court on the grounds that too long a time had passed for witness accounts to be reliable. I can think of many occasions when cases have been heard in court after much longer periods but then the police were not involved.

The Wapping dispute was a watershed in the newspaper industry, not because it introduced new technology, but because it marked the end of trade union power. I will not make myself popular with many former colleagues by declaring that this power had been abused. In the main the abuse did not come from the very top of the print unions but from the chapel officials.

In the mid 1980s the unions were beginning to tackle the power wielded by the Fleet Street chapels and as I explained, agreement had been reached between the NUJ and the NGA which would have allowed the introduction of direct input technology in the editorial area.

Unfortunately the changes came too late to prevent Wapping and in place of the abuse of power by chapel officials we had the abuse of power by management and 5,500 workers lost their jobs as a result. The removal of the highly organised production unions did not bring about the benefits predicted such as the growth of titles. The lasting testament has been larger profits for the managements.

19. David and Goliath

CHRISTMAS 1987 was approaching when Yousef Alan of the Trade Union Friends of Palestine entered my office on the fifth floor of Acorn House, the headquarters of the National Union of Journalists in London's Kings Cross.

Yousef was a regular visitor to my office. The NUJ supported the demand for a Palestinian homeland and in the past, as General Secretary of the union, I had written many letters to the Israeli Government demanding the release of Palestinian journalists detained without trial by the Israeli authorities.

Yousef's request on this occasion was somewhat different. The news bulletins on TV and radio as well as the columns of the daily newspapers were full of the Intifada which had been declared in the Occupied Territories on December 8. The Palestinians in the Occupied Territories of the West Bank and Gaza had risen against the Israeli Defence Force and our TV news bulletins were full of pictures of Palestinian youths throwing stones at soldiers who replied with live ammunition and beatings. Not surprisingly in this David and Goliath confrontation the casualties on either side were uneven. Few days passed without news of the death of another Palestinian youth.

Yousef asked if the NUJ would be willing to send a delegation to the West Bank to witness what was happening in the Occupied

Territories. I replied that I would put his invitation to our Executive. Yousef made one thing clear. He wanted myself as General Secretary of the union to be a member of the three person delegation. I cannot claim that I was terribly enamoured by this suggestion as I had no desire to be caught in a war zone, particularly as we would be guests of the Palestinian Liberation Organisation, for the Trade Union Friends of Palestine were an arm of the PLO. However I had a great deal of personal sympathy for the plight of the Palestinians and I agreed I would lead the delegation if the Executive gave the go-ahead. The union accepted the invitation and in February 1988 with the Intifada still at its height I flew on an El Al flight from Heathrow accompanied by Scarlett McGuire, joint President of the NUJ and Lionel Morrison, a former President.

We were met at the airport and driven to the American Hotel in East Jerusalem, which until the Six Day War was under Jordanian control and which of course is now disputed territory. The Arab quarters of the city were deserted, with steel shutters firmly down on all the shop fronts as the result of a general strike by the Palestinians in protest against the Israeli occupation and the brutality of the IDF forces.

Our hosts had arranged a busy schedule for our four day visit including a visit to the town of Nablus which was under curfew. Our driver for the visit we were told was 'George' and it was explained that as the IDF had placed roadblocks on all main roads into the town that we would have to sneak in by the back door down a dirt track. This made a mockery of my assurance to my wife Margaret that we would be in no danger and nowhere near the scenes of the riots being shown on our television screens back home.

Our hosts explained that the minibus we would be travelling in would have Israeli number plates which were a different colour from those issued in the Occupied Territories, and that both George and his companion spoke Hebrew, and lived inside the 'green line', ie Israel proper. We had not travelled far inside the West Bank when we noticed that our Palestinian friends kept a scarf lying on the dashboard clearly visible to passers-by. However one minute it would be a black and white checked scarf and the next it would be red and white. They kept interchanging the two scarves and when we approached IDF forces both scarves would disappear.When we inquired about the constant switching it was explained to us that the black and white version was worn by Palestinians and was identified with the PLO while the red and white was Jordanian. Our hosts displayed each scarf depending on the loyalty of the area we were passing through, and removing both scarves when Israelis were around.

The Arab villages we passed through on our journey were obviously steeped in the history of the area but showed few signs of prosperity with no evidence of any investment in public amenities.

It was a different story if you raised your eyes skyward and looked to the hilltops where often you would see modern houses, painted white, sparkling in the sunshine. These were Jewish settlements and nowhere was the stark contrast between oppressed and conquerer more stark. The Jewish settlements, like the castles dotted around Scotland, occupied the high ground so that they could easily defend themselves and also dominate the countryside around them. Needless to say these settlements had had a great deal of money invested in them.

This first hand view of the settlements in the Occupied Territories brought home to me the true nature of Isreal's presence in the West Bank. Earlier we had received a taste of this as we had driven out of Jerusalem and saw a bearded figure with a scull cap on his head standing at a bus stop with a sub machine gun slung over his shoulder. This is the reality of how the occupation is enforced, for the Arab population is not allowed to carry any arms. I could not help but think of the terrible irony of how a country, largely born out of the Holocaust of the Second World War imposed its will on Palestinian ghettos by armed force. Here were the very people who had suffered under the Nazi jackboot imposing their will on a subjugated people. Hitler believed in the Greater Germany and sadly many Zionists believe in a Greater Israel. They believe that the West Bank – consisting of the Biblical lands of Judea and Sumaria – is theirs because it says so in the Old Testament. Extreme Zionist and right wing religious Jewish organisations wish to turn a Greater Isreal into an an Arab-free zone. There is something intrinsically wrong with a system which gives Jews anywhere in the world the right to come to Isreal and be provided with subsidised housing in East Jerusalem while Arabs whose families have lived there for generations are not allowed to build new homes and whose existing homes have in some cases been bulldozed to the ground.

It was thoughts such as these which were passing through my mind as we drove past the main road into Nablus which was guarded by members of the IDF. Further down the road, out of sight of the soldiers we turned on to a rough dirt track.

The sky was bright blue and it was approaching noon when we arrived at Nablus, a town roughly the size of Paisley. Despite being mid-day there was an uncanny hush over the town. It was as if there had been a nuclear bomb warning and the entire population had fled leaving only empty buildings behind. We approached from high ground above the town and could see the flat-roofed houses stretching out before us. George explained the intricacies of an IDF curfew. My perception of curfews had been fashioned by Hollywood movies where the local population are ordered to be indoors by a certain hour each evening. Not so in the West Bank. An IDF curfew can last for days with the entire population ordered to remain indoors twenty-four hours a day. The occupying force lifts the curfew for a short period of one or two hours every second or third day to allow the 70,000 citizens to buy essential foodstuffs before the curfew is re-imposed. As we approached closer we could now see the occasional figure in flowing Arab robes standing on their flat roof risking the wrath of young Israeli soldiers who patrolled the streets below in order to breathe some fresh air.

Naturally in these circumstances the streets were deserted and it sounded to me that the noise from our engine could be heard all over town. I need not have worried about the engine noise giving us away, for as we turned right into a main street we came face to face with an IDF road block.

We all stiffened. Then as we slowed approaching the soldiers, someone spotted the black and white PLO-coloured scarf lying on the dashboard and hissed at George, "the scarf, the scarf." George hastily grabbed the scarf and shoved it from sight under his seat. George and his companion climbed out the minibus and began speaking in Hebrew to the officer in charge. There was a great deal of gestulating and raised voices while the three of us sat silently inside. It was fortunate that we did sit in silence for after about five minutes George and his companion climbed back in and we were allowed through.

None of us looked back, and we quietly asked George what he had said. Our Palestinian driver explained that he had told the young officer that we were American tourists, and that he was taking us to Bethlehem and had come through Nablus to avoid all the troublesome Arabs who were throwing stones at passing vehicles. The officer had inspected their documents, and seeing that they were Israeli, accepted the story and allowed us through.

Our first stop was a hospital which was full of Palestinian casualties of the Intifada, including three brothers who had been 'buried alive' by militant Jewish settlers. Once inside we were safe as the hospital only treated Arabs and had an Arab staff.

Suddenly everyone, including the doctors and nurses, began rushing outside. It was as if the fire alarm had gone off, but George informed us that the IDF had announced that the curfew had been lifted for an hour to allow people to buy food. The presence of so many people on the streets meant that it was safe for us to venture out and we mingled with the crowds who made Christmas shopping in Argyll Street in Glasgow seem like a quiet affair. We came aware of a certain frenzy in the crowd as shopkeepers began to slam their shutters down and cars began to speed off hooting their horns to clear a way through. An IDF jeep appeared, with a soldier speaking in Arabic through a loudhailer. George told us that he was saying, "People of Nablus, the curfew will be imposed in ten minutes time. Clear the streets."

Everyone he said was in such a hurry because if you were caught outside during the curfew the very least the soldiers would do would be to give you a beating with the long wooden clubs they carried. The scene has never left my mind. It reinforced how the Israeli forces were stripping the Arab population of any vestige of human dignity. The Palestinians – men, women and children – were just like rats escaping a sinking ship. They were certainly not treated as fellow humans with equal human rights by the youths turned into oppressors who act as the 'master race' in the Occupied Territories.

We returned quickly to the hospital then drove to the home of Shaheed, a Palestinian trade union leader, who had just been released from six months administrative detention. Such detention is Israel's equivalent of internment – imprisonment without trial. If caught meeting us, Shaheed would almost certainly have found himself once again imprisoned. Indeed within weeks of our return to London, George, our driver, and the other Palestinians who acted as our hosts and guides were all placed in administrative detention.

After enjoying tea with Shaheed and discussing the situation in Nablus, we made our way cautiously out of town and returned to Jerusalem.

Our Palestinian hosts also took us to the Beach Camp in the Gaza strip. My image of a refugee camp was once again proved wrong. In my mind the mention of a refugee camp evoked visions of a temporary settlement with makeshift tents or huts. Instead, when we drove in to the Beach Camp we found ourselves in a large permanent community – they had been there for almost forty years – of around 20,000 people. But unlike any other community which had been established for such a length of time, there were few utilities and no permanent roads. The houses were permanent. They had mostly been there since 1948 when the Stern and Irgun Zionist gangs had forced the Arab population to flee from their homes in Palestine.

In January 1996, film of the Beach camp was flashed up on BBC television screens when Baroness Chalker, Britain's Minister of Overseas Development, visited it. Nothing appeared to have changed since my visit – the dereliction was still obvious and viewers were told that little or no money had been spent on public utilities for forty years. Water supplies were contaminated from open sewers and there was a grave shortage of clean water. The British government along with the Americans, we were informed, were funding a new water supply system.

When we visited in February 1988 at the height of the Intifada all around us were the signs of recent disturbances with burnt-out tyres and the remains of roadblocks still making passage difficult. The banned Palestinian flag fluttered from telegraph wires or poles. Today, since the Oslo Peace process began in 1994 at least the Palestinian flag flies over Gaza and the refugee camps.

Our presence soon attracted attention. Obviously as we were accompanied by Palestinians we were recognised as sympathisers of the PLO. We were therefore in no danger, although we were constantly stopped and asked to help free Palestine. During one such conversation we were invited in to an elderly gentleman's house and our hosts told us that the man would be offended if we were to refuse. Inside the house we sat on the floor round the walls of a room. Several women of the household brought bowls of nuts and fruit accompanied by tea in thick stubby glasses. Arabs drink their tea without any milk and with copious amounts of sugar. Naively I asked if I could have some milk for my tea. One of my guides nudged me in the side and whispered into my ear, "In the camps the milk is kept for the children." Rather sheepishly I drank my tea, black without any milk.

The old man with a weatherbeaten face described how he had been a moderately well-off farmer in Palestine until the Jews had forced his family from their land in 1948. Since then he had been living in the squalor of the camp waiting to return to his farm. Like many other Palestinians during my stay he made clear the responsibility that the British Government had for the situation he and his people were in. He reminded me of the Balfour Declaration when in November 1917 AJ Balfour, then British Foreign Secretary wrote to Lord Rothschild, chairman of the British Zionist Federation, saying that "His Majesty's Government view with favour the

establishment in Palestine of a national home for the Jewish people."
Like others he also pointed out that the laws which the Israelies
used to suppress the Palestinian population were largely those left
behind by the British administration in 1948.

The population in the Beach camp had at that time little to
look forward to. Israel spent no money on the infrastructure of either
the refugee camps or Gaza itself. Indeed when the local population
attempted to create a small fishing industry in the Mediterranean
which forms one of the camp's boundaries the IDF prevented them
from fishing.

Since 1994 of course, Gaza has been part of the territories
handed over to Yasser Arafat's administration but the population
still live for the most part in relative deprivation. Most of the adults
who have jobs work in Israel, and almost inevitably any trouble
between Arabs and Jews is immediately followed by the border being
closed, depriving the migrant workforce of their wages. The Western
world will have to invest billions of dollars in Gaza and the West
Bank if there is to be any hope of Palestine creating a modern market
economy.

During our stay we also visited a small refugee camp on the
outskirts of Jerusalem. This camp, being actually part of the city,
was at the centre of the Intifada and was under permanent IDF
surveillance. During our stay while we were inside an Arab home
being shown damage caused by soldiers 'searching' the premises we
became aware of a rumpus outside. The camp it seems had suddenly
been sealed off by IDF troops and no one was allowed to enter or
leave.

The next thing we became aware of was a pall forming in the
air as the soldiers fired tear gas canisters into the camp. We had to
remain inside for almost an hour as the barrage continued, before
saying our farewells to the families who had to live constantly with
this form of harrassment. We spent part of our stay in Jerusalem and
were escorted around Old Jerusalem which is part of the Arab
quarters of the ancient city.

It was here that we witnessed at first hand Israeli bullying tactics yet again while on our way to Al Asqu, a Muslim mosque. In this ancient part of the town houses and shops are huddled together in alleyways. Suddenly we were confronted by armed members of the IDF who appeared to be guarding one of the houses. It was explained to us that Sharon, the Israeli Minister who had masterminded Israel's invasion of Lebanon, had bought the house by devious means. Attempts were now being made to intimidate Arab neighbours to sell their homes to Israelis, a move designed to slowly push Arabs out of the quarter.

As we approached Al Asq, our escorts informed us that it appeared that members of the IDF were not allowing anyone to enter the mosque which had become a focal point of Palestinian protests as people left after prayers. I tried to brazen my way in and walked past the guards pretending I had not seen them. The next thing I felt was the tap on my shoulder and turned to see a rifle barrel pointing at me while an IDF soldier made it clear that I could not go any further.

At the end of our four day visit we were driven to the airport. Our departure did not go as smoothly as our entry. Security at the airport asked where we had visited during our stay. We were at this time separated and had not prepared our answers beforehand as perhaps we should have done. I made a quick calculation and told them that as well as Jerusalem we had visited Ramallah and Gaza as both these towns were open. Lionel Morrison, however told his security questioner that he had never left Jerusalem. The security personnel after the initial questioning went into a huddle and compared notes. Both Scarlett and I had told the same story but Lionel's differed. They then began to question us again separately about who we had met while in Isreal, the West Bank and Gaza. I merely said Palestinian journalists without giving any names, and when asked the purpose of our visit I said to examine the censorship of the Palestinian media, which we had indeed discussed with journalists.

After about ten minutes Scarlett and I were told that we could board the waiting aircraft, but Lionel's luggage was by this time being dissected. The security personnel tried to persuade us that we should board the plane but we made it clear that we were not moving without Lionel. After a further fifteen minutes Lionel was gruffly told he could board the plane which had been delayed waiting for us to board.

On our return to London we arranged to call a press conference the next morning in Acorn House to describe the scenes we had witnessed. As a carrot we had told the news desks of the various papers that we had exclusive photographs of the three Palestinians who had been buried alive, as well as photographs of Nablus under curfew.

Before our visit to Israel we had bought a black and white film for our camera as in 1988 most newspapers were still published in mono. The first thing we did on our return to London was to send the film off to one of our freelance members to be developed overnight. On my arrival at the office the next morning I immediately asked where the prints were, only to hear that something had gone drastically wrong. It appears that the spool had not been turning in the camera, and that we did not have a single photograph. This meant we had to face a room full of journalists all with their hands extended looking for photographs and tell them there had been a slight hiccup in our plans. Oh dear, it was extremely embarrasing as General Secretary of the National Union of Journalists to inform a gathering of Fleet Street journalists, the vast majority of whom were our members, that nothing had been happening inside the camera while we snapped merrily away. Barbed comments flew, and we were left in no doubt what the gathering thought of us.

Despite this element of farce we managed to convey an accurate picture of the Intifada and several accounts of our visit appeared in the newspapers the following day. The visit was very depressing and although my spirits and hopes were lifted along with thousands of others when the Peace Process of land for peace began in 1994, events since then have left me wondering if Isreal has the political will to make a lasting peace on equal terms with its Arab neighbours.

The union's involvement in the Middle East reached new

heights when one of our broadcasting members John McCarthy was taken hostage in Beirut during the union's annual delegate meeting in April 1986, just a few months after I had taken up my position as General Secretary.

I must admit that it had not been my intention to take direct responsibility for the union's international affairs as I believed that there were more pressing problems facing our members at home.

However once I was elected, Aiden White, who was at that time the union's Honourary Treasurer persuaded me that as General Secretary of the largest journalist union in the world I should stand for election to Bureau of the International Federation of Journalists (IFJ) which has its headquarters in Brussels. I did this in June 1986 at the IFJ's Congress in Elsinor, Denmark and came second top in the poll for a seat on the bureau.

Another admission I must make is that the union, including myself, did not pay much attention to John McCarthy's plight until his girlfriend Jill Morrell, who was also an NUJ member came to my office on January 28, 1987 and asked for assistance.

I agreed to give the Friends of John McCarthy, the group of people who were campaigning to secure his release, a room in Acorn House. Jill refers to this in the book which she wrote with John after his release.

The room was to become the Friends' headquarters throughout the five year struggle to bring John back home. I would not wish to overstate the NUJ's and my own involvement in the campaign as most of the work was done by the Friends but I believe we played at times a crucial part in the battle to keep John's name in front of the public and politicians.

I have to say that the treatment of the hostages, and John in particular, by the British press highlighted a weakness in our media. The French media took a very active part in attempts to secure the release of their hostage, Jean Paul Hauftman who was also held in the Middle East. In France the broadcasting stations mentioned Jean Paul's captivity every day, counting the number of day he had been held whereas in the United Kingdom we had to dream up stunts in order to obtain publicity. The simple fact that John was still a hostage was not in itself considered newsworthy enough to broadcast or write about.

On his release Brian Keenan made it clear that he gave the Irish Government the credit for helping to secure his freedom and he flew to Dublin from the Middle East, not to London or Belfast. And of course both Hauftman and Keenan were released before John. All three were held together for a period during their captivity.

In February 1988 I went to Paris to take part in the events being held to mark the 1,000th day that Jean Paul Hauftman had been held in captivity. It was a very public occasion and a boat bedecked with banners cruised up and down the Seine. The French public expressed their concern that a French national should be a hostage and the French Government were actively involved in diplomatic manoeuvres with countries such as Iran to secure the release of the French journalist.

This was in stark contrast to the apathy which the British Government seemed to treat John McCarthy's plight. Time and again, the Foreign Office would make statements saying that they could not do any deals with terrorists. No one can deny that this has to be the public stance of Governments but the French, while publicly making the same noises, were active behind the scenes working towards the release of Jean Paul. Perhaps the British Government's head-in-the-sand attitude was illustrated by the different approaches between themselves and the Irish Government in the case of Brian Keenan, who while born in Northern Ireland, held an Irish passport and was therefore a twin responsibility of the British and Irish. The Irish government actively lobbied in the UN and elsewhere to secure Keenan's release.

On Thursday, December 10, 1987 the Friends of John McCarthy organised a series of events to mark the 600th day of John's imprisonment. It should be remembered that at this stage in the Friends' campaign no one could be certain that John was still alive. I eventually asked my PLO contacts if they could use their network in the Middle East to establish whether or not John was alive. The request went to the top of the PLO command structure in Tunisia, and I eventually received word that John was in captivity, and was alive. I immediately passed this to the Friends campaign and naturally they were lifted by the news. Jill Morrell, through the good offices of the NUJ, eventually visited the PLO headquarters.

In March 1988 I flew to New York as part of an IFJ delegation to meet Perez de Cueller, the secretary-general of the United Nations. The delegation was led by Mia Dooneart, a Belgian diplomatic journalist, who was President of the IFJ. Also on the delegation was Chuck Perlik, President of the American Guild of Journalists who was concerned not only about the journalists who were held hostage but also the American hostages, Terry Anderson and Tom Sutherland who was Scots by birth. A French journalist made up the fourth member of the delegation.

Perez de Cueller listened carefully to what we had to say in his office in the UN building high above Manhattan. Mia explained how the taking of journalists as hostages struck at the very heart of press freedom, and that if those involved in conflict, or who felt they had a grievance wanted to have their message heard then they should not threaten the journalists covering the conflict. De Ceuller asked if we would like to meet the Iranian ambassador to the United Nations. We immediately said yes, as it was widely believed that Iran had influence over the Hizbollah groups who were holding the hostages.

The secretary-general was as good as his word and a meeting was arranged for the next day, March 17. Mr de Ceullar pointed out that it would be better if only two members of the delegation met with the Iranians, as it was unlikely that they would agree to meet the entire group. It was decided that myself and Mia would be the ones who would meet the Iranian ambassador the following morning. I had been due to fly back to London on an early morning flight but we cancelled this as it was too an important opportunity to miss.

The meeting with the Iranians was strange. They listened in silence to what we had to say and we stressed that we were not asking for merely the release of our members who were hostages but all hostages. The ambassador addressed all his remarks towards me instead of Mia who was the leader of our delegation. This may have been because Mia was a woman. They made the point that many Arab people were held hostage by the Israeli Government and that therefore the problem was not one-sided. They also denied that their Government had anything to do with the hostage taking.

Both our meetings were very important. Perez de Ceuller promised us that he would draw our concerns to the attention of all the UN member states who had an interest in the Middle East conflict, and we also knew that a report of our meeting with the Iranian ambassador would be sent back to Tehran.

One unexpected bonus of my having to cancel my flight was that as it was March 17, St Patrick's day I was able to attend the world famous St Patrick's Day parade down Fifth Avenue. It will not surprise readers that with a surname like Conroy I have some connection with Ireland. All my great grandparents came from Ireland and I have spent many holidays in both Northern Ireland and the Republic.

Two months later I led the NUJ delegation to the IFJ Congress in Maastricht. In the intervening period between my visit to New York and the Congress at the end of May, 1988 Jean Paul Hauftman had been released. Jean Paul had agreed to come to Maastricht to address the Congress, but it was also arranged that I would meeting him personally to be fully briefed on what he knew about John.

The French journalist had spent a long time in captivity and he had only been freed a month before I met him in a private house near the conference centre. He was still recovering from his experience and appeared very gaunt. He spoke hesitantly but explained how he had been held in the same makeshift prison with an Englishman and an Irishman. This was John and Brian Keenan.

He described how their guards did not allow them to speak but that they managed to communicate in whispers and sign language. Brian Keenan had obviously not lost his sense of humour as Hauftman explained that Keenan told him that it was bad enough to be held a hostage but to be held with an Englishman made it worse. Keenan also told him that he objected to being described on the radio has a British hostage as he considered himself to be Irish.

Jean Paul was able to tell us that John appeared to be in good spirits and good health considering the conditions he was being held in. After our conversation Jean Paul left in a car escorted by friends, insisting before he left that he fill a bottle up with water. He was only going to be in the car for fifteen minutes, but one of the legacies of his captivity was that he refused to travel anywhere without water.

On Thursday, September 1, 1988 the union organised a No Holiday for Hostages Day to draw attention to the continued captivity of the hostages and John in particular. Realising that we would have to offer the media a gimmick, I organised to free white doves outside St Bride's Church in Fleet Street with Jill Morrell. The truth is they were actually white pigeons. I cannot remember the reason but we could not obtain white doves. I think it was something to do with the fact that the pigeons would fly back home to their owner while the doves would have just disappeared into thin air! Following the photo-opportunity we held a vigil for John in St Bride's Church. The campaign for John's release carried on and was still continuing when I was defeated in the ballot for re-election as General Secretary in July 1990 and left the union's employ in September. I was delighted when John was eventually released in August 1991.

20. Death on the Rock

I WAS ENJOYING a lunchtime glass of Frascatti in Smithy's wine bar when I first met Thames TV reporter Julian Manyon.

I had heard of Julian, as he was the reporter involved in the making of the controversial Death on the Rock documentary which the Thatcher government had been kicking up a stink about. The journalists involved, who were our members, had asked us to help defend them against the criticisms being hurled from the Government's front benches and from the Tory press.

Jake Ecclestone, the deputy general secretary of the union was handling the matter and Julian had come to Smithy's to talk to Jake about a major development – Thames Television were setting up an independent inquiry to look into the making of the programme.

Instead of Jake going into conference with our members to discuss this development I suddenly found everyone insisting that I became involved. I was reluctant to do so as I was already heavily committed on a whole range of union activities.

However I was talked into it and found myself sitting in a car beside Julian Manyon heading for Thames TV's headquarters near Euston Station, not far from the NUJ's offices at Kings Cross.

Julian had an attractive deep-timbered voice, but he spoke, as we say in Glasgow, with "jorries in his mouth" ie he appeared to speak with a cultivated accent rather than a regional dialect. On the short journey he exploded saying, "I voted for the damned woman you know!" He was referring to Prime Minister Margaret Thatcher who had made vitriolic attacks on the programme and its makers in the House of Commons.

I replied, "I guessed that," and Julian glanced over at me quizzically. We obviously came from very different backgrounds.

When we arrived at Thames I was ushered into a private room and introduced to Roger Bolton, editor of This Week who was responsible for the making of Death on the Rock. I already knew of Roger, because of his involvement when working with the BBC in the making of another programme regarding Northern Ireland which had also attracted criticism from the British establishment. Chris Oxley, producer of Death on the Rock was also present as was Alison Cahn, who was the researcher on the programme. All four were extremely concerned that Thames had announced that there would be an independent inquiry. Understandably they feared that they were going to be set up to satisfy Margaret Thatcher and her Foreign Secretary, Sir Geoffrey Howe, who were calling for blood.

Howe had tried to have the programme postponed before it was shown on April 28, 1988. He wrote to Lord Thomson, chairman of the Independent Broadcasting Authority asking for the showing to be postponed on the grounds that it could prejudice an inquest which was due to be held into the killing in Gibraltar of the three IRA terrorists, Danny McCann, Sean Savage and Mairead Farrell by the SAS.

The three terrorists had been planning to explode a bomb during a ceremonial parade of British soldiers. If they had succeeded many civilians who watched the parade would have been killed along with the soldiers. However the three dead terrorists were found to be unarmed and the car they were approaching at the time was found to have no explosives in it. Explosives were later found at another location. The programme raised disturbing questions as to whether or not the three IRA members could have been arrested, or whether or not the SAS were operating a "shoot-to-kill" policy. Julian Manyon interviewed witnesses who claimed that two of the terrorists had their hands in the air when they were shot and that a third was shot in the back as he ran away.

I did not see the programme when it was shown but I was not surprised at the reaction to it in the press. The Times headline said "Trial by TV," and the Daily Star had "Slur on the SAS." This was the traditional reaction to any questioning coverage of the British Government's role in Northern Ireland. Roger Bolton, as I stated earlier, had been lambasted for a Panorama broadcast he had made concerning Northern Ireland.

The same type of jingoism had been witnessed during the coverage of the Falklands War when television presenters were accused by the press of being traitors because they insisted on presenting an unbiased coverage of the conflict. We pride ourselves in having a free press but there is no need of state censorship if you have a media which censors itself as large chunks of the London-based press sometimes give the impression that they are willing to do.

After meeting the journalists I agreed to take their fears to management and insist that some safeguards should be put in place to ensure that the inquiry was not used as a means of getting the company off the hook in their relations with the Government and making the journalists scapegoats in the affair.

Thames TV made soothing noises and agreed to consult with us on what kind of framework the inquiry would work within. They of course denied that they were setting up the inquiry simply because of Government pressure. These denials have to be seen in the context of what was happening concerning television at that time.

The Thatcher Government were pushing through radical changes in broadcasting. The ITV companies were being faced with the prospect that they would have to make financial bids for their franchise, and for the first time in television history ITV franchises would be awarded to the highest bidder with some quality programme safeguards thrown in as a sop. Companies such as Thames already felt themselves under pressure from Thatcherite policies.

Our fears appeared to be confirmed when we learned of the identity of the first person appointed by the company to the inquiry team – Lord Windlesham, a Tory peer, who had served in the Heath Government as a Northern Ireland Minister. I immediately contacted Richard Dunn, managing director of Thames Television and told him that we now believed that our members should not co-operate with the inquiry.

This threat posed a real dilemma for Thames TV management. Without the co-operation of the journalists who made the programme it was difficult to see how they could complete any inquiry. The management could of course order their journalistic staff to co-operate but this could have exploded into an industrial dispute with press freedom at its heart.

Dunn finally agreed that I should have a veto on the selection of the second person for the inquiry team. This fact was kept very quiet for obvious reasons. It was agreed that Dunn would supply me with the name of any person being considered, and that if I objected that person would not be appointed. I rejected one name before Dunn put forward Richard Rampton QC.

I had to be very careful before coming to any decision as if I made a mistake and later discovered that the second person had a history of anti-press freedom, or had connections with the Government and was therefore likely to act in whatever way he or she thought would please them, then our members would be no more than sacrificial lambs.

I was on my way to attend an IFJ bureau meeting in Brussels when Richard Dunn phoned me, which made it more difficult for me to carry out my own personal checks. This caused Dunn some concern as his board of directors, who were not aware of our agreements, were pressing him to make the appointment. I spoke to some of my legal contacts in London and Glasgow about Rampton's background and finally set my mind at ease.

I was not looking for some left-wing radical but at the same time I did not want a right-wing reactionary. From what I was told Rampton, if he had any political leanings, was liberal thinking. Richard Dunn phoned me in Brussels to try and obtain my nod of approval. I was not able to give him it right away but soon afterwards I received a call which allowed me to phone Dunn back to give the all clear. Rampton did not have any knowledge of my involvement in his appointment.

Rampton was appointed on Tuesday, October 11 and we began preparing our representations to the inquiry. Our position was that there should be no inquiry. We made our feelings clear in our statement which was published in their final report which was published in book form by Faber and Faber.

Windlesham and Rampton said,

"It needs to be said that while co-operating with the inquiry, the NUJ told us plainly that it wished to:
'place on record its firm belief that it sees no need for any inquiry such as the one currently taking place. Such a development is a retrograde step for journalism in this country.

There are procedures and institutions already in existence to deal with any alleged journalistic abuses or mistakes, such as the NUJ's own Ethics Council, the Press Council or the Broadcasting Complaints Commission.

'We believe the inquiry was set up as a result of political pressure and is a method of harassment of journalists who are involved in the type of journalism which poses awkward issues.' "

Not surprisingly we were the only person or organisation to make such a reservation. I believe we were right to place on record such reservations. Under Thatcher's leadership the Government brooked no criticism and there had been several clashes concerning media coverage particularly on Northern Ireland.

In August 1985, shortly after I had been elected General Secretary of the NUJ, broadcasting journalists in both the BBC and in the independent sector withdrew their labour for twenty-four hours in protest at the Governors of the BBC agreeing to ban the Real Lives programme following pressure from the Government.

The measure of support we had for this withdrawal can be measured by the fact that for the first time in its history, the BBC's

World Service programme was not broadcast.

The Government had also introduced a broadcasting ban on Sinn Fein representatives being heard on TV or radio which meant the British public, until the peace process began, were treated to an actor/actress saying the words that the Sinn Fein representatives had said.

Other examples of the Thatcher Government's bad record on media freedom was its prohibiting newspapers from publishing information they received from Peter Wright, the former MI5 agent, whose book Spycatcher they had banned.

I personally came up against this restriction when I was due to address the TUC congress on the subject of the ban. I had a copy of the book, and it was my intention to read extracts from it during my speech which was going out live on television. I was almost put off my stride as I approached the rostrum and TUC chairman warned me not to read from the book otherwise the BBC would pull the plug on the live broadcast. Thinking on my feet I stepped up to the rostrum and began to paraphrase from the book. Just as I began I heard a voice shout from the cameras positioned in the balcony, "it's ok, ok," so I reckoned I had managed to escape censorship.

The Zircon episode in February 1987 was another abuse of media freedom under the Thatcher Government. Special Branch officers raided the BBC's Glasgow headquarters to remove material concerning the Zircon spy satellite project which was going to be screened as part of the BBC's Secret Society series until it was banned.

The Death on the Rock inquiry took up quite a lot of my time during the next three months ensuring that our members were being given a fair hearing and I had several run-ins with both Windlesham and Rampton over the methods they were using to conduct the inquiry.

Right at the outset I had to make my position clear to the members involved. All were highly qualified television journalists and very good at their jobs but this did not necessarily mean that they were good negotiators, politicians or tacticians. They naturally looked towards Roger Bolton for leadership but I had to explain as politely, but as firmly as possible that as General Secretary I was responsible for all negotiations with the management and/or the inquiry team. I did not want any polite chats taking place which might land us in deep water. Roger and the others accepted this position, although at times I think they sometimes wondered about this blunt-speaking guy who spoke with a broad Glaswegian accent.

I believe the final result convinced them they had made the right decision to go along with my strategy and ground rules. Both Roger Bolton and Julian Manyon wrote to me afterwards thanking me for my assistance.

While the inquiry was taking place a disturbing piece of information came into our hands. The main thrust of the Government's demand for the programme being postponed was that it could allegedly contaminate evidence to be given at the inquest in Gibraltar. When the inquest finally took place a police inspector told the hearing that he had just happened to be passing by the scene of the shooting when he heard shots and saw three bodies lying on the ground. Our information showed that the inspector was not quite the casual passer-by he claimed to be at the inquest. He was actually in charge of the transport used in the SAS operation which was given back-up facilities by the Gibraltar police force.

We realised that this information passed to the British press would probably be buried away at the bottom of a page. I decided to make the story public via Dublin and through one of our executive members made contact with Mervyn Taylor a member of the Dail. I met Mr Taylor in his office in Dublin and showed him the document I had in my possession which proved that the police officer was part of the entire operation and not a casual passer-by as he had stated.

The Irish Government had expressed their concern at the killing of the three IRA active service unit members. No one denied that they were terrorists but what was in dispute was whether or not in order to stop them it was necessary to kill them.

Mr Taylor agreed to raise the matter in the Dail at the appropriate time and his intervention was front page news in the Irish national newspapers. It was then picked up by London-based papers such as the Guardian and Independent.

After three months of investigation the inquiry issued their report on January 26, 1989. Lord Windlesham and Richard Rampton concluded in the report that the programme "did not offend against the due impartiality requirements of the IBA and the Broadcasting Act 1981."

In paragraph 50 of their report however Windlesham and Rampton noted, "We accept that the tendency of the evidence presented was to suggest a possibility that the terrorists had been unlawfully killed, perhaps murdered. Nor were alternative explanations canvassed in any depth. Yet these considerations do not lead us to believe that the programme concluded that the terrorists had been unlawfully killed. The true interpretation, it seems to us is that the programme pointed towards one possible explanation. By 'possible' we do not mean mere speculation or conjecture, but a real possibility suggested by credible evidence and requiring proper examination."

In this paragraph the inquiry team had hit the nail on the end. It was for the very reason given in the last sentence of the paragraph that the Government wanted the programme postponed.

This result was not the one that the Government wanted and when I last met Lord Windlesham to receive a copy of the findings he expressed the fear to me that he would now become the target of the Government's criticism. He was correct. Sir Geoffrey Howe rejected the inquiry's findings in the Commons before he had even read the full report. The Foreign Office and Ministry of Defence followed suit.

The publication of the report cleared the four journalists involved in the making of the programme of any unprofessional behaviour, but they had been put through the mental wringer by the attacks from the Government and from the Tory press.

The whole process was a method of harassment of journalists. No doubt in TV and radio stations up and down the country anyone who thought of doing a critical programme of Britain's involvement in Northern Ireland would think twice before going ahead. Who would knowingly subject themselves to the publicity, pressure and character assassination which our members in the Death on the Rock team were subjected to? We will never know how many questions have never been asked, or programmes never made because the programme makers believe it is not worth the hassle.

This state of affairs is damaging to democracy. One of the reasons that Ulster is in the mess it is today is because for sixty years after it was established, Stormont was ignored by the British establishment and British press. The Unionists in Northern Ireland were allowed to get away with the gerrymandering of seats and blatant discrimination against the Nationalist minority. Such silence must never be allowed to descend again which is why we need programmes such as Death on the Rock to be made.

The Death on the Rock saga rumbled on for a number of years with the families of the dead attempting to sue the Ministry of Defence. In April 1990 Foreign Secretary Douglas Hurd signed orders barring the families from suing the Defence ministry. Then in May 1991 a High Court judge in Belfast refused the relatives a judicial review of the Government's decision blocking their compensation claims. The families then went to the European Commission on Human Rights who in September 1993 agreed to investigate the shootings.

In September 1995 the judges at the European Court decided by a 10–9 majority that the killings were unlawful but rejected relatives' claims for compensation. They did however rule that the British Government should pay legal costs to the relatives. This result justified the Death on the Rock programme which as the Windlesham report stated, "In paragraph 50 we find that the true meaning and effect of the programme was that it pointed towards one possible explanation of the shootings, namely that the deceased might have been unlawfully killed."

21. Poacher Turned Gamekeeper

MOST OF MY JOURNALISTIC career has been spent chasing stories but from time to time I have jumped the fence and chased journalists in the nicest possible way – looking for media coverage. My earlier spells as poacher turned gamekeeper were all connected with my political leanings as a Labour Party member, trade unionist, and as a supporter of a devolved Scottish Parliament.

My first tentative attempt at producing propaganda material was during the famous UCS work-in led by Jimmy Airlie and Jimmy Reid in 1971. The Glasgow Branch of the National Union of Journalists agreed to write and edit a tabloid newspaper for the workers and I was elected editor. We met Airlie and Reid on several occasions with the other shop stewards and with the help of a team of reporters we produced *The Butchering of the UCS*. I had a talented team of journalists working with me including George McKechnie, until recently editor of the Herald, cartoonist Malky MacCormick, James Cox, now a political commentator with the BBC, and sub editor, Tom Cassidy who eventually became chief sub editor on the Daily Record.

Our newspaper contained a scoop as the managing director of UCS spoke to James Cox about the problems of the four yards at Govan, Scotstoun, and Clydebank, and came out in support of the workforce. We organised a press conference in Clydebank which Airlie and Reid addressed pointing out the support they had received from a most unexpected source. Not surprisingly the story appeared on the front pages of many newspapers the following day.

My next foray into public relations came in 1980 when the Daily Record management agreed to release me for a month to allow me to act as press officer for the Labour Party in the General Election. My main job was to produce election literature, help organise press conferences and handle calls from the media.

The Labour Party organisation in Scotland was on a high, something which could not be said south of the border. My first difficulty was to sort out the ludicrous proposal to print one million copies of the Labour News for Scottish constituencies at Plymouth along with the copies destined for English and Welsh constituencies. The production schedule would have meant that we would not have had our copies delivered to Glasgow until ten days before the General Election date. We would then have had to distribute them to 43 constituencies throughout Scotland when local party activists had then to distribute them to up to 40,000 homes in each constituency.

I informed Walworth Road, the Labour Party London headquarters that it was a recipe for disaster and that we would still be distributing papers the week after the General Election day. It was even more frustrating that I had already previously explained all these practical difficulties. Fortunately I managed to convince Walworth Road and I arranged to print 1.2 million copies of the Labour News, a four page tabloid, at the Scottish and Universal Newspapers' Irvine plant.

It was a massive operation. Forty three constituencies had agreed to participate in the exercise which gave them their candidates photograph on the front page along with their personal message. This meant that we had to produce forty-three different editions featuring each of the different candidates with their own 250-word front page message along with their photograph. A team of journalistic volunteers sympathetic to the Labour cause, led by Ron Bowie, a Daily Record sub editor and union activist, answered my call for help to write, edit and take photographs for the tabloid.

But it nearly all ended in disaster. Donald Dewar had agreed to accompany me to the plant on the day I finally put the paper to bed to ensure that we matched up the correct photograph with each candidate's message. I then asked the Irvine production manager, Jack McCrorie if he would run Donald's edition first to allow him to see his own copies coming off the presses.

It all looked very impressive as the machines built up speed and the first copies began to pass through. Then, as the printed copies began to be carried through the conveyor belt machinery to the despatch area, disaster struck. Papers began to become entangled in the wire conveyor belts and the machines had to be halted. Jack McCrorie clambered up the machines to clear the blockage, but the same problem occurred every time the presses were re-started.

Donald began to mutter, "What a disaster." At this point I told him rather sharply to go home as I had enough on my mind with more than a million copies of the paper to produce without having to listen to his gloomy predictions. The problem was identified as the papers being too light. The machinery was used to printing sixty page papers and ours, at four pages, was 'floating' as they passed along the conveyors. To deal with the problem Jack McCrorie had to slow the printing presses down to half speed which extended the production time but we produced the papers and distributed all forty-three editions throughout Scotland. It was a hectic four weeks.

In addition to the Labour News we produced half a dozen leaflets which had to be designed, written, printed and distributed to the constituencies. At the same time there was a press conference every day at Keir Hardie House and numerous calls from journalists to field.

In Scotland everything was going very smoothly under the overall control of Helen Liddell, who was expecting her first child. Alongside Helen was Jimmy Allison who has a tremendous feel for how an election is going. Alf Young, now economics editor on the Herald, was an outstanding research officer who supplied candidates with daily briefing notes and also helped me with publicity material.

The campaign was lightened by one particular episode which

occurred when I was asked to drive Denis Healey, then Chancellor of the Exchequer, to a press conference which I had arranged in Ayr for all the local weekly papers. However my car was a rather battered Avenger and I suggested that it would not make an impressive sight for the Chancellor to be stepping out of such a vehicle! Helen Liddell told me to use her rather more modern and better preserved Chevette for the thirty mile journey down to the seaside resort. Denis Healey and I set off on the journey in the borrowed car, closely followed by a car carrying two Special Branch officers who were the Chancellor's protection.

Denis Healey is an antiquarian book buff and he asked me first to take him to a bookshop next to Glasgow University, just off Gibson Street. I had never driven Helen's car before and it was taking me some time to get used to the clutch control. Before I had quite mastered it our car almost rolled into the special branch car behind as I tried to take off on a hill at traffic lights. Denis Healey's disposition was not improved when I indicated that I was going to overtake the car in front, not noticing that another car was overtaking me! A full side on collision was only averted by Healey shouting, "Watch, there's someone overtaking you!" However, we managed to relax in the bookshop as the Chancellor buried himself in various tomes while I anxiously checked my watch and calculated how long it would take for us to get to Ayr.

Eventually I had to order him to leave but only after I had presented him with an old copy of Robert Burns poems as a memento of his visit to Scotland. At last we headed for Ayr. It was a fine Spring day and it was a pleasant drive until I turned off the A77 at the wrong roundabout and headed for Prestwick instead of Ayr. As a result we temporarily lost our Special Branch escort who eventually caught up with us and ordered me to follow them, or else!

Healey was a pleasant fellow to speak to and during the drive I explained to him that my union, the National Union of Journalists, was holding their annual delegate meeting in Ayr, and that it was a pity we could not spare time to visit it, as he would have had the opportunity to meet 200 plus journalists under the one roof. I didn't know at the time that Healey was in fact a member of the Institute of Journalists, a right wing strike-breaking organisation numbering at most 2000 compared to the 30,000 members in the NUJ.

I am sure that Healey, although he was to the right of my personal politics was not fully aware of the nature of the organisation he belonged to. Several years later he applied to join the NUJ, but the union's rules do not allow it to accept new members who are already in full-time occupation outside of journalism and on this basis his application was refused.

On the serious campaigning front it became obvious that things were not going well down south. The party was suffering from the effect of the 'Winter of Discontent' as well as poor organisation. Despite the good canvas reports coming into Keir Hardie House we began to fear for the overall result. On election day there was little to do in the Keir Hardie House as all the activity was in the constituencies. I spent the day in my own constituency, Glasgow Cathcart where John Maxton was trying to oust Teddy Taylor the sitting candidate.

A myth had grown up around Teddy Taylor as the working man's Conservative who received the support of Castlemilk, one of Europe's largest housing estates. It was portrayed that the working class voters of Castlemilk voted for Taylor who was on the right wing of his party. The truth was that the constituency was pretty well equally divided between Castlemilk, a council housing scheme, and the owner-occupied areas of Kings Park and Cathcart. A higher percentage of middle class voters turned out to vote than the voters in Castlemilk and it was this pattern which had in the past given the Conservatives the seat.

John Maxton had a very good constituency organisation led by Gordon Craig, a full-time trade union organiser, who had organised the canvassing of Castlemilk to identify the Labour vote. On voting day Labour Party workers poured into Cathcart and there were traffic jams in the streets of Castlemilk as voters were taken to the polling stations. By the time polling had closed we reached our target of getting out more than 71 per cent of the Castlemilk vote and were confident of capturing the seat. I returned to Keir Hardie House where Jimmy Allison was watching the General Election coverage on TV. I told him I thought we had won Cathcart. Jimmy said he would believe it when he saw the result.

It quickly became clear that our worst fears had been realised. News of Tory gains flooded in and it rapidly turned into a very depressing night. It soon became obvious that Labour had lost the General Election and that Mrs Margaret Thatcher would become the Prime Minister. News of the victory at Cathcart came in shortly after midnight but it was the only piece of good news throughout the night.

The next morning when I arrived at Keir Hardie House the building was almost deserted. In place of the buzz leading up to election day, a feeling of gloom had descended and there was an eerie silence. I went upstairs to Helen Liddell's room and discovered Bruce Millan asleep, slumped in a chair. Bruce looked desolate. The image of him alone in the hush of Keir Hardie House will always remain with me. Less than twenty-four hours before he had been Secretary of State for Scotland and a member of the Government. Now, although still an MP, he was no longer the top politician in Scotland. It must have been difficult to accept as Labour had held its own in Scotland.

Another sortie into public relations came in September 1990. Shortly after NUJ General Secretary election result was announced I was approached by Allan Watson, who was then the Secretary of the Scottish Graphical Branch of SOGAT who asked if I would be interested in taking on the job of Campaign Director of the Scottish Constitutional Convention.

At the time it was like manna from heaven. I was still shattered at losing the election for General Secretary and Margaret and I had already decided to return to Scotland. We had never settled in Kent, and Margaret in particular had been unhappy. But I had no idea what I was going to do.

I realised that employers would hardly be queuing up to offer me a job as I had led and organised strikes in most of their offices and of course Robert Maxwell was still alive which ruled out any hope of my returning to my old stamping ground of the Daily Record. The Constitutional Convention position appeared to suit me down to the ground. I had long been a committed supporter of a devolved Parliament for Scotland. Indeed the first political party I belonged to was the Scottish National Party and I had rejoined it for a spell in the 1970s before returning to Labour. I flew to Glasgow to meet Campbell Christie, general secretary of the STUC, Canon Kenyon Wright, chair of the Executive Committee of the Scottish Constitutional Convention, and Isobel Lindsay, Convenor of the Campaign for a Scottish Assembly. They asked if I was interested in the job and I replied, Yes. I added that it was not the money which attracted me as, "I couldn't remember when I last earned £15,000."

Quick as a flash Kenyon Wright rejoined, "I have the same problem coming from the other end." After this little blip I was offered the job and accepted. The result was I left the NUJ on Saturday, September 1 and took up my new position the following Monday.

My first task was to find myself an office in Glasgow as the only money the Convention had was my salary which came from the Rowntree Foundation. The National Graphical Association gave me the use of an empty office in York Street, Glasgow while the Scottish Branch of SOGAT generously provided me with £1000 for office furniture and stationery. But there was no money for a secretary and no money for campaigning. For example, I had to ensure that any printing I committed the Convention to would be self-financing.

I was asked to draw up a strategy for a campaign to publicise the Convention's *Towards Scotland's Parliament* proposals which were being launched on November 30 – self-financing of course. Everyone, myself included, assumed that we were in for a short sharp campaign. The accepted thinking in political circles was that Maggie Thatcher would call a General Election by June 1991 – only nine months away, and one of the reasons why I had taken the job on was that I had, at that time, ambitions to stand for a seat in a new Scottish

Parliament. We had not counted on Mrs Thatcher being deposed and replaced by John Major which altered the entire political scenario. However we were not to know this in September 1990 and I drew up, with the help of Kathy Galloway, a Church of Scotland minister who for a short period was Associate Campaign Director, a We Say Yes leaflet.

Once again sympathetic journalists helped me to produce a four page tabloid paper, Scotland's Voice. I returned to the S&UN printing plant at Irvine where Jack McCrorie was still production manager to have 100,000 copies of the paper printed. The paper was paid for by supporting organisations taking out adverts. The departure of Mrs Thatcher and the arrival of John Major blew my game plan out of the window. It quickly became obvious that what was to have been a short sharp sprint to a General Election was now going to become a marathon over which I had to sustain a campaign, with no funding, in order to keep the Convention proposals in the public eye.

I must admit to allowing myself the odd shake of the head when I heard the leaders of the political parties who were members of the Convention pledge themselves and their parties to campaign vigorously the length and breadth of Scotland to promote the Convention's proposals. The reality was that none of the political parties put a great deal of their resources into campaigning for the Convention's proposals. The campaign in the main was sustained by the CSA, STUC, and of course Canon Kenyon Wright, the chair of the Convention's Executive Committee, who never tired of attending meetings. Isobel Lindsay, convenor of the CSA and Campbell Christie, general secretary of the STUC were also tireless supporters.

I managed, after some arm twisting, to persuade the Convention political leadership to attend regional launches in the North East, Dundee and Dumfries and Galloway but it was the CSA members and the STUC affiliates who bought and distributed the campaign publicity material, not the political parties whose leaders appeared on television expounding the worth of the Convention proposals. I fully understand that the finances of the political parties were stretched but if a Scottish Parliament was as important to them as they stated then more resources could have been diverted towards the campaign to ensure wider grass roots support and an understanding of the Convention's proposals.

It was ironic that throughout the actual period of the General Election when it finally arrived in April 1992, pundits accepted that there were two election campaigns in the United Kingdom, the England and Wales campaign around unemployment and the National Health Service, and the Scottish campaign which rarely strayed far away from the question of Devolution and the Union.

I could not help thinking during this period that if the Convention parties had paid more attention to the issue at grass roots level in the run up to the General Election then the Conservatives would not have been able to make so much of the running in the three weeks leading up to April 9. However despite the limited resources we managed a few successes such as the quarter page adverts we placed in the national Scottish papers on November 30 1991 to mark the first anniversary of the launching of *Towards Scotland's Parliament*. The £6,000 costs were met by public subscription with supporters donating £20 each towards the adverts. More than £2,000 of donations flowed into the Campaign funds from readers in amounts varying from 50p to £100 in the weeks following their appearance. We managed during the Campaign to cause the Tories some discomfort particularly when we organised a debate on Devolution at a fringe meeting at the start of the Scottish Tory Party conference in Perth in May 1991 where, with their usual lack of regard for democracy, the Conservatives did not intend to discuss the issue.

I invited three leading Conservatives to join our debate and laid down clear ground rules to ensure that they enjoyed fair play, but they did not accept our invitation. The meeting went ahead in the Salutation Hotel and we had three empty chairs on the platform to emphasise their absence. Our 'debate' helped to ensure that the Tories were unable to duck the issue and as a result devolution featured heavily at the conference.

My time as Campaign Director was revealing. It gave me an insight at first hand into the politics within the Convention membership as they struggled to reach agreement on issues such as proportional representation which in the end proved impossible. After the 1992 election the Liberal Democrats and the Labour Party did reach agreement on this matter. But for all its faults the Scottish Constitutional Convention had the support of a large majority of the Scottish people, and the parties are to be congratulated on the consensus approach they adopted when agreeing the proposals.

It was the first time to my knowledge that the continental style approach to political problems has been adopted in this country and we should not cast it aside too readily.

I had hopes of moving into Scottish politics in a more active sense if Labour had won the General Election in 1992 and a Scottish Parliament had been created. But it was not to be and I returned from whence I came – journalism, and began my fourth career as a freelance business writer. For a short time I did consider Cuba, but then I heard Castro was thinking about elections!

Yes it has been a funny old life so far, with many twists and turns, but I have few complaints for a wee boy from Pollok. If variety is the spice of life, I have certainly had plenty of spice, mixing as a journalist with hardened criminals as well as millionaires. My time as General Secretary of the NUJ was when the trade unions were under severe attack from the Thatcher Government which placed great strains on the movement.

I remain a Christian socialist. I believe that those who have should share with those who have not. The practical method of doing this is for those among us who earn more to pay more in direct taxation. Until society accepts this premise, the least well-off will continue to suffer and we will all be poorer as a result.